VOICE FOR
THE VOICELESS

VOICE FOR THE VOICELESS

The Uncelebrated Figures of Nigerian Modern Democracy

Dr. Olusegun Bamidele Abejide
(MSc, LLM, PhD)

Ambassador-at-Large
International Human Rights Commission
(IHRC-USA & NIGERIA).

ISBN 13: 978-1-7363987-2-2
ISBN 10: 1-7363987-2-5

Printed in India and published by BUUKS.

TO MY AFRICAN BROTHERS AND SISTERS

I once asked my brave grandfather why he was always afraid of sycophants in power. His answer was: *"because obsequious and manipulative people in society nowadays are in power, and by being the powerful minority, they silence the majority and install bad leaders. Hence, we are doom."*

What then happens when the powerful minority imposes a leader (President) on a nation? *"Destroying such a nation does not require the use of atomic bombs or the use of long-range missiles. It only requires lowering the quality of education, impoverishing society, imposing dissidents, and lowering all standards."*

Consequently, Patients die at the hands of doctors; Buildings collapse at the hands of engineers; Money is lost at the hands of economists and accountants; Humanity dies at the hands of religious scholars, Justice is lost at the hands of judges and the police, so, the list goes on. The collapse of economy, breakdown of law and order (security of lives and property) is imminent, and citizen may soon revolt, opinions are stiffened, and may lead to the collapse of a nation.

It is incumbent therefore, on citizens of such a nation to speak up, demand good and accountable governance. Because when good people keep quiet, the evil thrives, hence, they must stand up and demands their rights. They should always remember that sometimes, if there is no struggle, there will be no 'freedom'.

History has demonstrated that the level of development of any nation is determined by the demands citizens make on their leaders. But if citizens worship and fears their leaders as demi-gods, in such a situation, their rights will be trampled upon.

DEDICATION

This book is dedicated to my fellow Nigerians who offered their *"voices for the voiceless in our modern democracy."* And to those that have built and are building the Nigeria project but may have historically been forgotten, denied and/or deprived of the honor and recognition in their contribution to making Nigeria great. These are extraordinary people - actors, scholars, scientists, civic and political leaders, and many others. To these voiceless individuals, this book seeks to be an effective voice, instilling hope, motivating, and creating s/heroes that have helped and helping to build our country.

Nigeria is in dire need of more /heroes and for that reason, I equally dedicate this book to you that are willing to step forward to chart new thinking and newer ways to move this country forward, elevate us emotionally; heal us psychologically; transform and unite us; fight corruption; give us hope. You may not realize how much positive impact you possess but by stepping up to seek transparency and accountability of political leadership; greater freedom, rights, and participation for collective national development, I celebrate you.

TABLE OF CONTENTS

ACKNOWLEDGEMENTS

I am indebted to my friend and brother Mr. Obwin Owen Benjamin for encouraging me with this vision. You stood with me to the end, calling me daily to know how far I have gone in the writing and equally contributing ideas. You are a wonderful guy. Without you, maybe I would have lacked the motivation and may not have finished this book. Ben, I am grateful.

Thank you very much Patrick Alushula for going through the manuscript and your recommendations. This brother is just so awesome, he was there for me always. I thank you.

I owe many thanks to both Mr. Shaheed Ibikunle Sanyaolu and Mr. Babatunde Faniyan, who both handled the proof-reading of the book. These gentlemen made some contributions where needed. May the Lord bless the day I met them.

The editing was handled by Mr. Benjamin Okoh. Award-winning broadcaster and anchor of CLASSIC FM 97.3. #BookOnReview. Mr. Okoh performed wonderfully and also gave some expertise advice on the book. I am grateful brother.

Ms. Olabisi Adebambo Ojuade; my wonderful friend who rallied around for some important information needed for the completion of the book. You are the one. I am highly grateful.

I also could not possibly have written this book without the aid of Mr. Niyi Shittu, who tirelessly and dedicatedly supported me in those crucial areas of my job. Thank you. Dr. Ambassador Winifred Wanjiku Gitonga who stood with me throughout the writing with a lot of encouragement. Thank you, Your Excellency.

My gratitude for the success of this book would not be complete without the contributions of Oyeyemi Ogunmoyede, Olusuyi Adejoke, Pastor Ibukun Oyeyemi, Mr. Abolaji Kelani, Mr. Samuel Oliyide and Mrs. Olubunmi Oliyide. Their encouragement and prayers were effective as they kept motivating me to write this book with optimism and focus. Thank you all for standing and supporting me.

To Mr. Adebayo Olaitan, a brother in need and deed, his advice on Nigerian politics is unrivalled. I doff my hat to you, sir.

I am eternally grateful to my children, Eniola-Jessie, Olawande-Justice and Oluwole-Micah for your painstakingly reading and rereading the manuscript and fervently praying with me all the time for the success of the book you have in your hands. You guys are awesome.

Finally, I am indebted to the Director of Faculty, Public Health, University of Texas Dallas, Mr. Dark Denton, who allowed me to convert a class project to a book. This book. He warned me of the difficulties of such projects and the penalties of not meeting the standards. His supervision and support birthed this book. You are the best, sir.

AUTHOR'S NOTE

In comparison to 2015, the 2019 elections in which President Muhammadu Buhari got re-elected left many Nigerians pensive. I initially thought he would not contest because it was clear on his mind and the minds of most Nigerians, both home and abroad, that he had not performed excellently. To put it explicitly- he let Nigerians down. As a man who contested on the promise of Change - reforms, better economy and to fight corruption which has bedeviled the country for many years, I expected that he would resign as he did not fulfil any of his pledges.

Apart from the 2019 general elections, I saw notable men and women criticizing the All-Progressive Congress (APC) led government in nearly every area of the country. The criticisms were healthy in my view, but the apprehension of "dissidents" and corruption allegations on some Nigerians who are mainly not members of the ruling APC party left me wondering if the government was out to shut down opposition through false and selfish allegations. They rallied both elected and non-elected leaders into activism mode, who asked the government to be responsible and demanded the resignation of President Buhari.

There were sustained attacks on President Buhari, and I sought to know why that was happening.

I realized that these people throwing salvos at Buhari's administration were not doing it for political mileage or selfish purposes, but for the sake of their country. I said to myself: these are activists engaging in a cause that will, in the future, transform Nigeria for the better. Seeing what activists in the United States of America did to champion human rights, women's suffrage, and equality, I became hopeful. However, these Nigeria activists, often labelled by pro-Buhari devotees as "enemies" of the administration, are however engaging in a cause that I believe will develop Nigeria in years to come.

A few years ago, in America, it was inconceivable that people would advocate for laws that will protect the environment, end 'jungle justice' and push for human rights because they would be profiled. Also, an activist who could call for the protection of workers' right to unionize, to increase a federal minimum wage, and government-subsidized healthcare would have been labelled illogical idealistic visionary or 'dangerous socialist'. Now that a significant achievement has been made in these areas, rather than build on it, we unsurprisingly take such ideas for granted. Credit must however be given to these activists who took their campaigns from the margins to the mainstream. Presently, we stand on the shoulders of our former heroes who challenged the status quo of their days.

Every nation has its pioneers; the fathers of a country or the well-known individuals who made huge commitments to the advancement of the nation. Nigeria is not a special case to this standards. In our history, there are people who made lots of efforts to guarantee that Nigeria assumes her commendable position among the comity of developed nations. Their contributions earned them national and global recognition. These Nigerian legends are respected for their careful works, utilizing their initiative character-istics to fight for the nation's independence, democracy, human rights, and justice.

History is replete with stories of many leaders who actively moved people to a new way of thinking and acting. The names that come to mind may differ from person to person. And that is to be expected as we all see things from different perspectives. Commitment is a step up from sim-ply appearing. It is a step up from essentially showing up. Engagement is a step up from simply appearing. Engage-ment is a guarantee to accomplishing something and, for the most part, prompts action in a way to delivering on that promise. Doing this will more often than not, involve working with others and moving towards accomplishing a shared objective for the benefit of all. Nothing is wrong with this methodology. Activism is a continuous positive and an eager way of doing something. While commitment is to handle and basically do what we are encouraged to do. Activism pushes the limits to get positive results. Activists lead with a critical thinking mentality and with a collabora-tive spirit. They are practitioners and challengers.

I am writing about the contemporary heroes of our time. The list includes twenty-one individuals—listed in terms of their early importance and accomplishments—that helped on the journey for good governance in Nigeria from 2015. Their efforts are carried in a more progressive direction, pushing for radical reforms and popularizing reformist ideas that prodded others to activity. Most were not single-issue activists yet were engaged with expansive campaigns for economic and social equity, uncovering the numerous associations among various developments across different generations in the country. These individuals cut across different strata of society — senators, clerics, ordinary persons, a governor's wife, and an ex-governor. These individuals spent the greater part of their lives as activists for change, they are change-makers. Some of them were conceived in the twentieth century but became noticeable in the 21st century. These achievers serve as a start point for further discussion on the many uncelebrated courageous heroes and heroines that are positively shaping Nigeria, presently.

Every incredible dream starts with a dreamer. These people realize that we have within us, other individuals with great strength, patience, and passion who can also positively contribute development to the country. If these icons managed to do so much as it is elucidated in the book, much more could have been done had a thousand patriots of the same opinions and views become "voices for the voiceless".

One of the things that I worry about when it comes to any movement is that, when people think about activists, they only think of those who stand in the street or only those that got arrested. This might not be true. How about Festus Keyamo, among others? That young fella, who has fought for human rights on many occasions, mostly in the court as a legal luminary. I do not think he has once been on the street or been arrested, yet he has done so much for the benighted millions of the country and I believe that, even the heavens recognize his good deeds. But what I know to be true in protest is the idea of telling the truth to the public.

These honorable men and women used their bodies, brains, energies and whatever they had to tell the truth about the fact that the government of the day was not performing well or was losing bearing of what it had promised during campaigns. Some senators in this group of individuals spoke up on the senate floor, while others have disrupted boardroom meetings and other forums to let the government know it was not using its institutional power in ways that benefit Nigerian people. The clergies amongst these individuals made their voices heard in their churches and Mosques. They spoke truth to Power. And "truth-telling" it is said works everywhere, home, and abroad.

The role of activism is mostly rooted in the understanding that their stories are at the heart of all forms of social ill that are happening in the country. The government talks tough on corruption and nation-building, but many state officials act contrary to the government position, and none have been brought to book. Activists in the spirit of truth-telling will hold protests and tell off the government for talking tough without pressing charges or taking concrete action against the corrupt. Instead, these heroes are hounded and arrested. I have seen violent police action against peaceful picketers and civilians protesting against injustices.

However, we also have to remember that talking about or making the government know about the problems is not the end of work. That is the beginning of figuring out what the solutions are. Protest in itself is not the solution.

Protest creates space for the solution to happen, it drives the process. But what I often worry about is that activists sometimes get so addicted to talking about social ills that they forget to give government solutions to fix the problems. Whereas that should be a core part of the struggles. This is not an attack on the campaigners of democracy and good governance in Nigeria, but a personal observation. It is an eye-opener to them that they should not only talk about the current problems, but they should offer solutions as well.

But what is clear is that political, human rights and democracy activists know what is ailing their communities and would invariably convene a public forum to assail the perpetrators on their people. Of course, different people observe a similar subject in various manners; therefore, I hope it will not be disrespectful if the assessments of some certain characters might be inverse to other people.

I shall speak forth my sentiments freely and without reservation that the figures I will highlight in this book are the civic, political, human rights and democracy advocates and above all, the voices for the voiceless for the mendicant populace in the country at the moment. Many may oppose my choice of personalities in this book, but their opposition may not be good for our democracy at the moment. Many of us may have some negative reservations against some of these people on some corruption or fraud allegations but note; some of these accusations may have been used as a cudgel to mute the outspoken critics of the government. Evidence to those allegations is not yet served or presented against them. Nonetheless, who is that man in the political arena of the country that has the temerity to accuse another politician of corruption? I would like to see such a saint in the country called Nigeria.

In 1995 at a gathering, inside the Nigeria Institute of International Affairs, Lagos; Gen. Oladipo Diya, the then Chief of General Staff, literally embarrassed his audience. He challenged anyone among the elites (Politicians, mostly) in the gathering to raise a hand if he/she could boldly claim to have made his/her wealth through honest means. Alas! No one in the gathering had the guts to lift their hands, because we are all tar and mar with the country's problems. And it must be rightly said, the so called "elite" is the problem of our country.

The question before Nigeria now is, how are these outspoken leaders going to sustain calls for good governance and respect for human rights? It is normal for a man to enjoy the deceptions of expectation of hope as we battle for what is useful for our society. We can only be weak if we shut our eyes and mouths against an agonizing truth and move to the tune of oppressors, only to end up in the abyss. Are we disposed to be people who have eyes but do not see; who have ears, but hear not; and have a nose but smell not? The answer is no. For the democracy fighters, whatever anguish it may cost them, are willing to fight for the good of our society.

In like manner, these notable individuals mentioned in this book have yet but one light by which their feet are guided; and that is the *Light of Experience.* They know no other method for making decisions about the future but to utilize the past to caution us against regression. The Nigerian past has been dark, and the vibrant figures of democracy today warn us against allowing leaders to take the country back to the torturous past. Hence, I will assure you that the figures I will discuss in this book are democracy upholders. In spite of their efforts to fight for a cause that will strengthen Nigeria's democracy, I think we do not recognize their actions. We have not at one time or another celebrated or even recognized them as fighters for our modern democracy. I implore you to read this book with an open mind. The individuals discussed herein are Nigerians with vision for our country.

While they live, let us create time to celebrate them and support their vision. What is not appreciated, sadly, depreciates. We can avoid the African curse of only recognizing its noble men and women in their death, as was the case with Jesus Christ's tormentors who dismissed all His miracles and left it till the hour of death to declare: *"Truly, this was the Son of God."*

PROLOGUE

The story of Nigeria is as interesting as it is pathetic. Interesting because of its antecedents as the most populous, possibly the most naturally endowed country in Africa. Asides being the country with the highest number of black population in the world, arguably, also the most diverse in peoples and culture. Ordinarily, these are enviable assets upon which great countries and great civilizations are built. From the dogged and calculated manner in which Nigerian nationalists fought for and eventually achieved independence from the British colonial masters; coupled with the leading and courageous role it played in helping other African countries out of their challenges, it was no exaggeration to have tagged Nigeria as 'the giant of Africa'. That appellation endured justifiably for a very reasonable time, through the sixties and seventies. Then, it began to fizzle out by the 80s and 90s, bringing the country to the other leg of her story: the pathetic leg.

Easily, the most pronounced factor that dominates the pathetic side of Nigeria's story is its under-achievement. To whom much is given, as it is said, much is expected. Prior to her independence, the country had a successful agrarian setting, producing food crops, such as yam, cassava, potatoes, and vegetables for local consumption; and cash crops such as cocoa, groundnut, palm oil and rubber for export. Much later, the country was found to be home to several solid mineral deposits, such as coal, bauxite, zinc, and others. Nigeria was by reasonable definition a prosperous country by 1960 when her colonial masters existed. Education was being popularized and schools were expanding in size and scope.

The needs of the country were simple: to change the landscape from its bushy rural settings to the modern one with tarred roads, gleaming streets, and modern houses. Similarly, the needs of the citizens were minimal and basic food, shelter, and to be gainfully occupied. All along, politicians who took over from the colonialists ruled and the people cheered or booed as the case demanded. Nigeria prided herself as a unified country despite her diversity. The old National Anthem emphasized this point when it said that "though tribe and tongue may differ, in brotherhood we stand." The brotherhood, whether real or contrived, collapsed in 1966 when the Army forcibly took over the reign of government from the civilians. That set the stage for the beginning of Nigeria's problems.

Therefore, my fellow countrymen, ladies, and gentlemen, I take the liberty of addressing you upon a subject which so vitally affects the honor of our nation. These individuals with integrity and honor I single out in this book may likewise and proudly be called *unsung modern-day champions; the voice for the voiceless* who tirelessly fight to expand our democratic values. Thank you.

Arbitrary rule by military

Between 1966 and 1999, there were about six successful military coups, and some others that were foiled. Military adventurism in Nigerian political space marked the beginning of her constitutional crisis, which, between the 1970s and 80s, became deepened by the discovery of oil. At the time, crude oil was the modern equivalent of raw gold, but with much greater returns due to its relevance in the industrial revolution era. The sudden immense wealth that Nigeria found itself but was obviously not prepared for, though sorrowfully managed by some unsophisticated, uneducated, and anti-social leaders that ever govern Nigeria, changed her countenance, not just on the national economy but private orientation. The fact that there was so much money, without visionary leaders to make maximum use of the accruing funds, gradually led the nation into extravagance and greed by officers in vantage positions.

Every time the Army struck, the first thing they did was to suspend the constitution and instead promulgate decrees which were proclaimed to be superior to any constitutional provision. Decrees were excluded from suspension. This was the beginning of rule by arbitrariness, since many of the decrees rolled out were intended to achieve personal desire of the rulers, while at the same time, were oppressive to the people. The Decree 5 promulgated in 1966 by the military juntas that changed Nigeria Federalism system of rules to Republic as it is now and that of the 1999 Nigeria constitutions that is wholly base on tribal sentiment are two major of many of such satanic decrees. The courts were often inundated with suits seeking clarification of conflicting provisions of decrees and the unsuspended portions of the extant constitutions. Many times, the courts declined jurisdictions to entertain the suits, based on express provisions in decrees to that effect. But when judges tried to wriggle out of the dilemma occasioned by those decrees, the military immediately, sometimes within 24 hours of the court ruling, rolled out another decree that took the matter completely beyond the judicial intervention. The ensuing scenario was that of uncertainty and unpredictability in government and consequently, conduct of the people.

By nature, Nigerians are difficult to satisfy. Under colonial rule, they accused the rulers of favoring a section of the country in leadership position and for their selfish interest. They also accused the colonial lords of imposing leadership on the rest of the country. To be fair, the accusers were not imagining things, they based their criticism on logically presented facts. Those accusations were borne out of suspicion which effectively became ingrained in the average citizen and were carried forward to the post-colonial era, leading eventually to the 30-month civil war from 1967 to 1970.

All through the reign of the Army, the lack of trust continued and trailed almost every decision of the rulers. For instance, during the reign of Major General Muhammadu Buhari as Military Head of State between 1984 and 1985, some sections of the country believed that the government was discriminatory in allowing the passage into the country of 53 suitcases believed to contain undeclared foreign currencies, owned by a traditional ruler, an Emir, from the northern part of the country; whereas many notable people from the South were arrested and dealt with under a decree promulgated against such acts. Such was the arbitrariness that pervaded military governments in Nigeria.

By their nature, military personnel are intolerant of criticism of any type as it is antithetic to their command structure. Therefore, during military rule, opposition figures are largely silenced or existed only in few pockets. This phenomenon was promoted by the decrees of the military, some of which are simply irrational and illogical, designed as they were to satisfy personal caprices of the leaders. For instance, Decree N0. 4 of 1984, called Public Officers Decree (Protection Against False Accusation) was aimed at silencing the media. The Head of State at the time did not hide his personal hatred for the press which he had accused of often publishing false information and unconfirmed rumors.

Effects of military rule

By 1999 when the military handed over to the current civilian dispensation, the Army had ruled the country for 29 out of her 35 years' post-colonial era. What this signifies is that Nigerians, at the onset of civil rule in 1999, have had more military culture in them than civilian culture. The high-handedness of the Army, though often denounced, was to some extent, seemingly tolerated by the people, some of whom pointed out that civilians were no better in organizing themselves decently after independence, thus leading to election violence in many parts of the country. The phrase 'Wild, Wild West' was coined to describe the wide rampage, killings and arson that characterized elections in the Western part of the country in the early 60s. Incidentally, the Nigerian scenario was only slightly different from that of other African countries, many of which equally gained their independence at about the same time with Nigeria.

With hindsight, the long period of military rule incapacitated Nigeria from keeping pace with her contemporaries in the world; countries like Malaysia, India, Indonesia, Brazil, and many others which now have left Nigeria lagging behind in the international development index. Over the years, the military imposed a unitary culture on the country, ruled by fiat, summarily disciplined public officers by reposting or sacking them with or without full benefits. It is true that Nigeria had many conscientious public officers who performed their duties without fear or favor. But the fear of the unknown, and the desire to retire peacefully at old age, compromised to some extent the integrity of many public servants.

Having tailored the country along military structure where the Head of State is all in all, it was easy to dictate to any arm or organ of government, including the judiciary. It was a vogue for the military, particularly in the 70s, anytime they wanted to implement a decision which they knew would be controversial, to set up panel of inquiry which would be given terms of reference and a timeline within which to submit its report and recommendation. More often than not, the panel was a smokescreen, as government would announce its decision whether or not it tallied with the panel's recommendation. And of course, the public had no way of knowing what the panel recommended. They only got to know the 'White Paper', which is government's decision. The report of the panel is usually 'classified' such that it would be a serious offence for anyone to disclose it without government's authorization. Indeed, a news magazine, *Newswatch*, was once proscribed summarily because it published the report of a panel of inquiry apparently withheld by government.

Therefore, in the atmosphere of arbitrariness of military rule, and without a people-oriented constitution to guide affairs of government, the Nigerian society began to deteriorate. The judiciary tagged as the last hope of the common man, though worse today than before, tried its best for the people; but it could only interpret existing decrees. Where the decrees ousted the court's jurisdiction, the court would quietly withdraw from making pronouncements. With time, transparency and accountability waned in the public sphere. Key appointments were made not on merit, but on personal whims. Corruption set in and mismanagement became rife. The rot spread to all institutions, including law enforcement agencies. The economy suffered from hazy and often misinterpreted guidelines and, in the midst of impunity, produced millionaires overnight, including those with no visible means of livelihood. Contracts were awarded, paid for but not executed. Some contracts were abandoned under flimsy excuses. Sometimes, a new government cancelled contracts awarded by a previous government, just to spite that government or portray it as corrupt; whereas the ultimate aim of the new government was to create opportunities for its own self-enriching contracts.

The notion of 'anything goes' naturally permeated the youth, many members of who now believe in getting rich quick. They grew up worshipping wealth as an end rather than as a means. With all focus on crude oil production and export as the goose that laid the golden eggs, the country went into full importation of goods and items that could otherwise be gainfully produced locally, resulting in abandonment of the local industry. When oil prices dipped and production fell, the country began to wriggle in anxiety and pain. Many young people took to crime and the nation's value system took a nosedive. Under a pervasive official policy summersault, public institutions that were working began to crumble. Top on the list are the corporations for electricity, railway, post, and telecoms among several others. It was a question of time, therefore, for the Nigerian economy to suffer the current cripple.

Fallacy of civil rule

It is true that civilians have been in charge of Nigeria successively for more than 20 years since 1999, which ought to be an opportunity to rectify the wrongs committed under the military rule. That the desired change has not happened is partly a reflection of the lingering military mentality in government; and partly because the civilians failed to raise the ante of good governance and instead exploited tools of democracy to deepen the country's problems. In the past 20 years of civil democratic rule, Army Generals are still largely calling the shots. A former Military Head of State, General Olusegun Obasanjo was indeed the first to take the baton as civilian president, and he held sway for eight years. Within this period, retired military personnel held major positions such as state governors, Senate President, federal or state lawmakers, and Board Chairmen. Another former military Head of State, Gen Muhammadu Buhari is currently the president in his second term. Under that situation, it is no surprise that things have not changed much. Indeed, the more things changed, the more they appeared the same.

In any event, the basic laws of the country now governing affairs is the constitution, and in the case of Nigeria, a constitution bestowed on the country by the same military that is being blamed for most of its woes. But if the constitution is not perfect, why couldn't the civilian administrators rectify its defects, or explore ways of enthroning good governance? Sadly, proposals that the constitution be re-written or otherwise modified to truly reflect the peoples' desire have hit a brick wall because the people charged with re-writing the constitution are the same people, members of the legislature, voraciously benefiting from its imperfection. So, for 20 years, official and unofficial efforts to enact a people's constitution have borne no fruit in the national Assembly. The country continues to waste her resources and retard her progress. Indeed, corruption in the public sphere took an astronomic proportion compared to the military period. Worries expressed by writers and researchers on this have had no impact on the rulers who largely conduct affairs with the business-as-usual mentality.

The Nigerian spirit as factor

In 1995, the *African News Weekly* wrote that: *"Nigeria, the comatose giant of Africa, may go down in history as the biggest country ever to go directly from colonial subjugation to complete collapse, without an intervening period of successful self-rule. So much promise, so much waste: such was a disappointment, such a shame. Makes you sick"*. Powerful lamentation, but of little effect on the powers that be. At the time of the expressed concern, Nigeria actually appeared to be on the brink of collapse. Since then, there have been debates whether the country was a failing state or a failed state. Curiously, that debate has endured for perhaps 25 or 30 years, a strong suggestion that the country still has what it takes to keep going. It says a lot about the resilience of Nigerians who, some years ago were dubbed as the happiest people in the world. How anyone can be happy in the Nigerian circumstances beat imagination. What can be asserted safely is that the country somehow manages to do something right, even if these are followed by many other things done wrong: a case of one step forward, two steps backward. All the same, the question remains loud as to whether this winless situation is what Nigeria deserves, and the answer remains a resounding no.

Fixing the problem

The woes of Nigeria have been identified as the absence of visionary leaders to mobilize the people positively and utilize the country's resources judiciously for the benefit of the masses, which are categorized among the poorest in the world. Beyond this however, there is a clear perception that the state structure is deeply flawed, such that even if there is a visionary leader, he may not achieve much because of the corrosive effects and collateral damages emanating from the structure. The truth is that the country's problem is an admixture of bad structure and visionless leaders. Over the years, good and commendable actions have been taken under the warped structure; while untenable actions that were not necessarily instigated by the structure have also been taken. In seeking the way forward for the country, the two issues must be addressed.

It would appear, however, that the need to restructure the system is more pressing and of greater significance. The problem is that every government of the day, having met an amazingly comfortable situation for their selfish ethnic enclave, have been reluctant to embark on restructuring. Their lame excuse has been that they did not want to preside over the disintegration of Nigeria; or that the unity of the country is 'non-negotiable'. Meanwhile, it is business as usual. Corruption festers and mismanagement heightens. Government, both in the executive and legislature, is unwilling to sacrifice its opulent lifestyle for people-oriented projects. It has been shown that the Nigerian federal lawmakers are the highest paid officials in the world. They allocate monstrous financial largesse to themselves in disregard of public outcry or reality of the economy. Thus, only a handful of Nigerians consume more than 50 percent of the nation's resources. Elections are still not free and fair, while other institutions are weak. Good governance, therefore, continues to be a mirage.

There is a clear need to reform the institutions and make them perform their credible roles to check corruption, violation of human rights, provide functional infrastructure, provide basic educational and health care, and secure the lives and property of Nigerians. The nation's constitution should be jettisoned or trashed and I totally recommend that the 1963 constitutions be brought back in other to restructure the country such that state governments are given more roles and the prerequisites of office at all levels are reduced to emphasize service and eliminate the do-or-die affair associated with elections. Under the present setting, politicians sell their properties to get into public office, knowing that they can always recoup their loss, and gain more.

Institutional reform

Although the Nigeria 1999 Constitution is imperfect, the institutions can and should perform irrespective. In fact, poor governance, human right violation, vapid cases of corruption, all emanate from the absence or non-performance of the following 7 key institutions:

1. An autonomous National Assembly that provides oversight over the Executive and by this, checks and balances.
2. A free and autonomous media to guarantee the free flow of information, a smart system that would privatize the state-owned media, particularly the radio. This is the medium of the citizenry and has such power.
3. An independent judiciary is very essential for the rule of law. The Supreme Court Judges in the nation, for instance, should be rotated 'within the arena'.
4. A freestanding Electoral Commission that is comprised of representatives of every single ideological group and that of every political party, as against being filled with government appointees.
5. A free central bank: to guarantee money related issues, economic stability, fiscal discipline.

6. The establishment of an impartial and professional armed and security forces to ensure protection of lives and property, law, and order.
7. A productive civil service that executes strategies and convey fundamental social services to the people in a professional manner and not based on religious, ethnic, or political affiliations.

Each of these is basic in guaranteeing "good governance", antidote to corruption. The first six are prerequisites for a working democracy. The United Nations captures them as procedure for basic leadership through which policies are executed. They possess 8 significant qualities: Accountability, Equitable and Participatory, Responsive to the present and future needs of society, Effective and Efficient, Consensus-oriented, Transparent, and follows the Rule of Law. These help to fight corruption and ensure representation of all, including the minorities in policy formulation.

An analogy will better help the understanding of the concept of Good Governance. One may dislike the shape, the style or shade of a vehicle, yet all auto cars have a cooling system, brake system, an electrical system, suspension system, a transmission system, etc. Each framework of the car is independent of the other and has a specific capacity to play a vital role, and collectively contribute to making the vehicle run smoothly and can be said to be in "good working condition." So also, is a constitution albeit its imperfections. Constitutions recognize and empower institutions like the executive, the judiciary, parliament, civil service, and so on. Each institution has a specific capacity and function it serve to society. These institutions form the foundation on which society functions. Institutions to society are what systems are to a vehicle. So, when all institutions of society are functioning efficiently and professionally, good governance prevails.

Nigeria must be guided by words of wisdom established worldwide, as well as the experience of great nations. Former US President Barak Obama once said that *"Africa doesn't need strong men; it needs strong institutions"*. In Nigeria, strong institutions can emerge through restructuring of the country. Above all, the country must be guided by the rules of a functioning democracy as clearly enunciated by the United Nations to include participation consensus orientation, accountability, transparency, responsiveness, effectiveness and efficiency, equitability, inclusiveness, and adherence to the rule of law.

AMB. DR. WINFRED
WANJIKU GITONGA

I t gives me great pleasure and privilege to
introduce Amb. Dr. Olusegun Bamidele
Abejide's first edition of his book, "Voice
for the Voiceless" to the general society. It
is an understatement to say how delighted I
am to write the foreword for this extraordinary book as published.

I have known Amb. Dr. Olusegun Bamidele Abejide,
very well for the last five years as a comrade Ambassador,
a defender of human rights and a promoter of peace and
security internationally.

Dr. Abejide is a graduate of Criminal Justice (Homeland
Security and Counterterrorism), also Graduate of Science
of Law and also PhD. in Applied Health Administration.
Dr. Abejide has been very vocal in advocating for democratic governance, peace, security, and human rights. As a
Patriotic leader that Nigeria needs at this moment, mostly
in the area of Homeland Security, Anti-terrorism and Anti-
corruption and respect to human rights. Dr. Olusegun is

supremely professionally qualified for the task of writing and producing such an extraordinary book at this point, which in every other way resonates as the leadership governance guide. There is no fiction in the entire book as the characters are real. This is a nod to non-fiction writers around the world and a reminder that reality can be more remarkable than fiction, at least when someone like Dr. Abejide puts it into the paper. This book is notably unrivaled as one of the best sellers considering it is penned in a language that is understandable across the globe.

The book is a collection of strategies, but strategies designed to build understanding and provoke realization. The carefully sought and selected group of characters makes this book as unique as it pays homage to the true nature and characteristic behaviors of real-life leaders and the cadre of other actors as the editor sees them. In a world of silence, Dr. Abejide has courageously written a brutally honest book as he unraveled the notice of the few among many activists in Nigeria. Diverse cadre of activists that have been in the forefronts of voicing for the voiceless out of the muddy and stinking political system that has presently characterized the nation, called Nigeria. The whole resurrection of hope to the hopeless has been done in such a unique way and manner by digging deep into the wounds of their souls for the purpose of pulling back the blanket of silence.

But the real revelation is that Dr. Abejide's heart shines bright, like a lighthouse in the most profound fog. As an Ambassador and advocate supporting human rights initiatives, with gratitude, apart from being an academia with Ph.D. in his field, he has also immensely been honored and bestowed with Honorary Doctorates and Ph.D. honor awards, accolades, and other recognition awards for merit in the field of peace and humanity throughout the world. I am humbled to hold the same accolades as he also does.

Being conferred and receiving these invaluable honorary awards has given him more and greater exposure to a broad audience and given him the opportunities to spread peace and humanitarian messages further, including within most of the organizations and institutions enshrined in the United Nations and European Union Charters. With this, I congratulate Ambassador Dr. Olusegun Bamidele Abejide for a job well done.

Amb. Dr. Winfred Wanjiku Gitonga,
Ambassador-at-Large
International Human Rights Commission (IHRC-Kenya)

INTRODUCTION

The early heroes, heroines and great leaders of Africa have died or become inactive. Those still alive are lethargic and old age has caught up with them, making it difficult for them to speak with authority against poor leadership ailing Africa. Today, one would think that with the exception of few leaders like Chief Ayo Adebanjo, Wole Soyinka, Alani Akinrinade, Olusegun Obasanjo, Edwin Clark and others in Nigeria, there seems to be no towering figures capable of fighting for democracy, good leadership, and good governance. But a glimpse into Nigeria's political circle gives hope that heroes are arising even without much recognition and praise from the public.

With the flame of old freedom fighters diminishing, comes the blossoming of new set of freedom fighters, though with little recognition. Leaders with charisma, courage, and self-abnegation are getting their voices heard. We have seen leaders such as Barrister Femi Falana, Femi Fani Kayode, Senator Dino Melaye, ex-senate president Bukola Saraki, Senator Ben Murray-Bruce, Buba Galadima, Hon. Yinka Odumakin, Adeola Fayehun, Aisha Yesufu among others, empower and encourage citizens to stand against emerging tyranny, rampant corruption, or bad leadership in general. They are fighting for the rights and freedom of society in line with what our forefathers fought for until we gained independence, the gains which were trampled upon by the successive military regimes that imposed an autocratic rule on the political landscape and jarred our psyche.

With hindsight, no person with a sane mind would wish Nigeria to go back to the dark years of military rule, when the soldiers governed the country with an iron fist. Democracy gives citizens a sense of humanity, love, and freedom. On the contrary, dictatorship dehumanizes and infringes on the basic rights of members of the society. We are at a time when nobody is willing to let Nigeria relapse into autocratic leadership or misgovernment, not anymore. This is evident in the way some contemporary leaders are becoming perennial critics of the presidency they think is doing little to transform the country.

There are many people, principally, the educated but unemployed graduates and those who have been forced into extreme poverty due to corruption who are angry with the present situations in the nation. I mean exasperated at everything that they doubt if there are any genuine leader with their interests at heart. Such individuals would argue that there are no new freedom fighters in Nigeria at the moment, but a bunch of greedy people with no vision. I would urge such individuals not to lose hope because the current pro-democracy leaders, regardless of the positions they hold today, are as important as Nigeria's pre-independence freedom fighters of the 60s.

It is therefore germane that the current democratic mechanism of society efficiently and satisfactorily operates so it does not seem as if only those freedom fighters of the 60s were authentic. However, it will amount to fallacy to think that Nigeria does not currently have genuine individuals that are committed to democracy. The contemporary society of Nigeria can produce leaders of great ability and appeal if they continue advocating for social justice and hold accountable, state officers and public servants. While you may differ with my opinion, it is obvious that Nigeria has evolved; but we cannot expect the current leaders to be like the post-colonial freedom fighters, every generation has its opportunities and challenges to confront. Today, we are not dealing with colonial leaders, rather, we are fighting bad leadership, corruption, insecurity and attempts to reintroduce dictatorship as a means to consolidate power and silence opponents.

Of course, constitutional government with the maximum participation of citizens is the political objective with which we should aim. We should also understand that presently, the world urgently needs drastic political and social changes. I think that such personal leadership is needed for every enterprise of any kind, even for enterprises that are organized in the most democratic lines possible. Though, it is believed that the leadership of a democratic enterprise, organization or institution is a delicate and difficult task. Under a democratic regime, the leader ought to obtain his citizens' cooperation by convincing them rationally that the policy they are proposing is right and they ought to conduct a rational dialogue with them. Democratic leaders must prescribe the nature of systems and structures for the management of society. These systems and structures must be created by the tenets of democracy. When society is structured democratically, every leader will observe a sense of responsibility. The human heart, however, invariably harbors the greedy desire to stabilize and expand rights and privileges for themselves, even at the expense of others. When the man or woman in authority allows this desire to sway his or her thoughts and actions for individual gain, the system or structure of society deteriorates.

Look, the present situation in Nigeria is neither peaceful nor stable.

To effect solutions to the many challenges facing the country, leadership based on wisdom and high ideals is essential. We are witnessing police brutality on peaceful protesters, killings, kidnappings, and attacks on innocent civilians during elections. The country is not stable per se due to an array of negative happenings which, in my view, can be controlled if the leadership of the country is serious about its responsibilities and duties to the Nigerian people. A wise leader has ideas that will guide in developing solutions to the challenges bedeviling a society. Nigeria, one of the largest economies in Africa, runs a weak democracy and this threatens its peace and unity. However, if the current leadership, specifically the presidency, opts to pursue reforms focused on empowering democratic institutions to fight vices facing the country - (the total overhaul of the "so-called" military constitution of 1999 which largely favors one section of the country), Nigeria, within a few years, will significantly be peaceful and rapidly develop.

In a democracy, leaders must always be judged based on their leadership principle and the extent to which they can put those principles into practice. If applied sensibly and responsibly, can help prevent the emergence of autocratic leaders. If a democratic regime is to work satisfactorily, it needs a leader who is neither a trickster nor a demagogue. A leader with a high ethical and intellectual worth that fellow citizens would easily follow without coercion. This is what democratizing nations urgently want. This is what Nigeria needs at the moment. Sadly, such a leader is hard to find in a society where people want to take public offices and treat them as their personal properties. As far as I know, about the African continent, citizens are always willing to support a leader who stands for them and tirelessly fights vices like corruption, ethnicity, and the likes, I think in Mangufuli, the president of Tanzania and that of Paul Kagami of Rwanda to an extent, can we find that in the whole Africa. Please, forgive me if I am wrong in my judgement on this. Unfortunately, leaders of that kind are rare because of self-centeredness and the unwillingness to embrace democracy. In a working democracy, a leader's role is noticeable in their push for social importance. Leaders should prioritize public interest over private gains because leadership is about an altruistic phenomenon or self-sacrifice, purposely for the development of society.

Nevertheless, I feel that the power bestowed on leaders in a democracy must always be limited to avoid abuse of office. When a man's term in power is over, the people ought to judge his actions in office and decide whether to retain him in his position of leadership or oust him in favor of someone else. The kind of leader that Nigerians presently yearn, in contrast to a dictator, is one that will respect and serve the people.

I am firm in my conviction that there is nothing more disturbing in society than a politician who coerces the

people and adopts ethnic sentiments to secure his authority at all costs even in the face of ineptitude. Politicians
should be true and faithful to the people that voted them
into office. To qualify to be a good leader therefore, one
must have courage, integrity, courtesy, practical wisdom,
dignity and be fair. These values can only be manifested
if a leader is prepared to enter into dialogue with people
through citizen participation and to collectively solve challenges bedeviling a nation.

Citizen participation in the affairs of a country is critical since the people through their votes, are required to
'have a say' in the governance of their country and to
influence appropriately public policy. This is a vision the
likes of Femi Fani Kayode, Senator Sheu Sani and Senator
Eyinnaya Abaribe have when they speak to the public; it is
not that they are inciting the public against other leaders.
What they want is a corruption-free government, strong
democratic institutions and a speedily growing economy
that can benefit the entire society.

The leaders that I featured in this book, have lock stock,
and barrel to intensify the calls for good governance. They
have daringly assailed President Muhammadu Buhari
several times, not because they have a personal vendetta
against him but on the account that the country is ineffectively governed. Corruption, insecurity, police brutality,
ethnic/religious superiority, and intolerance, which I will
discuss extensively in the successive sections, are deflating
human rights and freedoms that are essential to democracy. Yes, every year, we celebrate Democracy Day, but there
is little to celebrate about that because the current state of
affairs contradicts what one would expect in a democratic

society. Having a Democracy Day in Nigeria without leaders living up to the tenets of democracy such as transparency and accountability, fairness, respect for human rights and freedom is meaningless.

＝‡ ‡＝

CHAPTER 1

DR. ABUBAKAR BUKOLA SARAKI

Many may wonder if Nigeria's democracy is anything to be proud of in over twenty years of civilian rule after successive military regimes. My interactions with people from different hues have allowed me to learn what democracy really is. My stay in the United States as well has given me an illustrious chance to experience American Democracy. My experience may not interest you, but it gives me the temerity to examine the people who have fought for my country's democracy from 2015.

Candidly, democracy is good, and I can say without an iota of doubt, it is one thing that the entire humanity should be proud of. There is this particular conversation I had with one of my friends about Nigeria's democracy. According to him, Nigeria has not realized any substantial democratic transition yet. To me, this is untrue. Don't we hold democratic elections? We do. I do not agree with anyone that thinks our country is wide off the mark to achieve democratic leadership. In recent years, Nigeria has had towering figures of democracy such as Dr. Abubakar Bukola Saraki. This is enough to certify that Nigeria is an emerging democracy. Recently, an Al Jazeera reporter, Hamza Mohamed asked a central question about our democracy: "In the 20 years of popular government, has Nigeria improved?" You have the answer. The reporter goes on to indicate pomp and color that characterized the transfer of power from the Generals to a civilian leader, the former President Olusegun Obasanjo who was in 1999 democratically elected as the president of Nigeria. The reporter's analysis shows a positive turn in our economy.

Likewise, as referenced by an Abuja-based financial specialist, Aliyu Audu who was cited by Al Jazeera, "the economy is improving now because there is the more noteworthy dimension of trust in our economic institutions. There are additionally, progressive foreign investments when contrasted with the military period". Essentially, what is abstracted from this reporting is that Nigeria's economy has grown markedly on accounts of democratic progression.

Let us not forget, Nigeria's democracy is young. And political personalities such as Dr. Bukola Saraki - Nigeria's ex-Senate President, particularly in the 2015-2019 period has contributed considerably to the growth of our democracy. For democracy to mature, some people must act with self-abnegation. Dr. Saraki, throughout his reign as Kwara State's two-term governor and Senate President, has shown us that sometimes we ignore our democracy giants. You may hold a wholly opposing view about him, but he remains relevant to Nigeria's democratic struggles. With all that stated, I dedicate this chapter to examine Dr. Abubakar Bukola Saraki's contribution, experience, and vision for this oil-rich West African Country-Nigeria.

Rough experience and party switch energized Dr. Saraki to fight for democracy

Although he has had failings, he is a human being - remember that! Dr. Saraki has epitomized what true democracy is. From being a governor and senator to trying to seek the presidency, he has proved that democracy creates space for freedoms and growth for everyone. He is not the president today, but his strive to reinforce Nigeria's democracy as Senate President will outlive him. In a democratic dispensation, people have limitless opportunities to achieve their reasonable desires. Saraki trained as a medical doctor, nevertheless believed that he could serve Kwara State and Nigeria at large in political leadership. Some people may attribute his success to political pedigree, but do not be blind to his struggle to build up democracy, particularly as a Senate president of Nigeria.

Now that Nigeria is not a one-political-party nation, political leaders have the liberty to decide where to belong. This gave room for a clear demarcation between progressive leaders and those keen on dragging behind independent Nigeria for their gains. President Winston Churchill once paraphrased this kind of situation this way: "some people change their principles for the sake of their political party, while others change their political party for the sake of their principle." If this is the case, then, there is no need for killing or hating ourselves unnecessarily because of party-switching. Only the intolerant people would perceive party switching undemocratic. We are more mature than that. Remember what happened between the NCNC and ACTION GROUP parties in the 50s and 60s. To the well-established societies like Europe and America, it was a brilliant move. But, to the immature society, this brought enmities within themselves and still exists today. This kind of dog-eat-dog in the realm of animality should stop in our society. In the realm of humans, pettiness is nothing, totally useless. However, human beings embrace each other and move forward.

In a personal struggle to seek political survival, Dr. Saraki demonstrated that party switch is healthy for democracy. He has exposed that party hopping is not indecisiveness, but a normal phenomenon in a functioning democracy. I say it again, this is good for democracy. In a civilized society, people are informed and should be free to belong to a political party that befits them or stick to their continuum of ideologies. In his quest for the top job in 2018, the ex-Senate President, Saraki defected to a major opposition party, Peoples Democratic Party (PDP), on grounds of incompatible principles with the ruling All Progressive Congress (APC). This rubbed his opponents the wrong way. All the same, this was probable. Nonetheless, it is unreasonable to bury heads in the sand by ignoring the individual liberty to belong to a party of one's choice.

Nigeria is a liberal democracy; though, a weak one. Elected representatives are bestowed with decision-making power. Dr. Saraki's decision to switch sides demonstrates that for Nigeria's democracy to blossom, nobody should be pilloried for leaving a party for another if they no longer align with their values, ideologies, and beliefs. In all fairness, belonging to a political party that aligns with an individual's belief system is all that politicians want, and that is flat. Party switches happen, not only in immature democracies but also in burgeoning ones. In the United States, the defection of boisterous and sturdy Southern conservative, Strom Thurmond in 1964 is one best-case scenario to justify Saraki's defection in a true democracy. Thurmond quit the Democratic Party to join the Republican Party. He was a South Carolina Senator, and once took a stab at the presidential race in the U.S. while riding on a segregationist party, Dixiecrat. In his book titled, "Making the American Century: Essays on Political Culture of Twentieth-Century America," Bruce J. Schulman views this as a historic shift in American national politics. Though it is unpalatable to agree with what Thurmond stood for as an advocate of Southern States' rights to oppress and dehumanize the blacks, he still epitomizes party switches as a touchstone of any liberal democracy. And many more have happened since then.

As earth-shattering as Saraki's decision to cross the aisle in 2018 is, it is central to see it as a democratic exercise. Leaving the ruling party, APC to join the opposition party, PDP puts him at loggerheads with Buhari's administration that set all guns blazing on him in all probability to bring Saraki down. This was expected, owing to the undeniable fact that many party leaders, especially in African democracies perceive opponents as archenemies. However, this was a tectonic shift in Nigeria's national politics; given that it was a high-ranking official third in line after President Muhammadu Buhari and his vice. Sometimes, party switches happen not based on ideologies, but to satisfy political ambitions. And this has happened in many democratic countries such as Kenya, where it is not uncommon for politicians to hop from one political outfit to another, with no care for principles within those political vehicles.

Political parties in emerging democracies are hell-bent on building a personality cult that can deny other visionary leaders an opportunity to transform their nations. In Africa, political parties have been personalized and there was no way President Buhari would have accepted a challenger in his ruling party. It is crystal clear that Buhari's first term lacked clout and vision that wiggled out his predecessor, Goodluck Jonathan from power. He rode to power as a transformational leader on 'Change' mantra and a roadmap to fight corruption, but that came short as Nigeria's economy dwindled. With a big man syndrome and cling-to-power obsession in Africa, Dr. Saraki had a slim possibility of carrying the APC presidential ticket. Perhaps this is one of the reasons that set him off to PDP.

Undeniably, Dr. Saraki was set to be one of the presidential frontrunners in 2019 hotly contested and tense race targeting to unseat President Buhari had he won the PDP ticket. Do not ignore that sitting presidents in Africa are very manipulative and scheming when their power is threatened. The rapid rise to prominence by Dr. Saraki had to be stopped through wild corruption and robbery allegations. Enmeshed in false asset declaration that attracted a considerable 18 count charges before the Code of Conduct Tribunal, Dr. Saraki's doggedness to ascend to presidency hit a snag. The charges were shot down to three, but it was not a sigh of relief for a presidential candidate. The police dragged him into Offa bank robbery scandal that took place in his home Kwara State with a laughable piece of evidence. In their uncultivated assertion, the police said that a gang leader connected to the burglary was pictured at the wedding of Saraki's daughter in Kwara State. Besides, the gang leader was said to have been clad in similar Ankara clothing at the nuptials. These were attempts to contaminate Dr. Saraki's expanding political influence and to block his ascent to the presidency. Still, there is hope even though the ride to Nigeria's presidency was a depressing one for Dr. Saraki considering that he lost the PDP ticket and had charges tagged on his back.

Competitive politics is healthy for an emerging democracy; however, Nigeria has to slay the impending monster. The ogres of a political witch hunt, false allegations and personal attacks directed at political opponents have to stop if we are going to move forward. Democracy requires that political actors sustain competition through policies that are pro-development instead of character assassinations. What does a man have to gain by holding onto power instead of creating a favorable socio-economic environment where all and sundry have equal opportunities to succeed? This is a fundamental question that all Nigerian leaders should look forward to answering as they consolidate power. By answering soberly this question with an abstemious mind, Nigeria will have a political environment where true democratic leadership will be exercised.

I do not doubt that if Dr. Saraki supported President Buhari, charges that were pressed against him would not have seen the light of the day. The presidency would have felt that their policies would sail through the senate and in effect nobody in the government would have dared accuse him of any wrongdoing. As a man of principle who is gritty to fight for true democracy where every Nigerian could choose to belong to a political party of their choice at any time, he could not give in to threats. He stood firm and protected the independence of the senate, something that rarely happens in Africa. If he were obsequious, he would have swiftly allowed the presidency to destabilize the independence of the senate.

While I am bighearted to say that Dr. Saraki had a rough ride following the aforementioned allegations, I would say that this is a leader that was not threatened by intimidations from the executive. He allowed his conscience and the public interest to supersede individual interests that stubbornly sought to weaken and persuade him into supporting corrupt and non-performing leaders to secure "undisturbed life." In contrast, endless threats and investigations from the police did not deter him from serving the public. He walked and worked as a free man amid bludgeons from the police who no longer exercised their semi-autonomy to carry out their duties.

In truth, one interesting thing to me is that this man was unmoved by accusations and threats canalized to him by a government that tried to use anything humanly possible to implicate him. The courage Dr. Saraki displayed by standing his ground to serve the senate with bipartisanship justifies his undeterred devotion to growing our democracy. He has shown Nigerians that, in the face of intimidations to support a cause that you do not believe in at all, the best thing to do is to remain adamant. You ought not to be a namby-pamby kind of a person if you are a democracy advocate in a nation where leaders are devotees of dictatorship. You should be firm in what you believe in and if that would mean switching to another political party, you must do so. We need not stick to a place that no longer supports the values and principles that are critical for democratization. We must willingly switch parties and stay in a party that accommodates us as well as grows democracy. Besides, we should not be demoralized when championing democracy even if we are threatened regularly by the government or the police.

Dr. Saraki's perspective on Nigeria's democracy

Democracy building is not a one-day event and by all means, it is a political and institutional process. The epochal transition of the military to civilian rule in 1999 set a stage to cultivate Nigeria's democracy. National Democratic Institute (NDI), (a non-profit organization working to strengthen democratic institutions in emerging democratic nations) has been at the heart of supporting and fortifying democratic institutions with a view to making Nigeria a true democracy. Since 1999, NDI has not relented in growing Nigeria's democracy because it understands that it is a process that needs a fundamental transformation of the constitution, judicial system, and respect for independent institutions.

Nigeria, on June 12, celebrates *Democracy Day,* not "Dictatorship or Authoritarianism Day," on account of the desire to be a democratic nation. While acknowledging the successful direction to democratize Nigeria, Dr. Saraki holds the view that it is within the realms of possibility for our country to nurture its democracy. In the run-up to 2019 general election, the former president of the eighth Senate, Federal Republic of Nigeria, Dr. Saraki said this in a Democracy Day Lecture at the International Conference Center held in Abuja, "Our democracy is very fragile. It behooves on us to strengthen it as a nation."

There is no lie here. It is an absolute truth about our democracy; Nigeria's democracy is indeed fragile, though its fragility can be overcome. In its feebleness, our democracy can fall to either side. It can lose headway or take a positive turn. This is all dependent on the political leaders and the will of the people. In his own words, he thinks it will take people from all walks of life across beautiful Nigeria to fortify democracy. Of concern is whether Nigerians are prepared to obey this clarion call. In his capacity, it is difficult to strengthen democracy, especially when working under a President of the Federal Republic of Nigeria that has put aside the rule of law.

Democracy can become a cropper in a political ecosystem where the president can fire judges at will or strangle other arms of government. Regrettably, President Buhari sacked Nigeria's top judge and head of the judiciary, Walter Onnoghen. This was seen as an attempt to muzzle and weaken the judiciary in the run-up to the 2019 presidential election. Justice Onnoghen had previously adjudicated electoral disputes independently, and the fear for his effrontery stands to be a reason for throwing him out. It was a direct insult to the efforts of building Nigeria's democracy-a blow to the principles of checks and balances and separation of power. So, those who tongue-lashed Dr. Saraki were blind to the reality of the intricate power play and deft political maneuvering that confronted him. This is a man that stressed the need to respect the principles of checks and balances.

Progress of democracy is hinged on how the arms of government respect each other, without disregarding edicts of the constitution or rule of law. As Senate President, Saraki asserted that the executive, judiciary, and legislature must exercise independence, but within the dictates of the constitution. Even as he held the position of Senate President, he exercised independence of the legislature even though the executive used the police to intimidate vocal opponents. Senators such as Dino Melaye and Saraki himself were dragged to court to answer to charges, which were widely perceived as a political witch hunt. Mr. Saraki presided over a legislature that he believed is the bedrock of democracy. He further insisted that the legislature must stand true to its independence. He once reiterated to the senators-elect and members-elect of the 9th assembly at an event convened at Nicon Hilton Hotel, Abuja by the National Assembly management: "In its constitutional role, the National Assembly carries out oversight, makes laws and ensures constituency representation. In carrying out constitutional functions, lawmakers must always recognize that the independence of the legislature is non-negotiable".

Mr. Saraki envisioned a Nigerian government that will treat the Senate as co-equal partners in advancing democracy. He equally lobbied for members of the National Assembly to protect the principle of separation of power as a basis for enhancing democracy and good governance. It was a powerful message that Nigerians have recently witnessed from leaders like Dr. Saraki. His coming out of the woods to ask legislators to stand their ground and act independently to make laws that brace democracy is an apparent testament of his push for democracy. Despite being required to be a co-equal arm of the government, Dr. Saraki called for a change of tact. The change involved altering of perception of the legislature. The public thinks the legislature is the weakest branch of government when it is the one that makes laws, oversights, and represents the people.

In his vision, Dr. Saraki regarded the legislative arm of government as crucial to the democracy of Nigeria. Dr. Saraki remains on record for fighting tooth and nail to keep the legislature strong and independent to counter well-calculated attempts by the executive to control it. However, many ordinary people do not realize that that is how to promote or support democracy. In Saraki's leadership at the Senate, key bills that are important for the democratization of Nigeria were passed. To enhance transparency and accountability, Dr. Saraki through his decision-making power made NASS' (National Assembly's) budget a permanent policy. This followed lengthy engagements and pressure from civil society organizations. An 'open' NASS became a permanent policy and allowed the public to know the nitty-gritty of the budget of the National assembly. I think we should see this as a step in the right direction. It will ensure that the financial resources of Nigeria are handled in an accountable and transparent way.

As momentous as Saraki's decision to make NASS budget public, more institutions in Nigeria are likely to follow suit. In a democratic society, citizens expect public institutions to perform their tasks transparently and Saraki put his country on that path through the opening of NASS permanent policy. In modern Nigeria, the federal government tables its budget proposals before the Senate for deliberations. This is something that was not previously given much attention. Transparency and accountability, no doubt, are central to democracy. Although budget transparency for the National Assembly was a failure given that the budget lines were not disclosed, Saraki strove to enhance transparency. Budding democracies have a phobia to be transparent and accountable to the public. But Saraki considered the NASS budget as a tremendous decision that will in many years to come promote transparency and accountability.

Over 290 bills passed under Saraki's Senate Presidency, which was a great achievement. The preceding (7th) Senate passed only 128 bills, but under him it was exceptional. Sorry to say, many will not consider it as a great success for democracy. Has anyone in the country commended him for this fantastic achievement? Importantly, Saraki came in as a visionary senator and Senate President with his eyes set on raising the bar high for the legislature. He envisioned it as the bedrock of democracy that is fundamental in making Nigeria a freer society.

Today, through the Not-Too-Young-To-Run bill, a person who is 35 years can run for president, a significant reversal of the 40-year age limit. Also, those interested in the gubernatorial seats can run at the age of 30. Before Saraki, the age limit to seek such a position was 35 years. You ought to regard this as a move to allow the Young

Turks to drive Nigeria's democracy in the right direction. Lest we forget, Saraki also led other senators to address security challenges facing the nation. Security is the role of the executive, but as a leader of the senate, Mr. Saraki led senators to address rising insecurity in the country. In the course of his term, he convened security meetings and presided the passing of resolutions to address security crises. The executive never paid attention to them, but the North East Development Commission Bill which is in effect today was passed to help victims of insurgent attacks. In genuine terms, Saraki's Senate was effectively led, and it sought to strengthen democracy of Nigeria. His record of passed bills is proof of vigor and determination to use the legislative body to make laws that will shape Nigeria's democratic space for many years to come. Little attention is paid to his successes as a Senate President.

However, modern democracy needs leaders to make policies and laws that create an environment where human rights and freedoms are respected and observed. Mr. Saraki championed a democracy where different leaders can cooperate and support each other instead of brewing enmity that hurts the public. Cooperation and respect for every institution, in his mind, were significant for improving public service delivery and bolstering good governance.

Saraki senate leadership

In previous pages, you must have come across the phrase "Saraki leadership." The context of this phrase is hinged on how he led Nigeria's senate. In the preceding topic, Dr. Saraki's perspective on Nigeria's democracy, I underscored his insistence on the independence of the legislature.

Here, let us delve deeper into his leadership at the senate. Because of his stellar performance and determination to keep the senate independent, he attracted aversion. In some scenarios, one would have expected him to be the President's "errand boy." But never was he obsequious. He is absolutely a man of principles. He treated the Senate with lots of decorum, but not without intimidations and forgery allegations coming his way.

President Buhari and his operatives wanted a man they can control, a senate president they could manipulate and use to sail their agenda through the Senate without scrutiny. Saraki did not budge. He never caved in, instead, he chose to stand firm and repelled the selfish gains that usually come with bootlicking failed regimes. He stressed to the executive that the National Assembly will exercise its independence and push for public interest. Is this not laudable? By withstanding tribulations and unending legal and political battles, Saraki remained indomitable. He remained unmoved, on course to move Nigeria forward. Very few people can fall out with the ruling party and still succeed in their mandate.

In some political tumult, some leaders can opt to pursue individual interests for political survival. Saraki was not that type of a gullible leader. He stood his ground to lead the senate in the right way. As a democratic leader, Mr. Saraki was invariably bipartisan; he was not biased at all. He gave every senator an equal opportunity as he fostered cooperation. It is collaboration and team building in the Senate that made it possible to pass 298 bills under his watch. As I said earlier, the seventh senate only struggled to pass a paltry 128 bills. We all agree that the buck stops with top leadership. With all due respect, it was Saraki's democratic governance or leadership that inspired those enacted laws. In any case, the Senate under Saraki focused on enacting laws that centered on democracy, security, and economy.

In many years to come, Saraki's laudable contributions to use his power as Senate president to enact laws will dominate national discussions. Democratic institutions in Nigeria are set to become stronger, courtesy of Saraki-led senate. For instance, in July 2017, senators passed the Whistle-blower Protection Bill. It was a critical bill that empowers Nigerians to disclose corrupt practices in either public or private companies. Other bills such as NASS Budget (OpenNASS) and FOIA (Freedom of Information Act), although passed after serious civil society activism, they are key in bolstering democratic institutions. The coming into effect of these bills will expand transparency and accountability in Nigeria. These important bills were passed immediately Mr. Saraki took office; he showed readiness to support any transparency reforms in the country.

Before Saraki, an institution like the National Assembly ran undisclosed budgets. The public was not in a position to know how a legislative body entrusted with the power to enact laws was spending its financial resources. Under Saraki's leadership, the situation changed and today, Nigerians can scrutinize the National Assembly (NA). Please, do not ignore that kind of magnificent achievement. Saraki did not oppose the release of the NA budget; instead, he supported all efforts that could make the senate transparent.

Saraki's vision for Nigeria's democracy and economy
Democracy allows a nation to grow its economy. It is a generally held notion that when a nation is democratically governed, people can work indefatigably to grow their economy. Saraki shared the same reasoning. Nigeria's economy has grown six-fold since the democratic government took overpower. It has facilitated development in Nigeria, even though some people may argue that a democratic government has hindered development or to a larger extent leaned towards rewarding political cronies. Amid differing perspectives whether democracy can fuel development or not, Nigeria has proved that it can. In the school of thought of democracy, it is capable of enhancing development. Saraki embarked on making laws that can create a favorable investment environment. Under his leadership in the Senate, Mr. Saraki oversaw the passage of Economic Priority Bills: The Company and Allied Matters Act (CAMA) and Investment and Security Act (ISA). These Acts are crucial in making Nigeria a democracy with a rapidly growing economy. Mr. Saraki believed that through CAMA and ISA, Nigeria was destined to become conducive for investments. When assuming the office of Senate president, Dr. Saraki indicated that his office was going to commit efforts to build the country's economy.

Conspicuously, this economy was not going to grow under a dictatorial regime, but under a democratic environment. In his official statement on Twitter about the two bills, Dr. Saraki claimed: "the core issue is still the issue of the economy; we need to get it right by creating jobs for our youths, more investments in the private sector, and empower our people through new opportunities. ISA and CAMA will help do this."

Many of the comments that followed this tweet were positive. This is an affirmation of support for Saraki's dedication to pushing for bills that will grow the economy. A performing economy will create jobs for the youth or generally the jobless. From the economic perspective, investors line up to pump their capital into a country that upholds democratic tenets. An economy is not likely to thrive in a dictatorial or authoritarian regime.

However, this is debatable, given that economies such as China, without a considerable level of democracy, have a remarkable economy. It does not rule out the fact that investors from Asia and the Western part of the world are investing in peaceful developing democracies in Africa. That said, it was under the leadership of Dr. Saraki that such significant bills came to the fore. As a leader that cares about the young generation, Dr. Saraki had to pursue avenues that could bolster the business environment. The benefits of these bills may not be felt immediately, but there is hope. Things will look up for the Nigerian youth seeking employment. In which way can a leader contribute to modern democracy than that?

In the current democratic societies, leaders grow democracy by making pro-public laws. It is because of this contribution that Saraki comes out as a strong fighter of modern Nigerian democracy. Dr. Saraki on several occasions urged leaders and all Nigerians to work hard to build a stable economy for the sustenance of democracy. When an economy is performing well and creating jobs for a majority of Nigerians it becomes feasible to sustain democracy.

Democracy and economic growth are proportionally related and affect each other. From a personal school of thought, democracy can be used to build an economy because it supports economic institutions. It attracts both domestic and foreign investments directly. A strong economy is equally needed to maintain democracy, and this is only possible through having the right people in a leadership position. Democracy has a price to pay, and selfish thinking cannot build a government to serve people through people. Despite Dr. Saraki's exceptional leadership in the upper legislative chamber, he sadly became a political reject, following the 2019 general election. With his democratic credentials, push to reposition Nigeria's economy and democracy through legislation, he lost his senate seat. He steps out of the political sphere as a man who fought for his people. Forlornly, his people saw nothing of that. He put his people first, and a sane person would not have imagined him missing out in the Nigerian power equation.

In his home Kwara State, he remains a former governor, medical doctor, and former Senate President and former senator. Everything is now former, though, for a little time, when the lion will roar again - mark my word he will be stronger. It is saddening. It is saddening to learn that he lost the bid to capture PDP's presidential ticket but ran to retain his Senate seat which he unfortunately lost. He wanted to continue representing Kwara Central District as a Senator and Senate President. All that came short. As Saraki left office, he got out of elective office with a fractured image. Allegations of corruption and forgery will follow him. In a pensive way, his loyalists and pundits can question why such a brilliant leader was rid of. Couldn't voters see the foundation he laid for Nigeria's economy and democracy by allowing and supporting the passage of critical bills?

All is not lost, as there is always next time. As tumultuous as his exit from the Nigerian power equation could be, there is still much to celebrate about Saraki as highlighted in the aforementioned pages. In terms of enactment of laws and strengthening of democracy, Saraki will always be applauded. He is sturdy. And deserves respect as a long-standing civil servant and democratic leader. His contribution to Nigeria's modern democracy, which is akin to the second liberation, is indelible. He is rich in ideas but denied power; he still ranks much higher than those with power but facing acute shortage of proper leadership.

CHAPTER 2

FEMI FANI-KAYODE

Femi Fani-Kayode is a familiar name, particularly, to Nigerians who understand the reforms in the Nigerian aviation industry. He is the man that led the industry open-mindedly. The reduced airplane disappearances and crashes in Nigeria are because of the transformation he brought into the department. I am old enough to know that Fani-Kayode is a dedicated leader. He is not perfect per se, but there is a lot that he has done to transform Nigeria. His contribution to the nation may not bother some people, but what is evident is the reformist nature in him.

I learned about Fani-Kayode during the reign of President Olusegun Obasanjo. It was during this time that Nigeria had come from a dark era of military leadership. This president had to bring in individuals with transformative minds. It was then that I came to learn about Fani-Kayode.

I remember his brief stint in the ministry of culture and tourism. During cabinet reshuffle, he was moved to the ministry of aviation. This was one ministry that was crashing, and urgently needed a right-minded person at the helm. The trust President Obasanjo had in Fani-Kayode is a testament of his transformational leadership. The country's aviation needed some radical changes, which could only be effected by a reformist that Fani-Kayode was.

I observed him lead and communicate his agenda. Although he was not an all-publicity-seeking leader, someone could feel his presence in the aviation ministry. Aviation being an area a majority of Nigerians do not bother about; we cannot ignore the fact that it is a crucial industry to our economy. Nigeria is a populous and large country; people have to fly from one state to another, from here to and fro other countries. We need to connect with the world and trade through air transport. Our air transport was in coma before this dedicated leader came to the office to bring change.

Any well-meaning leader will always do his job. That is seemingly the guiding principle of Fani-Kayode. When given a task to perform, he diligently does so. He is not a person interested in profiteering or getting into graft deals like a majority of leaders you see around with luxurious vehicles. This is a person concerned about his country, and people. Holding a public office requires nothing less than effective and efficient service delivery.

As I said above, Fani-Kayode made many changes in the aviation industry that reduced plane crashes and other challenges that bedeviled it. He landed at the aviation ministry following a minor cabinet reshuffle that saw him leave culture and tourism ministry. As a transformational leader, he, Fani-Kayode had to burn the middle night oil to restore efficiency in the ministry within the shortest time possible. He was up to the task, he moved with speed to put in place structures and safety measures to ward off loopholes that had led to plane crashes and mistreatment of Nigerian air travellers. As a loyalist of President Obasanjo, Fani-Kayode had his full backing as the aviation minister. Even though there were some persuasions that he bends the rules in favor of some powerful people, he went ahead to execute his agenda. This is one trait that puts him on a higher pedestal when it comes to integrity, a value that is missing fundamentally in government officials. We know our country has been unable to develop significantly due to lobbying and graft. There are some people in the system who do not want things to run smoothly. They will do whatever they can to keep the system skewed for their personal interests.

Fani-Kayode, a brilliant lawyer understands that a leader should put ahead public interest. Regardless of lobbying, intimidations and persuasions, a transformational leader will go with the agenda that will serve society in the best way. Prior to his coming to the ministry, air crashes were common in Nigeria, and this can be attributed to poor radar coverage. There was a project on radar coverage that had been stalled due to some personal interests. As a good leader, he went ahead to implement the project so quickly to safeguard air transport and airspace.

Knowing Femi Fani-Kayode

He may be a stranger to some, but a household name to many. Knowing him lays a basis on which we can all agree that this is a leader qualified to lead us in different fronts and as a matter of fact, my main knowledge of him is that he is a voice for the voiceless. Identity is an important phenomenon to my people. Nigerians like titles and they are proud of their backgrounds. This makes a case for telling those who do not know him, who exactly he is to our great country.

Fani-Kayode, born in Lagos to Victor Babaremilekun Adetokunbo Fani-Kayode. His father was a prominent figure in Nigeria towards and after our country gained her independence. His own great-grandfather was an Anglican priest, with an incredible educational background. He is a great grandson to Rev. Emmanuel Adedapo Kayode, who was lucky to study in England. His great grandfather also pursued his further studies from the University of Durham. Fani-Kayode hails from a family, where people knew the value of education. His own grandfather Victor Adedapo Kayode was educated in Cambridge University. It was there that he studied law, and later became a sought-out lawyer and judge. His own father equally studied at Cambridge University, where he was conferred with a degree in law. Fani-Kayode's father was a prominent political figure in the early years, when Nigeria was getting on the right footing after many years of colonial rule. His son, Femi Fani-Kayode pursued law as well. Law runs in this family, and this could be the motivation behind Fani-Kayode's decision to pursue the same career. It is commonplace in our society for children to pursue some careers to emulate their fathers or immediate family members.

Today, Fani-Kayode is a senior lawyer and he is sharing his knowledge and experiences with supporters through poems and essays. Fani-Kayode can now be identified as a politician, lawyer, essayist, and poet. He is a leader that is blessed, and his broad experience in public and private sectors has cultivated his imagination and worldviews. The essays and poems he wrote are thought provoking. They persuade his followers into developing a new way of looking at things. As a poet he looks into issues that undermine our efforts to be democratic. He understands that as a father he has to fight for a better country for his children.

I find this one interesting because sometimes many parents do not bother about the country, they leave behind. In the near future, I see a possibility of many Nigerian parents recognizing they should fight for a country they can leave us in. A good parent will fight for a better society that will offer their children opportunities and safety. Fani-Kayode is accepting that he has to utilize his knowledge and available resources to positively change Nigeria, so that his children can have a country that will support their dreams and ambitions. His law studies have been crucial in resolving conflicts in the country. Even though his own first marriage collapsed, I still find Fani-Kayode a man of family values, which drive him to lead to deliver positive change. As an educated man, has a realization that he has to use his education properly to empower his community, society, and the country. His own family looks up to him. Similarly, a considerable number of Nigerians still want him to play a role in shaping the agenda and development of their country. Fani-Kayode recognizes the obligation he has for his country, and many have witnessed him deliver in areas that he has served before. However, he has been a party hopper, something that has angered some individuals. Some people could view him as an ordinary politician seeking political survival, with little to offer to citizens. But let us be candid, people change their political positions sometimes when they realize the other side does not have a transformative agenda.

Fani-Kayode's political standing

At the end of 1980s, Fani-Kayode jumped into politics as a member of NNC (Nigeria National Congress), where he became a national youth leader of the party. His appointment to the position was due to his vibrancy and determination. However, at the turn of 1990, he shifted to NRC (National Republican Convention) to become its first national chairman. Within two years, Fani-Kayode had stamped his authority in Nigeria's politics despite the high-handedness of the military. He became an active player in Nigerian politics, but with potential threats to his life, he had to leave the country. After leaving Nigeria in 1996 following a polarized political atmosphere, he became a member of NADECO (National Democratic Coalition). The coalition was running its affairs from abroad, but with keen interest in Nigerian politics. Although the then military rulers could not give space for democracy to grow, the pro-change faces had to fight against autocracy tirelessly. The political atmosphere in the country was not bearable under General Sani Abacha, who trampled upon any opponent. Knowing that he could not win against the military junta, it was reasonable for Fani-Kayode to fly out of the country to mount a strong opposition against his tyrannical leadership.

When the civilian rule came into power, Fani-Kayode felt the need of coming back home. In 2001, he was with

President Olusegun Obasanjo. He worked for the president and became a prominent figure in his re-election bid in 2003. The inner circle of the presidential campaign team is never forgotten. After President Obasanjo's victory, Fani-Kayode became the minister for Culture and Tourism, before heading the ministry of aviation. Nevertheless, since President Obasanjo left office, Fani-Kayode went back to the private sector for legal practice.

Fani-Kayode's political journey has been a brilliant one. Nonetheless, he has never won a political office through an election. His decision to go back to legal practice, justifies his commitment to serve Nigerians in the corridors of justice. Shocking is the fact that he has not sought a political office since he served with the incredible President Obasanjo. There could be a reason underlying such a decision. With his boldness and constructive criticism of leaders, the expectation would be that he could seek a public office. That is not happening, but he seems to consider his legal practice as one way of delivering services to his people.

To be a leader, one does not necessarily have to hold a public office. Fani-Kayode certifies that assertion, by sticking to his legal practice. He must be happy serving Nigerians so that justice can be served. More important is that his voice still matters, and there are people who still look up to this great leader. It is possible that he can get into politics to seek a higher office to deliver his agenda to Nigerians. A great leader does not cow but will proceed to do what is good for the public. In his entire reign in the ministry, he tried to do what was right for Nigerians. He effected some reforms painstakingly, but he was still dragged into the mud.

He was accused of money laundering when he left office. The charges were brought to him by Economic and Financial Crime commission, but they were ultimately dismissed due to lack of evidence. There was no smoking gun in the charges, in some quarters it was considered to be intimidation and harassment of the former head of aviation ministry. The misappropriation of Aviation Intervention Fund, which he was accused of led the Senate committee on aviation to demand that he should not be allowed to hold public office for 10 years. However, things took a positive turn when he was acquitted of any wrongdoing in the ministry.

Running a public office is a test of integrity. In some scenarios, leaders that do not bend the rules to favor some individuals - big boys in street language, find themselves in difficult situations. Crimes against them can be cooked up to dirty their images and put them under unnecessary pressure through the corridors of justice. It was challenging for Fani-Kayode to pull through post his service in the aviation ministry, but what remains clear is that he is a leader of high integrity.

From what I have learned about Fani-Kayode I got no doubt that he is a good man with interests in serving Nigerians genuinely. Although he does not hold an elective office, there is a lot to admire from this great man. He is a person that Nigerians can rely on to defend them against any evil perpetuated by authority against them. Many Nigerians have lost trust in the country's leadership, but there is inspiration that some people like Fani-Kayode are committed to fighting for what is good for society. Through his legal practice he fights for justice and goes to any lengths to see justice is served in the country.

At present, Fani-Kayode is dedicated to creating public awareness, particularly on leadership. He is crisscrossing the country for political sensitization for his people to make right decisions and demand better leadership. He goes the whole hog to defend his people and seek unity in the country. He understands the deepening tribal differences that if left unattended, can plunge the country into animosity. His messaging is clear; people should fight for their freedoms not as tribesmen, but as Nigerians. That is the only sure way of vanquishing authoritarianism and progressing Nigeria's democracy. Being human, it is undeniable that he runs short of wisdom in some circumstances, but his reliability when it comes to serving the public is outstanding. Nigerians can bet on Fani-Kayode, who is willing to serve them despite the consequences. Going into the future, I see him become more committed to defending Nigerians and fighting for what is good for our society. He is a freedom fighter that will tirelessly, speak out for Nigerians and demand justice.

Fani-Kayode is your voice

Fani-Kayode has been trashed, threatened, and dragged through the mud for speaking and advocating for the truth. He speaks what the power-wielding figures in our country hate. The powerful elite loathe truth-tellers because they rub them the wrong way. They are a threat to their existence, underhand dealings. They want pushovers, and sycophants, which Fani-Kayode will never be. In several situations, we have witnessed this lawyer come to fight for us. He has spoken critically against the oppressors, and he gives us the power to hope for the best even in the worst of circumstances. He is a fighter for our rights and freedoms, and he is unmoved by critics. He is moving forward to fight for our rights, regardless of the many difficulties he is facing. You may have a different opinion on this, but I assure you that this is a voice for the many voiceless Nigerians. I like him because of how he stands for us. He is a shining example of a Nigerian politician, and he embodies democratic values that are critical for our success as a country. He is loud and emotional sometimes when things get out of order, but fortunately he knows where the fault lines are. He is the sort of fellow you will want in your camp when everything has come down to guttersnipe.

I insist that Fani-Kayode is a voice for us, who because of us, suffered in the hands of authorities that are bent on silencing him. This advocate has gone through torturous experiences for fighting for us. His own family has suffered; it has been subjected to psychological suffering. In an interview, Fani-Kayode raised fundamental questions that give us an insight into the challenges he is facing as he fights for the good of his country. Do you know what horrors my first wife Regina and my daughter Remi were subjected to by a PDP government? Do you know why they had to go into exile and live abroad? Do you know what hell my ex-wife Precious and first son Aragorn were subjected to by the APC government? Do you know the tears we shed secretly and the number of times we suffered and were forced to go underground for no just cause? Do you know the kind of stress and torment this put us through? Do you know that all our bank accounts were frozen for five years? Did all that stop me or stop us from standing? Did we not endure and bear it all with dignity for years and still continue to make our contribution to national affairs with zeal and passion?

These questions reflect the agony that Fani-Kayode has gone through as a family figure. His innocent family has been dragged into the dirty world of politics. All this has been done to him by the government, not because he has stolen. It is just for one reason. He is advocating for Nigerians who for an exceptionally long time have been neglected by the government that is supposed to serve them justly. It is difficult for a person with the interests of people at heart to keep mum, and this is what is causing all these troubles to Fani-Kayode. The persecution of his family and himself underscore the significant cause this man is pursuing. There is no way the government could harass him, if he is not a threat in any way. He is a threat, and the government is threatened by him, and that is the reason they feel he should be silenced through intimidations on his life and family.

The government cannot target people that dine with them, it targets the opponents. Fani-Kayode is viewed an enemy to a government that is oppressing its own people. Unfortunately, despite the selfless efforts by Fani-Kayode he is always abused and hated by some ordinary citizens he fights for. We have seen this great leader come to our defense and standing for solidarity for those who speak the truth. His persecution is because of Nigerians and should be respected as a freedom fighter.

Not a hair must fall from Kukah's head!
Chief Femi Fani-Kayode recently defended Bishop Kukah when the Muslim Solidarity Forum issued threats and give quit notices and ultimatums to Bishop Kukah. As a voice for the voiceless, Chief Fani Kayode said "It is most

disconcerting when a handful of mischievous, recklessly dangerous, and hopelessly misguided religious zealots and ethnic bigots that ought to know better like the Sokoto-based Muslim Solidarity Forum, issue threats and give quit notices and ultimatums to leading members of the Christian community like Bishop Matthew Hassan Kukah". This is disappointing and unacceptable and, if not handled properly, can lead to a major religious conflagration and crisis. I say this because Kukah is deeply loved by millions from all over the country, and the Christian community revere and adores him. The Muslim Solidarity Forum is seeking to undermine the great work that the Sultan of Sokoto has achieved in creating peace in the Caliphate between Christians and Muslims over the last few years.

I oppose those Muslims who issue such quit notices and threats against Christians and their fellow Nigerians, just as I am against any Christian or Christian group that issue quit notices and threats or give ultimatums to the Muslim community members. We must all learn to get on with one another and avoid any inflammatory language or unnecessary confrontations. I say this because Nigeria belongs to us all. No-one has the right to tell another to leave his territory simply because he delivered a sermon that sought to highlight the failings, dangers, and evil of the Buhari government. As a matter of fact, no-one has the right to ask his fellow Nigerian to leave his territory for any reason.

Human rights defenders like Chief Femi Fani Kayode are people who champion and fight for human rights of other people. They challenge brutality, oppression, and injustice in every part of the world, often risking their lives to expose abuses and hold powerful people to account, while supporting the survivors of human rights abuses. They are invaluable in creating a world where all of our human rights are respected - their efforts benefit all of us. Human rights defenders are defined foremost by their efforts to stop human rights abuses and make sure that everyone has access to their universal rights. They come from all walks of life. A defender's human rights work might be fulfilled through their job - they could be a community worker, lawyer, teacher, journalist, or activist working for human rights change. In this as before, Chief Femi Fani Kayode qualifies as both human rights defender, activist, and a voice for the voiceless.

As a Voice for the Voiceless, Chief Fani Kayode is not obliged to fall into decline. He is not obliged to be miserable. He has the right to be happy. The honest and true have a right to triumph. No wonder he despises the arrogant. Irrespective of their status or celebrity, they will remain strangers to a genuinely fulfilled life. He loves people who sincerely work on their continuing growth and development. How sublime it is to look up at the heavens and converse with the stars after a discussion meeting with the lowly and helpless people in our society, either on sweltering dry season nights, on cool nights, and on harmattan nights. His voice comes with, "I have won again today. I have savored life's essence".

Seeing those controlled by earthly desire succumb to the countless vices that plague society and be tossed by fate, Chief Fani Kayode knows with confidence that he stands on the victory tower of the greatest possible life. No wonder, Chief Fani Kayode says about himself: "I am a product of divine prophecy and a fulfilment of God's promise. I am the axe that cuts down the evil tree. I am the wind that parts the dark waters. I am the shining light that resists the terrors of the night. I am the warrior that never falters or falls in battle. I hate injustice and oppression. I am the servant of truth, the voice of the voiceless, and the champion of the oppressed. I am a King, and the royal blood of the Holy One of Israel flows through my veins. I am a conqueror, and the Holy Spirit of the Living God guides my steps. I am a deliverer, and the Lord of Hosts emboldens my heart and sharpens my sword. I am a living manifestation of the grace of God. I am a beneficiary of His manifold blessings, His love, kindness, and infinite patience and mercy. I am a favored son of the Ancient of Days, and it is my calling and destiny to affect His will. For this great commission, He lifted me up, and He forged me in the fire. For this noble cause, He taught my hands to fight and my fingers to war. I am a terror to tyrants and a friend to the subjugated.

I torment those that abuse power and that visit evil upon the innocent. I am a shield to the weak, an inspiration to the despised, and comfort to the vulnerable. I am a scourge to great and mighty dictators. I am an adversary to men of blood, and I am the defender of the righteous, the poor, and the persecuted. I am Oluwafemi, the Beloved of the Lord, the champion of the Highest, the favored of the King of Kings, and the son of the Alpha and the Omega. I am FFK, the one whose hand is strong and mighty and whose angels wax strong in battle. I am the Odum-Agu of the south, the one who has the heart and strength of the lion and the courage and soul of the tiger. I am the Odogwu N'agha of Christendom: the strange and mighty warrior who is covered by the blood of Jesus Christ and who fears no adversary in battle. I am David, the anointed: a mighty Prince of the Kingdom. I am irrepressible, indestructible, and unbeatable. None can stand against me. I am FFK: he that knows no fear and that bows before no man".

Though people may call him a nobody, he may be slandered and maligned, others may plot and scheme against him, through his powerful, overflowing prayers, he stands with dignity as an undaunted victor. How wretched is the smug? How pathetic the avaricious and dark-hearted? How horrible is the appearance of the fearful demons whose all-consuming jealousy drives them to seek others' downfall? In the words of Leo Tolstoy, "You can neither weigh nor measure the harm done by false people". No matter how such malevolent forces may try to torment or harass Chief Fani Kayode, he is filled to the very core of his being with supreme happiness. His life shines with an eternally youthful spirit. This fresh, vibrant spirit, burning with great, burgeoning energy, conquers the future's uncertainty. Continue brother. Always #SoroSoke.

⊷✢✢⊶

CHAPTER 3

SENATOR BEN MURRAY-BRUCE

S enator Ben Murray-Bruce, a man popularly christened "Common Sense" is a successful business magnate. Born February 1956 in the Nigeria's richest city, Lagos. Years later, he rose through the ranks to become a successful motivational speaker, entrepreneur, and politician. Through hard work and determination, he has tremendously succeeded in politics and business. He founded his own company, Silverbird Group and served in various companies as a director in the U.S.A, the UK, and France. He threw himself into the political arena when he ran for a gubernatorial seat to become Bayelsa State governor but was floored. Though he failed at his first attempt in politics, he did not lose determination to fulfil his political ambitions. He ran for senate in Bayelsa East Constituency in 2015 and won resoundingly.

Before joining politics, under his status and influence in the entertainment industry, he inspired people from all walks of life. His public speaking skills are top-notch, and his story of success is certainly something to admire. He is a man that inspires. He instils hope and encourages his audience to dream. Murray-Bruce knows how to have a better and prosperous society; the mindset of its members must first be changed. He stayed true to that belief. And manifestly, this was seen by his commitment to educate and inform Nigerians.

He has spoken at various auditoriums addressing a raft of issues on economy, politics, and entrepreneurship. Murray-Bruce has shared world stages with Leaders of Thought and substance, politicians, and other prominent individuals. It is no mean achievement to be allowed to speak at national and international events. But because Murray-Bruce has the interest of every member of society at heart, no event organizer could refuse to invite him. His message of hope and understanding of issues is what is required to empower the browbeaten in society.

This distinguished Senator, who doubles as a media mogul and statesman, is a player with a crucial role in empowering the Nigerian society. Democracy and good governance are easily realized when society is empowered. For society to overcome autocracy, it must be empowered. Leaders are not likely to mess up a country if the people they are leading are empowered. With that in mind, Mr. Murray-Bruce has been keen on empowering Nigerians and spoke inexorably about bad governance.

African leadership, for a long time in the post-independence period, has been frustrating. The ruling elite has been wielding power and amassing wealth at the chagrin of voiceless citizens. If there is something hard to achieve in Africa, evidently, it is a democracy. People have been weak enough to not stand up against greedy leaders. Successful personalities like Senator Murray-Bruce now feel that they are indebted to give a voice to the weak. In all certainty, motivating and inspiring give power to people. It makes them strong at the ballot.

Calling out Nigeria's poor planners for the economy
Although Nigeria has made fundamental progress since the end of the military rule, there is still a lot left undone. Progressive personalities in Nigeria accept this as true; that the country is capable of becoming a developed nation. It is feasible only if the democratically elected leaders consider themselves as servants as opposed to demigods. The rigidity and thoughtlessness of Nigerian leaders, unfortunately, are putting the country on the precipice. The incompetence and sycophancy displayed by the political class are what is ailing Nigeria and other African countries.

But all is not lost yet. Nigeria has recently witnessed the rise of gutsy figures like Senator Ben Murray-Bruce. They are calling out incompetent and ineffective leaders out to shape up or ship out. Murray-Bruce, a long-time and well-meaning critic of the government, is on record dressing down Nigeria's top leadership. In his informed perspective, these people we call leaders are naïve and unwilling to pursue change. Rather, they want to maintain the status quo than pursue a transformative agenda that benefits the entire society. For the many that follow him, on July 16, 2017, on his 112th episode of Common-Sense series that airs on YouTube, Murray-Bruce called on the government to restructure Nigeria. The episode gave intriguing information on the future of the Nigerian economy. The great Senator fore-sees this and says that less than 20 years from now, the larg-est economy in Africa would probably crumple if nothing were done to diversify it. This claim is the utter truth.

The world economy is changing. Technology is trans-forming economies. For a country to develop, it should equally adopt and support innovations. It is lamentable the Nigerian headship is not farsighted enough to steer the country in the right direction. When leaders do not open up their minds, it is within the obligation of influential peo-ple to pinpoint grave weaknesses and alert the public. As a Nigerian, I fully understand in this country how the elected leaders have taken for granted, the electorate. However, cir-cumstances are changing on account of influential persons of Murray-Bruce's stature to say enough is enough on this behavior. That is why Murray-Bruce spends adequate time to admonish a leadership that robs from the poor and goofs about.

Murray-Bruce never retreats but lays it on the line. It is the government ordinarily that determines, develops, and streamlines an economy. Government policies influence the economy. As things stand, Murray-Bruce is among the few transparent leaders. Genuine enough to say Nige-ria's federal government has not been swift and creative enough to revolutionize the country's economy. The rul-ing elite with the majority egocentric has instead put their interest in oil money. They do not give a hoot that soon the oil economy will be on its knees due to decreasing depen-dence upon it.

Let us face it. For many years, only a few people in Nige-ria have been amassing wealth so callously without minding about the future of the economy. It is this horrific leadership in Nigeria that has failed to recognize that soon, the country's economy that is dependent on oil risks going into coma. Lest restructuring, this economy is done, this oil-rich country stares at bankruptcy. As constituted today, the global economy is on a paradigm shift. The manufacturing industry for many decades has relied on fossil fuel. At present, the situation is changing as we are on a different trajectory that requires reforming the economy. The dependence on clean energy and the manufacturing of electric cars, according to Mr. Murray-Bruce, should be a wake-up call to Nigerian leadership. Conversely, because our current leaders are deliberate non-thinkers, it would be a tall order for them to plan for the future of the country. This is not just a claim, but a fact that any leader should not ignore.

Countries such as France have vowed by 2040, they would reduce significantly or eliminate petrol cars. Then again, manufacturing companies such as Tesla in the same vein are making electric cars to replace oil and gas reliant vehicles. Technology is fast revolutionizing the global economy and as a people, we must accept the truth. Nigeria has a great potential to have a better economy, without necessarily relying on oil. The Senator is confident, for this potential to be realized, the leadership must transform, be more visionary and ready to embrace change. However, going by his constant criticism of Buhari's administration, he believes the current crop of leaders seem not to think that the economy needs a shake-up. Instead, they want to thrive in an oligarch-like government where they control oil proceeds for self-enrichment. They do this without any vision and mission for the country.

Murray-Bruce as a bold leader is speaking directly to a leadership that is resistant to change. Having plucky people who can openly disapprove of bad governance and encourage it to take a positive turn is all that Nigerians urgently need for a prosperous country. A few people cannot be allowed to thrive and put the lives of many at risk. To have social justice, equity and democratize Nigeria, the famous senator notes, it requires political goodwill and an aggressive overhaul of bad leaders. The political will and people-centered vision are generally absent in Nigeria's executive arm of government. Murray-Bruce does not have to speak to the government to move with speed to restructure its economy to avoid going bankrupt if there is good governance. The absence of a people-focused government is what exasperates any well-intentioned people like Murray-Bruce.

Some individuals may think that this statesman throws barb at the government because of his political affiliation. In actuality, assailing the government for obvious reasons like failing to provide proper leadership needed to rebuild, reorganize, and transform Nigeria into a green economy is constructive criticism. It hurts to observe the government not using common sense. It is common sense that, for the Nigerian economy to be sustainable, the federal government should be at the heart of transformation and embrace change.

As a member of the People's Democratic Party, a major opposition party, Murray-Bruce is a sober leader. He does not allow political affiliation to rob him of rational thinking. From his standpoint as an entrepreneur, he wishes his country rebuilds and redefines its economy. He does not condemn the government for no reason, but because he feels the government is not level-headed, as it is presently constituted, to bring change.

What is happening in Nigeria is a replica of the events occurring on the African continent. In Africa, systems of government and reforms have always hit a snag owing to corruption and selfishness. Corruption has been a monster that has rendered Nigerian leaders unreasonable and senseless. They no longer reason beyond themselves but are much absorbed in stealing public resources rather than in policymaking. Murray-Bruce has decried corruption and bad governance for they are the primary source of the problem. It is most improbable for the corrupt to accept change, which most likely can put them in trouble. This forward-thinking leader has been unhappy for the inflexibility of Nigerian political leaders to transform the country. It is hardly clear for myopic and corrupt leaders running the government to accept that the global economy in a few years to come will depend on electric cars and clean/solar energy. Those who for many years have benefited from the oil economy through dubious ways are resistant to embracing a diversified economy for fear of losing oil money.

In his own words, Murray-Bruce has come out so visibly posit that it will only require one leader to transform the Nigerian economy. A critical analysis of this claim exposes the current leadership of the country as non-innovative and visionless. That one leader the media mogul is referring to is the President. He sees President Buhari as a rudderless leader that plans less on how to diversify the economy to match up the ongoing transition to a green economy. This is a leader that is convinced that it is not rocket science to take Nigeria forward, on account that the country only needs progressive policies and commitment. These policies will be developed by the brainy.

Plausibly, to develop and progress requires progressive policies. However, Murray-Bruce, a truth-teller, thinks Nigeria is not likely to progress because of bad policies, rotten leadership, and negative ethnicity. When the government hires people based on ethnicity and religion at the expense of merit, the best brains are likely to be lost. The bad brains will certainly be hired because merit does not matter. The bad brains are not a think tank that is committed to proposing and directing the economy of Nigeria. The consequence of this is visibly retrogression.

The criticism that Senator Murray-Bruce directs at the government of Nigeria is not treasonous. This is a man that truly and patriotically loves his country. He wants the best for his country. It is the state of affairs in the republic that he detests. He wishes that the present leadership transforms the economy and strengthens institutions. If that is done, Nigeria will realize its abilities and develop fundamentally. That is healthy for democratization efforts in the country. When all sectors of the economy are functioning effectively, every citizen will be blissful. Murray-Bruce is right to throw salvos at such an administration whose President cannot seek health services in his own country, instead, flies out to a foreign country.

In furtherance, Murray-Bruce asserts that building Nigeria can be achieved by exploiting our prospects rather than relying on foreign aid. Sad to mention, African leaders including that of Nigeria have since independence relentlessly relied on foreign aid. They overlook the fact that when they put systems in order, their economies shall be self-sufficient. The foreign aid which the Western nations donate is meant for development, unfortunately, observers note that it is a reliable source of wealth for the governing elite. By stealing foreign aid, the corrupt elite perpetuate poverty, authoritarianism, and hopelessness in the continent for self-fulfillment. According to Murray-Bruce, this needs to stop. The big question is: how? Possibly, by electing creative and selfless leaders that are dedicated to serve people altruistically.

For Nigeria to be awake from self-induced slumber where warlords and corrupt leaders enrich themselves to a point of crippling their home economy, leadership has to change. I have never seen a leader that is so angry at bad leadership like Murray-Bruce. Really! The reason he pillories bad governance is that he comprehends that Nigeria can only exploit its potential with good leadership. The only hindrance to achieving the Nigerian Dream is bad governance. The country is in the hands of leaders who are obsessed with power, not good governance. Murray-Bruce does not just trade meaningless accusations. He speaks to Nigerians and their leadership. It is time that citizens agree that the development, employment, and full democratization they so anxiously desire, need good governance. The Senator's simple choice of the title "Common Sense Revolution" in his published book is a disclosure that as a country, Nigeria does not need to seek foreigners to develop her economy.

Foreign support, not necessarily financial, nonetheless is indispensable. But leaders ought to use common sense. It is common sense that, diversifying the Nigerian economy and fast-tracking efforts to shift to a green economy, is unavoidable. It is something that the National Assembly, the executive and other agencies in the country should cozy with. Unexpectedly, there is less willingness to accept change. The situation may be sad today in the Federal Republic of Nigeria because of unhinged leadership. As a hopeful leader and entrepreneur, Murray-Bruce is confident that with time things will look up. It is this "vicious" though healthy criticism of the Nigerian government that will awaken citizens to make informed decisions at the ballots in the future. As an advocate of good leadership, Murray-Bruce justifies his criticisms as constructive.

Pathetically, a lot of Nigerians toady and pour praises on a leader that is taking his country to the dogs. Constructive opponents against Buhari's administration and other leaders attest to Mr. Murray-Bruce's love for Nigeria. He was not simply criticizing, but he did so with a purpose. As an individual that wants his country to be better and to lift most people from poverty, it was justified to express disapproval of incompetent leaders. This is a bloke that wants greatness for his country. He is a leader that speaks honestly without any fear. He laments the direction the country is taking. At some point, he was saddened by the fact that his own country is pushing more people into extreme poverty. The solitary reason that is happening, is due to ineffective leaders who are not using their power to empower Nigerians.

Holding power as a public office holder, demands that a leader improves lives of citizens. This is a dream that Murray-Bruce lives on. It is unacceptable that leaders flaunt wealth while their compatriots cannot afford basic needs. The senator blows up when he imagines that the current leaders are so callous to live sedentary lifestyles at a juncture the masses are mired in abject poverty.

Good economy and socio-economic pillars of democracy
I am saying this for the umpteenth time; democracy is not confined only to freedoms like speech, expression, and voting. It is about socio-economic empowerment. It is improbable for a country stuck in extreme poverty to promote democracy. After all, and the question is: what kind of democracy does the mendicant populace want? Poverty is not a tenet of democracy, but it is its undoing. The efforts by Murray-Bruce to advocate for good leadership are keen on strengthening Nigeria and her people through economic democracy.

Political scientists agree that economic development facilitates countries to become democratic. When people have better lives and the economy favors everyone, immoral vices like corruption which are obstacles to democratization, can be tackled head-on. There is vast literature to support this possibility. Yet, powerful dissenters always suppress such discussions. They argue that there are exceptions where countries have a good economy, but democracy is elusive. And contend that one cannot repress the truth or research findings that point to a good economy and socio-economic empowerment as pillars of democracy.

Authoritarian states like Russia are strong economies worldwide. People are empowered, yet their freedoms are limited. President Vladimir Putin, a strongman silences all dissenting voices and even recently argued that in the Western nations, people are rejecting liberal values. Perhaps using this example, a dissenter of this school of thought that a good economy does not promote democracy can have ground to sustain a debate. Nonetheless, in Russia, there are opposition leaders and citizens that are yearning for their human rights and freedoms. Long-time when President Putin is gone, there is a high chance the situation will change. The point here essentially is that good economy and socio-economic empowerment that Senator Murray-Bruce fights for can set a stage for mature democracy in Nigeria.

"It cannot be forgotten." A tweet with a tinge of cynicism, Murray-Bruce lamentably claimed, "The fastest growing business in Nigeria is poverty and the second-fastest-growing is corruption." This mirrors a society that is benefiting a few people while the majority helplessly gazes at poverty. A hungry and poor society is vulnerable to political manipulation and conmanship. Tellingly, African leaders have subjected their people to unending poverty, benefiting from the very series of crises that befall citizens. Hopelessness and poverty have been used as a cudgel to silence society so that the mighty in the ruling class can plunder public resources at their comfort. The degeneration into extreme poverty in Nigeria, which ultimately can widen further the gap between the haves and have-nots, will weaken the ongoing calls for a strong democracy. That is why Murray-Bruce is emerging so powerfully to push for a strong economy and poverty alleviation. Within the tenure of corrupt leaders and dictators, people can become vulnerable and defenseless. But here in Nigeria, influential people like Murray-Bruce are wholeheartedly advocating for a better and diversified economy. He does this not for self-interest; it is for the sake of democracy. He is seizing the opportunity to point out the wrongs within the government, but nobody is recognizing such efforts.

It is no wonder, therefore, that a poor citizenry is weak to demand political accountability and respect for the rule of law. African leaders have mastered the art of impoverishing to rule. With a poorly doing economy, many Nigerians will be jabbed into penury. In a state of pennilessness, it will be beyond the realms of possibility for the poor to hold their leaders accountable. Poverty weakens not only the physical body but also the psychological wellbeing of an individual. With knowledge of how African leaders use poverty to weaken citizens, Mr. Murray-Bruce has come out to assail such ploys.

In retrospect, Patrick Lumumba, a professor of Public Law and distinguished lawyer and Afro-optimist from Kenya, once underscored (in a speech delivered at the close of Ceremony of African Congress of Accountants) the vision of Africa early post-independence leaders. He noted that Kwame Nkrumah wanted a United Africa, warning that if that were not achieved, colonizers would confuse African leaders and disunite people. He goes ahead to assert that the colonizers indeed confused Africa. The African leaders have been using this line of thought blaming colonizers or Europeans so to speak about the problems ailing Africa. Nevertheless, Professor Lumumba sees this as a diversionary tactic because, for more than 50 years, it is illogical for African leaders to boldly blame foreigners for lack of fruits of independence. The African leaders are apportioning fault to escape political and economic accountability. In truth, with this line of thought, they are describing Africa as rising. Some describe it as a sleeping giant. Some would call it, resource-endowed continent. With lofty expressions, some shameless African leaders do not want to take responsibility for poverty, dictatorship and slowly performing economies. There is no way a continent can be a sleeping giant for more than a half-century.

Having known the trickery employed by African leaders to scapegoat their failure on colonizers, Senator Murray-Bruce has been insistent on demanding actions that will improve the Nigerian economy. He understands that some visionless African leaders only want to seat in office and enjoy the trappings of power as bestowed by their positions without caring about the masses they lead. Any voice that offers constructive criticism is as a rule suppressed. But in the new dispensation of Nigeria, people like Murray-Bruce will not go silent. He castigates non-performing leaders, not to disparage them, instead to help them get their act together. For instance, he has gone the whole hog to describe President Buhari as a health tourist. This is on account of Buhari seeking treatment in a foreign country after failing to elevate his own country's public healthcare system to London's standard.

Nonetheless, his vicious challengers and sycophants of the ruling elite are coming with well-crafted language armed with statistics that, it is poor prices of oil that are pushing people into poverty in Nigeria. This is a trick to blindfold the public so that it does not place responsibility on the government. It is a big cover-up or a cursory explanation to persuade the vulnerable society to accept the situation while their leaders loot hardheartedly.

Murray-Bruce is a man among the few pro-change and people-focused leaders that educate and empower the public tirelessly. As he dismantles propaganda and opposition, he encourages citizens to be keen on salvaging their economy from plunderers. This economy has to be saved from imminent bankruptcy. This is not done with self-centeredness. It is done with one primary objective of streamlining an economy to lay a foundation necessary to advance Nigeria's democracy. Senator Murray-Bruce intelligibly understands a developed economy and empowering people economically is paramount in promoting democracy.

Murray is fully in accord that directing efforts at rebuilding an economy will fruitfully fortify democracy. However, he asserts that corruption, which is a growing business, is also a stab in the back. Corruption flourishes when leaders are openly callous. As a monster as it is, graft must be slain and removed from us. It is a sad state of affairs for leaders whether in the National Assembly or Executive to oversee graft and perhaps be direct beneficiaries. It is no secret that a majority of political leaders not just in Nigeria are crafty. They participate in massive corruption as a way of self-enrichment. For many, the very essence of holding public office is to plunder public coffers; not to be servant leaders.

However, Murray-Bruce believes that there are other genuine ways of becoming rich. He is on record as saying; "it is possible to create wealth in a genuine way". This assertion is well established in the introduction. Murray-Bruce is a business magnate and wealthy, not through corruption. He has been able to create his wealth through his companies like Silverbird Group. With him as a perfect example, it is time that the African leadership becomes innovative to create honest wealth. By stealing from the public, literally those who pilfer, cripple the economy and democracy.

Going forward, Murray-Bruce who did not seek re-election in the 2019 general election is focused on using his influence to empower his followers. There is a lot he can do, not necessarily by being in the senate. The ex-senator is not taking a softer line but is going to punch harder until that time when poverty and corruption are defeated. He is still determined to influence public policy, defend democracy and drum up for it. However, whatever the case may be, let it be remembered that this is Nigeria. This is Africa where leaders are manipulative. Citizens should not cow but should join Murray-Bruce, and likewise, celebrate him for protecting their country from dictators and looters. From this time forth, citizens should also, and always, elect good leaders, probably like Senator Murray-Bruce. If that is done Nigeria will self-assuredly be a flourishing and legitimately democratic country as Senator Ben Murray-Bruce envisages.

CHAPTER 4

AISHA BUHARI

The First Lady of Nigeria, Mrs. Aisha Buhari, in 2016 caught my attention when she picked on her husband, President Buhari, accusing him of poor governance and incompetence. She surprised many with the disapproval of her husband's administration, leadership, and performance. She joined many Nigerians who were not pleased with the way her husband was running the country then. Let us quickly refresh our memories with the BBC interview that Mrs. Buhari had a year after her husband assumed office. In it, she lamented that the President's government had been hijacked by some "few individuals." She said the President did not know the large portion of the people that are administering the government. In other words, she was referring to those that are working for him. To be exact, in the BBC-Hausa interview with Naziru Mikailu, Mrs. Buhari stated: *"The president does not know 45 out of 50 of the individuals he*

delegated to the government affairs". She does not have any acquaintance with those people either, despite being his wife of 27 years. She further said: *"people who did not share the vision of the ruling party, the All-Progressives Congress (APC) were as of now, named to top positions of the administration because of some "influential people" in the administration. That some people plunk down in their homes, with their arms folded, just for them to be called to come and head an organization or a ministerial position."*

Mrs. Aisha Buhari also uncovered the huge money extortion in her husband's government. Responding to the analysis of misrepresentation on the N500 billion meant for social investment programs (SIP) of the government. Mrs. Buhari said the SIP failed in nearly all parts of the country, mostly in the northern states. Mrs. Buhari challenged the special adviser to the president on Social Investment Programs, Mrs. Maryam Uwais, of incompetence in her duty. *"I was anticipating that the N500 billion should be used in various methods and for the purposes it was intended to accomplish. I don't have the foggiest idea about the technique they used to utilize the money, yet the greater part of the northern states didn't get it"*. She spoke. *"Possibly it worked in some certain states in the country. In my state, out of the twenty-two local governments, it was only one that benefitted. I did not ask what happened and I would prefer not to know, nonetheless, I can say that it failed woefully in Kano. More demoralizing is that the said funds were intended for the welfare of the poor people in the country of whom Mr. President had consistently professed to speak for or represent in the government."*

Shockingly, these poor Nigerians have been waiting endlessly for the social investment program that was guaranteed to them by President Buhari, just to have their expectations dashed as the money provided for the program was stolen according to the revelation of Mrs. Buhari. Mrs. Buhari's choice to open up to the world about her worries stunned many individuals, both in the nation and worldwide. Yet it demonstrates the degree of discontent with the President's administration. To be sincere on this, it is her fundamental right of choice to make these significant facts open to the public. As the President's spouse, she was determined to see her husband serving Nigerians equally, instead of serving the interests of a few. Also, as a member of the party and a citizen of the country, she has the obligation and the right to be the whistle-blower for her compatriots. We should not overlook also that Mrs. Aisha Buhari campaigned vivaciously for Mr. President in the 2015 race, as she organized various town hall gatherings with women and youth associations across the nation. So, she is no doubt, a key stakeholder.

It was a significant blow to Mr. Buhari who has been known as an intense, no-nonsense person. Mrs. Buhari still remembered the yesteryears of glory her husband had when he was military head of state. How the Army carried out a coup in 1983 and General Muhammadu Buhari became the head of the nation and ran an authoritarian regime. General Buhari returned looted state assets; executed drug dealers caught and sent soldiers to the streets with whips to enforce traffic regulations. I still remember what he did to save the Nigeria's economy from the decreasing oil prices that happened within his 20 months in power. That was when Nigerians were saying that foreigners were depriving them of work. The reaction to that was when Mr. Buhari and the late Idiagbon regime ordered an estimated 700,000 illegal immigrants out of the country. Have we overlooked how he treated his administration or govern-ment workers who showed up late to their workplaces, how they had to perform squats or frog jump?

So, when President Jonathan was running a dysfunc-tional kind of regime that made some Nigerians sick at the time. Or do not you remember the growing corruption in the Jonathan administration! The Boko Haram syndrome under Jonathan's administration! Now, to have someone like Mr. Buhari, a man known with his image of honesty and strictness–for all intents and purposes, was what the country needed as a savior at that time. Furthermore, his experience in the military was viewed as significant in the battle against Boko Haram. This made Nigerians to troop out in high numbers to vote in Buhari "to save Nigeria and Nigerians from the dungeon that Dr. Jonathan put us".

And now, to have seen a man of such high caliber to have used his first four years as the president to consoli-date his tribe alone was an embarrassment to me and I think same for Mrs. Buhari. Well, I still believe in him. Old soldier, they say, never dies. Maybe his giant will wake up this time around. And use his remaining four years to wipe out those embarrassments and at the same time saving the Mendicant populace. We need someone like him to help us out of our present abyss. Nigeria is in trouble. Compare to Nigeria of yesteryears; what a hell is this! Look at Ghana and Rwanda for Christ's sake. Only the erudite will see the wisdom in Mrs. Aisha's behavior. She is our mother; I doff my cap to her.

Mrs. Buhari was provoked to stand up with an end goal of ending those hegemonistic practices of some selfish individuals in the government so that the party followers, who contributed so immensely to the president's election victory, could profit from their good deed. Nonetheless, as the closest individual to the President, she must have exhausted all opportunities before reprimanding the president in the media. This caught the attention of political analysts because this was something extraordinary in the Africa context, where such behavior from women is considered unorthodox. Bearing in mind what is generally known of First Ladies in different countries of the world; her act sets her apart and will be remembered for good. First Ladies, accordingly, are supposed to support their husbands even if they disagree politically. In some instances, First Ladies assume a low profile to avoid being dragged into making statements in public that will seem disagreeable with their husbands who are occupying the highest office. The remarks of Mrs. Buhari must have marked the defining moment for an administration that has unmistakably attempted to manage the economic recession of the country and the growing restlessness within the ruling party.

Let me bring this closer a bit. Conventionally, a husband would expect his wife to support him unconditionally especially in public. In the case of Mrs. Buhari, she went against the grain to assail the leadership of her husband, who she bears his name anyway. I am cocksure, it surprised you as well. Without doubt, her entire family is in APC and she is supposed to be a behind-the-scenes policymaker. If her husband is someone that listens to her at the same time, she seems to be reminding her husband of his promises to Nigerians and the world, that; "I don't belong to anybody; and I belong to everybody." Anyway, I would not dwell so much on how Mrs. Buhari's reaction shocked people like me. However, let us be insistent on how important she has been at holding her husband accountable by daringly pinpointing his weak spots in the handling of the affairs of the country. All said and done, I would like to recommend to the first lady to direct her attention at supporting female education which, from my perspective, is one of the problems in Nigeria especially the northern part of the country. If properly done, it will take Nigeria forward immensely.

Our eyes in the presidency

First, I would like to make it crystal clear that Mrs. Buhari is an independent thinker who has the right to express her opinions as she wishes. With that in mind, her decision to assail her husband's administration should be looked at objectively so that we do not lose the basis for her protest against the APC-led government. Therefore, I would not expect anyone to think that the action to protest was meant to undermine or disrespect her husband; rather, it was to expose the cabal in her husband-led government. It was in no way a sign of a wife disrespecting her husband or a sign that she is in the opposition party. As far as this is concerned, I strongly believe that she understands her husband better than anyone else. This should lead us to conclude that when she speaks against his administration, it does not mean that she views him as completely weak; it is only that she thinks that the president needs to roll up his sleeves and fulfill the pledges he made to Nigerians in 2015.

In retrospect, the Niger Delta debacle and Boko Haram palavers are problems that the Buhari administration inherited. But since it promised to solve them forthwith, we trusted the president. As we have observed, the very challenges that the president was trusted to resolve, including the ravaging farmer-herders' crises, are still facing us till now, making people more disillusioned than before. Ethnic restiveness, growing violence, shedding of innocent blood everywhere in the country, corruption and hopelessness are becoming more ingrained in our livelihoods. It seems that the president does not have a clue on how to solve those problems facing the country. Mrs. Buhari also became disillusioned like any other Nigerian who voted for President Buhari with the optimism of a dazzling future. We all trusted him to be a man that will reinforce our democracy and tackle head-on insecurity. As he took over from President Goodluck Jonathan, we grinned everywhere with our eyes set on a bright future. The glittering future seemed closer because we thought President Buhari, as we knew him previously, was the solution to our problems. Our hopes to restore security re-emerged and the fight against corruption was reignited. Insecurity and corruption were gradually washing down against the sanguinity that we cultivated for so long after a transition to democratic governance. Quintessentially, Mr. Buhari's coming to power at first made us feel that things were going to change, but months afterward, we learned that he was not ready for the country, but for his close friends-sad indeed. In consequence, our hopes have been shattered and we shared a common feeling with Mrs. Aisha Buhari that the president has seemingly turned against the very people he promised to serve selflessly when he took the reins of power in 2015.

When you hold high hopes and trust in someone, such expectations are generally high. That was the case of Nigerians then. Aisha believed that her husband would stick to the promises he made to Nigerians and work for them assiduously. Conversely, that was not the case in President Buhari's first term. That was what prompted Aisha to take up issues with her husband. It was the right thing to do as the first lady or mother of Nigerians who has the interest of the masses at heart. Even though the consequences of her utterances against the president were undisclosed, it remained evident that Nigerians were angry at their President. Having a first lady speak publicly against her husband shows how she cares about her fellow citizens. Even though her husband downplayed her public eruptions, the message was delivered. I remember while in Germany with his host Chancellor Angel Merkel, journalists raised the question regarding overt criticism of President Buhari by his wife. His response was tragic. Instead of the President giving a plausible response, he disparagingly asserted that "she belongs to my kitchen and my living room and the other room." This response was beneath the office of the President, even if some people treated it as humor. There is nothing humorous here. What I see here is what I can describe as downplaying some critical issues his wife was raising.

Publicly, the president underestimated the First Lady's outbursts. I am persuaded to think that he must have pensively taken the point that things are not good on the ground. I think the president wanted to bring an abrupt end to a debate about what his wife was complaining about. However, there was this imperative point that Mrs. Buhari raised that I think must have woken up the President conceivably to get him serious on his job. His wife claimed that her husband was not in total control of his government, something that is deplorable and points to why he is failing. If the president does not know his appointees very well, it is something that should worry citizens. It means the person they elected as their leader is not competent enough to call the shots. This was a powerful assertion that helped Nigerians draw great insights into why President Buhari turned out to be a turncoat on the very people who trusted him the most. This revelation is a direct indictment of the President who knowingly or unknowingly, allowed powerful and influential individuals in his cabinet (tagged "the cabal") to run the government against his own will, and against the interests of Nigerians.

This elite minority does not have the will of the people in mind at all, and it is the one that I think strangled Buhari's efforts to constitute an effective government throughout his first term in the office. Since this did not happen, these appointees, who most likely represent the few people, failed the President and the country in its entirety. They felt that they were not accountable to the President, but themselves or their ethnic groups.

Empowerment of women and helping the Boko Haram victims was of utmost interest to Mrs. Buhari and Nigerian women. She promised to stand and fight for that rather than pamper her husband who unfortunately allowed 'conmen' to manipulate his first-term leadership. She preferred being called "Wife of The President" to "First Lady", perhaps because she did not want to get involved in the drama that Nigerians were treated to by Buhari's government. Being the First Lady is not merely a title, but it makes one feel that they have a responsibility to the country. Given that the Buhari administration was compromised from the onset, it was implausible to be part of it. If you believe that your vision and aspirations can be shattered by a certain selfish group of people, it is reasonable to do things that one considers valuable and transformational in society that will be positively remembered after you.

Her earlier delinking from the Buhari-led government and criticism affirms the left, right and center assertions that the once tough and ready-to-perform President had been cornered. When you have a First Lady who does not mince her words and believes in truth-telling, it allows the citizenry to understand the Presidency inside out. Behind the scenes, she must have tried to persuade her husband into focusing on the agenda that will benefit Nigerians. Since the president became compromised and succumbed to the persuasion of the establishment, it was reasonable to go public to disclose his government's inadequacies. As First Lady, Aisha is obligated to protect her husband against those handlers she thinks are harmful to the President's success. It is in that line that I think she had the honorary obligations to caution her husband in the appointment of great and credible citizens into his cabinet. She was right to be angry. It is only fair to speak out when she sees that there is something wrong happening while her husband does not take stern action that could restore order.

First Ladies do not need to hold public offices to influence policymaking in their husbands' administrations. It is in this spirit that Mrs. Buhari chose to attack the administration for undermining party democracy through tampering their primary purposes and failing Nigerians. Her husband as a party leader should have focused on implementing the party's manifesto and committed to serving the people. Aisha believed so much in serving Nigerians because she held a belief that her husband was the solution to the problems the country was facing. On this basis, I would always consider Aisha as a voice for the voiceless for speaking against misgovernment by her husband and his appointees on behalf of Nigerians.

It is clear that Mrs. Buhari stands for good leadership and service to the people. In her view, it was wrong for the President to promise people that he would tackle nepotism and corruption whilst appointing visionless and corruptible people to government. This kind of criticism ignites the impetus for people to hold their leaders accountable for whatever they do in office. Mrs. Buhari energized us to ask the government to do what is right. In fact, in 2016 she vowed that if her husband could not change tact, she was going to withdraw her support in his 2019 re-election bid. Fortunately, for the president, his wife supported his re-election by informing Nigerians that her husband is going to come back forcefully in his second term to fight poverty, corruption, nepotism, insecurity and to support the young men and women of the country in their bids for employment in the next term.

Time will tell. Perhaps President Buhari will save his face, image, and his tomorrow from those apparent failures in his first term. Probably this time around the few men who Aisha believed caged and emasculated her husband, making it hard for him to perform greatly to the expectation of Nigerians, will not be allowed to influence the appointment and the government affairs this second term. It is now upon the president to decide to be in charge of his government and correct his mistakes by nurturing democracy, eradicating poverty, rescuing the economy from imminent recession, tackling corruption and to restore security. If that is done, Mrs. Buhari and all Nigerians would possibly be a happy lot.

Legacy is on empowering society through women education

Now, if the First lady, Aisha Buhari is committed to empowerment of Nigerian women and the youth, she should seize this opportunity to promote female education more than anything else. Girls in the north and south have equal abilities, and education is the only tool that will level the playing field for them. The northern part of the country has girls with huge abilities whose potentials can only be realized through education. The First Lady should champion the cause in her husband's last term female education, particularly in Northern Nigeria. Doing so will leave an indelible mark on her history as someone who used her position to empower women in the country through education.

Let me take you down memory lane a bit, perhaps to put to perspective reasons why female education should be something of urgency by our First Lady before her husband leaves office. Commonly, men and women can be compared to two sides of a coin - without one, the other cannot exist. They help each other in the circle of life. A child's education starts with his or her mother at home. Indira Gandhi argues, *"When you educate a man, you have educated an individual, yet if you educate a woman, you have educated a whole family."* Along these lines, education ought to be given to both men and women in equal measure. Further, women are the mothers of generations and if they are denied education in a society, future generations will be uneducated as well. For this reason, the Greek warrior, Napoleon, once pointed out that *"give me a few educated mothers; I shall give you a heroic race."* In the past, it was a social and basic practice for women not to get any education whatsoever. They are, for the most part not permitted to venture out of the four walls of their homes. Domestic works were essentially their portion throughout their entire life, then.

Surprisingly, in some parts of the world, men just do not like the idea that women should be educated like them. This should be considered a global problem that we must confront as a people if we have the determination to make the world a better place. It is an undeniable truth that in Nigeria, Boko Haram's terrorist agenda is to see that no child, mostly women in Northern Nigeria gets an education. They specifically loathe the idea that women are going to school to acquire education which according to them is evil and immoral. You will wonder where such kind of reasoning emanated from, given that a society without education cannot make any substantive development. We cannot innovate or offer any skilled labor without education and it is ridiculous to view education as something evil or a thing for men alone. Sadly, some people or communities in our country have no sense of the value that education offers to our society.

Let me make this one considerably basic: if women are educated, they can solve their household problems by themselves. Imagine a scenario where working men with families become handicapped in unfortunate accidents. In that situation, the complete burden of the family rests on the women. To meet this exigency, women should be educated and employed in different spheres. Women can work as teachers, doctors, lawyers, and administrators and in other careers that are largely dominated by men. It is presently accepted that women's education can be useful in eradicating numerous social ills at any known point. Education helps people in every society to guarantee their privileges and to understand their potential in the political, economic, and social fields.

Education is known to be the best single most dominant approach to lifting society out of poverty, but such society must include women to enjoy its full value. Education assumes an especially important role in society. Mrs. Buhari is an intelligent leader and fully understands and acknowledges that education is a fundamental right that no woman should be denied. Fundamentally, it ought to be an inherent piece of any procedure to address the sexual orientation-based discrimination against women and girls that remains prevalent in many societies. The accompanying connections will further clarify the need for women's education. It is universally known that everybody has the right to education; this has been recognized since the Universal Declaration of Human Rights (UDHR) in 1948. The right to free and compulsory primary education, without discrimination, has been reaffirmed in all major international human rights conventions. A significant number of these equivalent instruments encourage, yet do not ensure post-essential education. These rights have been additionally explained to address issues like quality and equity, pushing ahead the issue of what the privilege to education implies and investigating how it very well may be accomplished. At the minimum, states must guarantee that fundamental education is accessible, adequate, and adaptable for all.

We should ensure that girls in the north have access to education as other girls in the southern part of Nigeria and in the western world. As we consider the benefits of education, we must not lose sight on our culture and tradition. Some cultural and traditional practices stand between girls and their prospects for education. These lead to missed opportunities later on in life. Improving educational opportunities for girls and women create skills that enables them to make informed choices and impact community change in their society.

Another reason behind denying women and girls their entitlement to education is that those in power dread the powers that women will possess through education. There is still some protection from the possibility that young ladies or women in general can be trusted with education. Education evokes a few apprehensions. And now with globalization, the fear turns out to be considerably bigger to the loss of cultural identity, fear of moving towards the obscure or the undesirable, and the fear of dissolving many other norms.

Education is not luxury, but a basic need that both men and women need for their health and development. Specifically, basic education provides girls and women with an understanding of health, family planning, and nutrition, while giving them the power to choose over their own lives and bodies. Women's education leads legitimately to better reproductive wellbeing. It also improves family, health and prosperity, economic advancement for the community and the general public. It is the key in the fight against the spread of HIV and AIDS.

Women are more than half of the world's population. Sadly, equal opportunities have not been offered to them in several parts of the world. The development of feminine ideas has helped a lot and improved the condition of women across the world. The feminine ideas have given much importance to women's education and our First Lady should see this as an opportunity to empower Nigerian girls and women. Educating girls is not a burden. It is clear in my mind that our First Lady believes it cannot and will not be a burden to educate girls. It is something that we should cherish and pool resources to support if we want to leave a mark in the lives of Nigerian women, particularly in the northern part of the country. In certain parts of the world many people do not know about women's privileges. Along these lines, they believe that young girls are subordinate to young men, not realizing that young girls are of co-equal standard.

There has been tremendous progress in the field of media, information technology, science, and others. But unfortunately, there has not been coordinating advancement in the area of educating women up to the obligatory standards. Female proficiency and education have an immediate effect on the general improvement of a country and its development. The UNESCO studies demonstrate that female education in the developed nations is 96 percent while in developing nations, it is at 55 percent. However, in the underdeveloped nations like Nigeria or

Africa in general, it is 27.9 percent. Countries with high levels of basic education do better economically, mostly, when female education goes in pari-passu with that of men in society. If Nigeria wants to be one of the developed nations within Africa and in the world, it must concentrate on female education.

The major cause of all issues confronting women in Nigeria and other African countries is tied to education. If all women became educated, issues like domestic battering, infanticide, malnutrition of women and her child, female suicides, early marriage, rape, prostitution, and other related atrocities would significantly reduce, if not vanish, from our communities. Education gives us the fundamental capability to satisfy certain political, cultural, and economic needs. At each age and level of life, education improves the social and emotional intellectual advancement of women and empowers them to meet their fundamental needs of daily life. It brings a reduction in inequalities in society. Mahatma Gandhi once alluded to women as *"respectable sex."* He said: *"If our ladies are powerless in striking, they are strong in suffering".* He once depicted women as the epitome of sacrifice and motherhood. Women are no way different from men, except in marriage when the Godly orders must be followed –that the man is the head, it is time the contemporary women grappled with that. In marriage, he is the head, period.

As men are commonly feeble in showing love, women are commonly powerless in demonstrating physical norms as well. Women are solid in demonstrating affection, sacrifice, and sympathy. For instance, if we ask a child, "Who do you like the most, the person who corrects with adoration or the person who amends with beating," the kid undoubtedly would say the person who rectifies with adoration. Since this is true, for what reason do we disregard the education of our women who are likely the most skilled in running the general public with their adoration and sacrifices? Do they not submit, cooperate, and collaborate, adjust to the given task from their high authority?

I am immensely proud of Nigeria as my country. I am so joyful to tell anyone that our mother tongues are of Yoruba, Hausa, Igbo, Efik, Fulde, Urhobo and others. We were conceived in our mothers' bellies, have been naturally introduced to this world through them, have suckled their milk, have been ensured by her at the hour of anguish and perils and have been cherished by her constantly. Yet, we neglect them when we are adult and oppress them with regards to some specific uniformity. We see other ladies especially "white ladies" as our Demi-god. But we ill-treat ours and carry out moral, religious, political, cultural, educational, social, and economic injustice against them. Why?

We regularly overlook that we all originate from the womb of a woman. We are alive in light of their unequivocal love towards us. A woman can even love a terrorist who happens to be her child, who no other being can do. Having got these awesome women in our world, why are we overlooking the education of the female child in our society! Are we doing this deliberately without insight? The appropriate response is, we are doing it intentionally to keep up male domination. Therefore, men ought to have a receptive outlook to respect the adjustments in our society of educating female children. If only men participate, they can have every one of the women educated sooner than later. This would improve the economic wellbeing of our present and the future Nigerian mothers. Nobody walks with one leg. Nobody prides himself on one hand. For a man to be socially balanced in this contemporary time, he should marry an informed woman.

If a female child became educated, any place she goes and whichever field she works in, she will surely advance her intellectuality there. Similarly, if a woman becomes educated and gets married and has her children, she will understand what to be done at every stage. She will realize how to conscientiously raise a solid child or recognize what to do when such a child becomes sick or challenged in any way. They would additionally advance education for every one of their children through which the family and the general public would eventually benefit. However, if such a lady is not educated but gets married, she will be greatly handicapped. She would do anything without thinking and harm herself and her kids. And towards the end, the family would horrendously languish over it. As she is not educated, she would generally believe that education is just for the male and not for the female and in this way, instill in her female child that they are inferior as compared to their siblings.

Let me use the India preliminary educational system as an example here since India ranks in peer with Nigeria and Africa when it comes to female education. Article 45 of the Indian constitution says: "The State will endeavor to give, within ten years from the commencement of the constitution, free and obligatory education for all children until they complete the age of fourteen years." I believe the Nigerian constitution on education has a related Article of such. If not, it is the job of Mrs. Aisha Buhari to rise to this and rally the leadership and make sure such is recommended and made available for our women in Nigeria. The Government alone does not have the sole responsibility in a situation like this; parents to play a major role. Parents should always support female education and ensure their girls go to school. To do so, we must educate them through songs, street plays and cultural dances in every village.

Are we ready to give our women, daughters, and sisters in our family proper education as we did to our male children? Can we begin to teach that women are not inferior to men in all ramifications in our families and our society? Can we treat them with equivalent right in our homes and at work? Can we allow ladies to exercise their privileges and authorities at home with no limitation?

If one female child is educated in a home, a family is certainly educated. The female barbarities will be eradicated, and women would be similarly competent to the posts which men hold and demonstrate equivalent rights. At that point, impeccable correspondence would be kept up among people in our informed society. If all these happen smoothly, Nigeria and Africa at large would become a developed nation in its social, political, economic, and cultural realm. Unto that goal, First Lady's legacy is premised.

CHAPTER 5

SENATOR DINO MELAYE

B etween 2015 and 2019, Nigeria has witnessed a new breed of campaigners of democracy. This breed is bold, fearless, unfaltering, and adamant. This mirrors a new era in a country that about two decades ago was under stratocracy. We have observed lately, scholars and analysts warning that democracy is dying while authoritarianism is intensifying. The caveat is pegged on the rise of autocratic global powers such as China and Russia. The United States as a global power undeniably has been instrumental in sustaining democracy and global peace. Under President Donald Trump, sorry to say, we are on a dangerous trajectory that threatens democracy. Since President Trump took over the U.S. Presidency with the nationalistic slogan: "America First," China has been observed to wrest global leadership from the West. The dwindling global influence of the U.S. which is a champion of democracy and the rise of China

which on the contrary is authoritarian, are now shattering the dreams of hopeful Nigerians to live as a democratic nation.

Contrary to growing worries in many quarters, democracy is not dying in Nigeria and by extension-Africa. Instead, it is expanding under energized young, educated, and visionary leaders. Bukola Saraki and others as voices for the voiceless were featured in previous chapters as great advocates of democracy. It has not been their lonesome battle. To win, combat and possess territory, you do not fight alone. You will require foot soldiers. Similarly, promoting democracy is not a one-man battle. It requires concerted efforts, especially in a murky political environment that is characteristic of the political landscape across Africa.

Senate President Bukola Saraki pushed for democracy with other indomitable and energetic political leaders like Senator Daniel Oluwagbenga Melaye a.k.a Dino. He was born in 1974 into a proud Christian home and grew up in Kano which was then an aggressively Muslim city. Daniel (Dino) Melaye is arguably, one of the most misunderstood personalities in the country today. His unique, bold, and flamboyant lifestyle - which he had worked hard for all his life - cast him as a controversial figure on the political landscape. However, the truth is that those who hate him do not really know him.

In his book, *"Antidotes for Corruption – the Nigerian Story,"* Melaye recounted how his father struggled to keep his job at the Ministry of Agriculture in the hostile Kano environment at the time. His father was in the position of what is called a Permanent Secretary today. *"On Sundays, they would say the governor was coming to the ministry to do some inspection.*

Our father, a staunch Christian would instead go to Church to worship his God. Ultimately, his trick was later exposed, and was sacked; hence, life became harder for the family'. Fortunately, the experiences toughened the young Melaye and kept him determined to make a success in life – and to fight for social justice, and against Corruption in whatever form. Melaye's father also remembered how he won a scholarship to a Secondary school in Kano but was denied admission because of his Christian name. His father refused to change his name, and instead took him down to Okene, in his Kogi State.

Dino Melaye began his active political career while studying at the reputable Ahmadu Bello University (ABU), Zaria, where he became Students Union Leader. After, ABU, Melaye started the National Association of Democratic Youths In 2005. Later, he became the Chairman of the Grand Alliance of Nigeria - which was the umbrella body campaigning for Obasanjo's re-election. And that was how he earned his way to national politics through the PDP. Some of his life's guiding principles are couched in his popular statements such as:

- *Political maturity is not measured by how many grey hairs are on your head. It is measured by your ability to listen to your conscience above Money.*
- *Integrity gives you freedom because you have nothing to hide (and fear).*
- *If we speak the truth, we will die; if we lie, we will die. I prefer to speak the truth.*

Senator Melaye has been a vibrant warden of Nigeria's frail democracy. He has been active, boisterous and all ears on addressing essential national issues. Notwithstanding, his opponents have perceived him as a controversial, dramatic, theatrical, and abrasive politician. It all depends on how a person looks at his personality. Those who truly recognize his promptness to sacrifice himself for public interest highly regard him as an unwavering fighter of democracy.

Dino Melaye is a Senator and member of the 8th National Assembly, representing Kogi West Senatorial District, under the People's Democratic Party (PDP). With Dino's re-election in the 2019 general election, he was expected to maintain more vibrancy in the 9th senate. He juts out as an unconquerable political revolutionary to reckon with. Nobody can deny the truth that he is at the forefront to champion human rights and freedoms of all Nigerians and to buttress democracy in his country. Dino's re-election in the 2019 general election in the face of threats of recall by a section of his constituents is an evidence of confidence a majority of his supporters still have in him.

As Bukola Saraki whom he passionately supported exits Nigeria's Senate, Mr. Melaye still exudes buoyancy in the 9th senate leadership. He believes it will shore up democracy, economy, and favorable policies. In Nigeria's political circles, he has demonstrated top-notch respect and defense for democracy. With a valiant and audacious personality, Melaye has been able to grow politically. He speaks not only for his Kogi West constituents, but also for the entire nation. In the 8th senate, the world heard him loud and clear speaking with poise about security, economy and domineering policies perpetuated by Buhari's administration. His opponents throw salvos and nitpick at him because they disagree with him or dislike his public display of dramatic character. But that is a sign that he is a simple leader, a kind that has the same attribute of the public. But do not lose the major focus. His private life which has been on the radar of his political enemies should not be the focal point. His dress code and ostentatious lifestyle-which for long have been in the limelight, can swerve us from regarding him as a humanitarian and champion of democracy.

But only if we stick our nose into pettiness, advanced politicians have moved beyond that. Luckily, many Nigerians have matured and overcome the age of trivial mindedness. They are now informed and hardworking individuals that no longer surrender to dictatorship. Let us look at this Senator from a broader perspective. Does Melaye speak about issues that are significant to the common man? Without prevarication, the answer is, a big YES! I think we should ransack our minds on this and let us focus on the bigger picture, but not on unnecessary character obliteration. We should not engage ourselves in the character assassination of others, which will not help. What helps is Melaye's resoluteness to defend Nigerians. It is to defend our fragile democracy.

Across the continent, democracy has been elusive. The major impediment to democratization in Africa is lacklustre criticism from the gloomy-gus and the naysayers so to speak. In Africa, as we know it, we sometimes criticise vehemently on very flimsy grounds. Leaders that take the better part of the airwaves for good reasons usually receive destructive criticism from opposing quarters. I know you seem to think I am digressing. I am still on the case of Senator Melaye. Africans in some circumstances, consider anti-government or outspoken individuals as saboteurs. On this, I am speaking to those who are wired to downgrade a leader of Melaye's stature. He is absolutely a human rights defender. He is a Nigerian defender. His dedication to democratize Nigeria and promote an egalitarian society is no mean feat.

Melaye Aficionado of Nigeria democracy

Those who live in Nigeria and take time to follow our politics will candidly acknowledge Melaye as a fighter. He frankly envisions living in a democratic country. He is a selfless "hombre" that is determined to push for a democracy that works for everyone. In a free society, people are liberated to express themselves liberally without the fear of condemnation or threats to their lives. That is a country that Mr. Melaye is fighting for. Democracy thrives only in a space that is accommodating, and free speech is the core. Nobody can doubt it. Democracy grows only in an environment that is tolerant of dissenting voices directed at the oppressive governments.

Senator Melaye, in a personal description, calls himself as a "democratic evangelist." It is incontrovertible that he is. Fighting for democracy commands that leaders put the interests of the people they serve first. On several occasions, Senator Melaye has come out as a firebrand politician committed to speaking for the average Nigerians. On the floor of the Senate, for instance, on December 21, 2016, he introduced a new philosophy into the political domain that senators, and indeed other leaders, are only "honorable and distinguished" when the public is joyful. Precisely, this is what citizens expect. A leader that stands in a reputable house such as in the senate floor to speak in such a way is genuinely democratic. In this new philosophy, Melaye argues that legislators, including other leaders, deserve the two titles only if the needs of the citizens are met. Yes, that is what characterizes democracy. It is a no-brainer; he is a voice for the voiceless.

In his firmness and strong conviction, Senator Melaye puts public interest before self.

Unquestionably, this is healthy for democracy which easily flourishes with selfless leaders. Leaders make sacrifices. Politicians, in the wildest circumstances, put their lives on the line while protecting the public interest. We should not see this as a lie, but absolute truth. Mr. Melaye, a gallant and democratic leader, has put his life in danger to pursue what he thinks is right and good for Nigerians. His stinging criticism of Buhari's repressive policies is the only attestation of Melaye's altruistic commitment to social justice, democracy, and governance. Incontestably, if you monitor Senator Melaye you will make intriguing conclusions about him. Senator Melaye passionately believes that the absolute power belongs to the people. Such recognition of reality is good for democracy. The public can appear so weak and helpless to resist suppressive laws as they were during the military regime, but that does not mean that it is powerless.

Society is made up of people who donate power to leaders. Even though they can look powerless to take back power, it remains theirs. By acknowledging that power belongs to society, politicians and other leaders are likely to exercise restraint. Political happenings around the world reaffirm that power is subject to abuse. The trappings of office or the power bestowed upon leaders, in some way corrupts their minds. As a consequence, some leaders misuse power, ignore the poor masses and concentrate on self-enrichment. Melaye does not fall in such a callous category of leaders. In his leadership, he recognizes that we come from different schools of thought, but we stand on the same pedestal when identifying where power belongs. Power belongs to people regardless of their socio-economic status. Sadly, if people are not empowered, the ruling elite can abuse and reduce them to road-kills. Today, Nigerians are becoming more vocal because of inspirational and empowering leaders like Melaye. In the presence of promising leaders like Dino, power-elite theory as conceived by C. Wright Mills (1956) is not practicable.

The power elite practically worked so perfectly during military rule. As visualized by Mills, the power-elite theory states that the ruling class (government, military, and big corporations) controls society usually horrendously and high-handedly. This ruling class protects its interests and does little to empower society. Senator Dino Melaye is specifically keen on fighting against the re-emerging power elite years after Nigeria's democratic rule. In one fell swoop, average Nigerians are getting up determinedly, to strengthen democracy.

According to them, there is no turning back to older days of dictatorship, high-handedness, and self-centeredness. In practice and in deed, the aspirations and needs of people have evolved. Today, people desire to live in free societies where they can independently express themselves fearlessly and gain socio-economic empowerment. These very people, including Nigerians, have social power that gives them the temerity to question leaders. In another scenario, people can side with leaders that value their social power.

Melaye as an unwavering supporter of social power, demonstrates unrelenting tackle of re-emerging power elite. His audacity to rub shoulders with leaders undermining democracy is why in modern Nigeria, he is a beacon of hope among the youth. The youth are rallying behind him to reinvigorate his quest for a socially just society. The youth, in modern democracy, is becoming active. The Nigerian youth is not taking a back seat. They are up in arms to influence governance and prop up democracy in their country. Just as a reminder, In Africa, the Republic of Sudan and Zimbabwe are perfect examples of youth power.

The long-serving dictators like late Robert Mugabe and Omar al-Bashir – former presidents of Zimbabwe and Sudan respectively have recently been forced to step down from power through peaceful protests and demonstrations. The same has been witnessed in Algeria where President Abdelaziz Bouteflika resigned on April 2, 2019, following sweeping protests in Algiers. Demonstrations unceremoniously ended President Bouteflika's 20-year rule. Here, I am not justifying the removal of leaders from power, but I elucidate the active role that young people have played in such countries to secure their democracy.

Senator Melaye, as a good observant, is shrewdly capitalizing on the youth power; hence, he is positioning himself as a leader of the pack. Indeed, a leader of the youth. Vibrancy among the youth in demonstrations and protests as seen in countries such as Sudan and Algeria, confirm that the modern youthful population yearns for democracy. On that basis, young Nigerians see Senator Melaye as their dauntless fighter. I do not doubt that a leader that fights for the rights and freedoms of the youth at all times wins their power. Efforts to recall Mr. Melaye prematurely notably became futile after the youth passed a vote of confidence on him. The representatives of the youth chiefly from Kogi West during their Youth Assembly Meeting in one voice acknowledged Senator Melaye's marvelous job of representation. Was this not youth power? It was. The support for Melaye by the youth cannot be rubbished. When they speak positively about a leader, they must have seen something positive about him. And Mr. Melaye intelligently capitalizes on that.

On advocating for Nigeria's democracy, Melaye does not back down. He comes out as a visionary leader. As knowledgeable as he is, he speaks intrepidly. His mastery of the rule of law and unflinching support for Nigeria's democratic system is something his political supporters reckon with. He has sufficient erudition on democracy. His understanding of issues is what projects him as a dedicated supporter of egalitarianism in the public eye.

Holding doubts whether Mr. Melaye is a towering figure or not is baseless. As the appetite for democracy grows by leaps and bounds, this honorable Senator certainly has a long life in Nigeria's leadership. He is a typical modern freedom fighter. The voters who are majorly youthful and educated match up with this Senator. They see him as a transformational leader with long political life in our power equation. He shares similar liveliness with young democratic leaders in mature democracies such as U.S. congressional representative Alexandria Ocasio-Cortez

(AOC) who represents New York's 14th Congressional district. Her courage, notwithstanding her young age, in the 116th United States Congress has made her popular and a politician to take seriously. She addresses important issues of national importance ranging from economy, migration, American values, and democracy.

Senator Melaye is on the same pedestal as her. Interchangeably, she is like Mr. Melaye. I am not digressing here-just giving a perfect example that shares a similar vision on a democratic system with Melaye. Nigerians of all walks of life are geared towards supporting leaders like Melaye. In his quest for a free society, the best that Nigerians especially the youth can do, is to continue supporting him. It is abundantly clear that Melaye epitomizes how representation and constitutional democracy works. In the Senate, someone cannot doubt or undermine the fact that Melaye has substance. He proposes laws that will stay with us for a long time; strengthen democracy in a country that thus far, is the largest economy in Africa.

Senator Melaye's superlative performance in senate
The roles of senators in the Federal Republic of Nigeria are well underscored in the constitution. Some of the roles include making laws, amending laws, approving judicial and federal appointments, managing public funds and removal of President and his Vice from power. A good leader will perform these roles excellently and do more to empower constituents. Melaye is directly answerable to his constituents of Kogi West Senatorial zone. But for national interest, he does more than what the constitution sets down for him. The senate is a powerhouse of Nigeria's

democracy. Melaye sufficiently uses the power vested in him as a Senator to legislate with his eyes set on enhancing democracy, good governance, and economy. The many bills he had pushed in the senate are crucial to holding constitutional democracy. When the laws are in place, the ruling party cannot limit or abuse the rights and freedoms of the masses.

As a reminder, in 2012, United Nations General Assembly-UNGA, stressed that democracy, rule of law and human rights are interconnected. In the context of this affirmation, Melaye tabled bills that reinforced the rule of law and human rights. As a protector of human rights, Melaye sponsored Anti-Jungle Justice Bill 2015, which later passed. The bill prohibits extrajudicial executions or mob lynching. The law stipulates that everyone is equal and presumed innocent and has a right to be served justice. The right to life as well as dignity provides statutory protection for all Nigerians. Melaye sought to use this bill to address extrajudicial killings that were rampant in Nigeria. Extrajudicial killings cannot be condoned in a liberal nation. The passage of the bill was a great achievement that will protect Nigerians from losing their lives unlawfully. The rule of law in a democratic state is unquestionably supreme. That has been crystal clear to Mr. Melaye. He envisaged a country where suspects can be subjected to fair trial. Jungle Justice cannot apply in a democratic nation.

Senator Melaye sponsored other bills such as Ethnic and Religious Hatred Bill 2017, Protection against Domestic Violence Act (Amendment) Bill 2015, Economic and Financial Crime Commission Bill 2015, among others. All the bills he sponsored are vital in strengthening Nigeria's democracy.

Although his opponents may underrate his role in promoting democracy through legislation, Melaye remains a celebrated leader. In the modern history of Nigeria, he is the Senator with the highest number of bills as at the time the author is writing this page. With 35 bills, 29 Motorized and hard Drilling Boreholes, 15 electrical projects, and 19 road projects.

As heterogeneous as Nigeria is, it has to guarantee religious liberty, which is a significant tenet of democracy. To pre-empt ethnic and religious discrimination, the dazzling senator moved in swiftly to table a bill that will hold accountable any Nigerian that will profile others ethnically or religiously. We cannot say plausibly that we live in a free society when ethnic or religious animosity thrives amidst us. In modern Nigeria, ethnically and religiously motivated hatred does not have space to boom. Holding people accountable for their actions and behaviors will be the cornerstone of a budding democracy in Nigeria. It is pointless to live in a country where people are targeted for being different from us because of their religion or ethnicity. Democracy asks us to live harmoniously, as we acknowledge and appreciate the diversity of society. Of course, many people may not see the essence of this important piece of legislation. But a person who is plausible enough will praise Senator Melaye for sponsoring such a bill. It is a bill that will help the police as well as execute their mandate principally when handling cases of ethnic and religious hatred. Yet, the Nigerian constitution protects the freedom of speech, not in absoluteness. Exercising freedom of expression does not guarantee sane people the liberty to perpetuate hate speech. Uttering words that will spark ethnic or religious hatred is not freedom of speech. It is discrimination that is not condoned anyway. However, as a person completely entrenched in democracy, the bill is a step towards building a free society. Senator Melaye deserves accolades for directing Nigeria in the right direction by promoting religious and ethnic tolerance in this bill.

These days, no partner should be allowed to suffer domestic violence. Family harmony or happy domesticity is all that people wish every couple. The necessity of Protection against Domestic Violence Act (Amendment) Bill 2015 is drawing attention to the Bill of Rights. In Melaye's logic, amending this bill was central to protecting partners and families from domestic violence. It is preposterous to think that a country can become democratic and free when domestic disputes are tearing people apart. By amending the Act, Senator Dino Melaye was determined to make the most basic unit of society, which is the family, strong. It is also one way of keeping society off violence.

The integration of the disability bill is notably the underlying principle of the Bill of Rights. Senator Melaye was always aware of the problems deterring Nigeria from becoming a fair and just society. As a leader who understands what ails the Nigerian society, he sponsored this motion. According to this Senator, it was long overdue to live in a society that discriminates against others. It was no longer tolerable to see people with special needs discriminated against. Mr. Melaye admits that he does not like calling "the disabled, disabled." He prefers them to be regarded as special citizens, and that they deserve the right attention. It is wrong, in all dimensions, to neglect disabled people. The Integration Disability Bill was driven by the desire to protect the unalienable rights of disabled

Nigerians. There has been less attention to integrating this group into society. Special interest cannot be denied to the disabled community. The bill was well-intentioned to give a voice to this special group of people in Nigeria. What else can people want if not a leader that is focused on creating a non-discriminatory society?

Melaye has been a hawk-eyed senator who stood out by sponsoring bills that have a far-reaching impact on Nigeria's national life. He was voted the best senator in 2016, a year after assuming office. His work and efforts were noticeable. He has set the bar high in legislation for other senators. In a representative democracy, people expect their leaders to make laws that improve their lives and create a favorable environment for thriving. All the bills he sponsored and the contributions he made in the senate will not go in vain. They will impact lives and make Nigeria a better democracy. The democracy of Nigeria is heavily dependent on the legislators. They are the ones that make laws and if they slack in their job, the executive can be dictatorial. Melaye never wasted any single opportunity that he had to legislate. As a leader, he took his work seriously. Even though he faced multi-dimensional challenges, he never tired. He was arrested on several occasions for being vocal and against the Buhari administration.

Senator Melaye at crossroads with police

In spite of his stellar performance in the Senate, Melaye has been an embattled Senator. The police, literally and figuratively, have been on his neck. Allegations of all kinds, from homicide to fraud were tagged on him. The mainstream media and social media were awash with stories of

Melaye's apprehension. The manhandling by police left Melaye, a fighter of democracy, a bruised man. His home was under siege. His residence was cordoned off, as police "hunt him down." It was not a good spectacle at all. Some people felt that the allegations were baseless and politically motivated. His opponents, particularly the political ones supported the police harassment. He was accused of shooting a police officer in his Kogi state, operating a bank account overseas and forgery of academic documents. He was in detention for about 120 days. Comically, while on a police van, it is alleged that he attempted escape, another conspiracy theory, I believe.

Becoming a champion comes with pain, agony. It is impossible to avoid wild accusations, especially if you are a critic of the government. The police are habitually used to torturing government critics, silence any dissenting voice. As a law-abiding person, he complied with the police, possibly with the hope of overcoming the ruthlessness of the unrelenting police. Every time the police attempted to bring him down, he stood firm. He looked energized and undeterred. He never lacked popular appreciation. The youth who like his ideas and indefatigability to strengthen democracy supported him unconditionally, urging him to keep fighting. Perhaps that spurred him. He gave a voice to the voiceless.

Freedom fighters rarely find happiness because they step on the toes of top leadership of a country. It was absolutely tactical for the government to make Melaye go through trouble, tumult, and torture. It was one way to cow him. But because this is a leader with a bigger dream, it was difficult to stop him. Melaye is a man of steel whose vision for Nigeria overrides his interests. This is crystal clear in the way he continues to fight for our democracy. Senator Melaye's dream for Nigeria is huge. His performance as a leader, will, in all possibility transform Nigeria into an established democracy. Roadblocks to creating free Nigerian society where the rule of law is respected are numerous. But with leaders like Melaye, there is optimism that Nigeria's democracy will not wither, but mature. Even though Melaye may be uncelebrated in some quarters, his contribution to democracy may appear nothing to the doomsayers. The truth will prevail, Senator Melaye is a transformational leader. Having a genuine democratic Nigeria is not only good for her citizens, also for the African continent. As such, Senator Dino Melaye remains a fighter, a defender, and a genuine devotee of modern democracy in Nigeria.

A majority will agree that the police action on Dino Melaye is a return to the military era. When the police make up charges against government critics who they perceive as threat to democracy. No politician or political leader should use the police to terrorize their opponents, particularly in a democratic nation. It is hard to believe that the police act with neutrality when Nigerians observed them beating up Senator Melaye. No right-thinking man can celebrate police brutality against others who spend their time to expand democracy. Such tyrannical Police actions are undoing the very democracy that Nigerians fought hard to achieve. In an effective and functioning democracy, police cannot be a law unto themselves. It was observed that when it came to Melaye, the Police acted with impunity and arrogance. In the public eye, they acted under the instructions of leaders taking Nigeria back to the dark era of military rule. Senator Melaye fundamentally desires a nation where rule of law and national cohesion are entrenched and such a fellow cannot in any way be an enemy of the Federal Republic of Nigeria. Instead, those who use the police to silence vocal politicians doing an excellent job to bolster democracy are the ones dragging Nigeria behind.

In some part of Africa, the world has witnessed the Police maiming and killing innocent citizens whose only call is democracy. Sudan, DR Congo, Uganda are countries lagging behind in achieving democracy owing to brute force from non-independent police. They have been quick at launching terror on political activists and nonconformists. The underlying justification for uncalled action by the police is that they are maintaining public order. This is a cover-up to their brutality. Meanwhile, the Police are central to democracy but can threaten democracy if they 'hand in' their independence to political persuasions by dictators. The Police in a democratic setting should protect and serve the people without favor, comply with the rule of law, and treat everyone equally. The fundamental principle in law is equal application. The investigation carried out on the Russian meddling allegation in the U.S. 2016 presidential election in favor of President Donald Trump epitomized how democratic police should act. This is what senator Dino Melaye is fighting for, to see all of Nigeria's democratic institutions perform independently. He remains the voice of the voiceless in the National Assembly.

Melaye a misunderstood personality, but a man of principle

The perception of the personality of Senator Dino Melaye attracts attention. At one point, he is taken as a showbiz guy whilst his adversaries consider him corrupt, stubborn, and obstinate. All these views emanate from political affiliations or the misunderstanding of him. To his adversaries, Dino Melaye is a thorn in the flesh. He rattles them from enjoying the excesses of power. Very few leaders will condone their rattlers or challengers.

Senator Dino Melaye is loved and hated. The love and hate are not on equal measure. His haters are few, just a small group of the ruling elite who do not want a healthier Nigeria that works for all. As petty as it is, some of his haters do not like his showbiz life. Senator Dino Melaye literally entertains having devoted his social life to entertainment. He lives large. However, in my opinion, he does not steal from the public to live lavishly as it is the norm in Africa. He has appeared in several music videos. So, why should it be an issue of concern? His opponents, strangely, believe that it is immoral for a leader to do that. Let us face it. We all live life differently. The theatrics of Senator Melaye about his social life should not be the yardstick to measure him, politically. Why criticize a man who is nurturing his happiness by engaging in a social activity that he thinks is good for him? If his social life impacts his delivery in the Senate, then we could raise an accusing finger to it!

Politics nevertheless is murky. Political challengers in all probability, look for anything to undercut another leader. Although people hold differing opinions, which is allowed, Senator Melaye in all sureness is a man of principle. He is a person who adamantly wants leaders to stay true to a cause that is good for all and sundry. When Nigeria yearned for good leadership, Senator Melaye believed in former President Dr. Jonathan Ebele Goodluck. He rooted for him. He rallied behind him because he had confidence in him to lead the country in the right path, a path that will give Nigeria a strong democracy. But when President Goodluck failed to stand true to his commitment to foster democracy, sustain graft purge, protect Nigerians, and serve his people diligently, Mr. Melaye fought tooth and nail to have President Goodluck voted out of office, regardless of his previous steadfast support. In his view, the Goodluck-led government was a promoter of massive corruption. He campaigned to have Goodluck voted out for the clear-cut failings - increase in insecurity, underperforming economy, and increasing corruption - and shifted support to President Buhari who, according to him, was the best to fight corruption. He later became a consistent critic of President Buhari. In the same vein, he locked horns with his own Kogi State governor for ignoring his subjects. His decision to disagree with the leaders he once supported is on account of disappointment in the people he so believed to be pro-change. You would allow me to confine my references to Africa.

In this continent, many politicians come with progressive policies during campaigns. They promise to deliver and commit to good leadership to change lives and shore up the economy. After assuming office, all the pledges made during electioneering are swept under the carpet. This is what senator Melaye abhors. It hurts to be betrayed. In any case, we expect leaders to walk the talk. True leaders will keep their promise. Even if they do not deliver everything as pledged, they commit themselves to doing the right thing. In this vein, what Senator Melaye envisions for President Buhari when he was supporting him, went into the abyss. Power is transient. It comes and diminishes at any moment. As such, elected leaders ought not to slide into their comfort zones, leaving the people who elected them to wallow in poverty. What is wrong for a patriotic citizen to pillory officeholders who are non-performing? The Kogi Senator thus far has proved that he is dedicated to the masses. Senator Melaye deserves commendation for his honest devotion for sponsoring key bills that will help us overcome ethnic, religious and disability discrimination. Other leaders should emulate him, act decisively and courageously in opposing tyranny that is slowly creeping back into Nigeria and swaying the country from the right path.

As Kogi State governorship elections draws near, Senator Melaye may take a stab at it. In no way should good leaders be denied an opportunity to serve in positions that are vital in influencing policies and building democracy. If Dino Melaye is given a higher office in Nigeria, that will be the turning point to our democracy. I am not campaigning for Dino. However, as a person who supports democracy and wants Nigeria to thrive democratically, I unswervingly root for good leadership. By and large, he has shown the world that he truly supports democracy and dreams big for Nigeria. In my informed assessment, Senator Melaye has a long life in Nigeria's politics. He has shown the willingness to lead selflessly whilst fighting for the disadvantaged in society.

The Senate where he is a lawmaker principally makes laws that are geared to address equality, economy, and other rafts of issues. It does not have many financial resources allocated to it to initiate mega projects that can significantly uplift the poor. Perhaps it is the desire to seek more resources and commitment to serving people that in recent times inspired him to declare his interest to unseat Governor Yahaya Bello. The governorship seat which is up for grabs this year allows him to manage resources and diligently serve his constituents as he positions himself strategically for national politics. Though, the electioneering system in Nigeria cannot be trusted but I am particularly afraid and concerned if the system will not turn the table against him.

⊷⊷ ⊷⊷

CHAPTER 6

SENATOR SHEHU SANI

Nigeria, beyond doubt, is a great country. However, her history is painful in particular for people who devotedly fought for freedom and democracy in the early years. After several years of back and forth to push for democracy in the country, some freedom fighters went through tumultuous experiences. Senator Shehu Sani is one. Born in 1967, he was the Senator for Kaduna Central Senatorial District. Aside from being a politician, he is a renowned playwright, human rights activist, and author. In his struggle to defend civil liberties, he has served in senior positions, such as the Chairman of Hand-in-Hand in Africa and as President of the Civil Rights Congress of Nigeria. Throughout his country's determined struggle to defeat stratocracy, he was a foremost figure that lobbied and campaigned for democracy. With the ruthlessness and

callousness of the military regimes, he was unlucky. Brutality was meted out on him. He was apprehended, dehumanized, and jailed. From prison, he did not give up on human rights activism. He walked into freedom from torturous confinement in 1999 when the democratic government was handed power. He stood firm to defend the rights and freedoms that Nigerians are considerably enjoying today. His fight for human rights and freedoms was universal. He protested the invasion of Iraq by the United States, and Gaza by Israel. Essentially, his activism was not confined to Nigeria, but worldwide. As a believer of equality, civil liberties, and democracy, he wants every person in the universe to be free and dignified. This justifies his universally broad-shouldered activism.

Activism inspired him to author books on peace, dictatorship, poverty, and corruption. This is a man that has wholeheartedly dedicated his life to defend the rights of all of us. With the history of the state of affairs of the African continent at his fingertips, he has extensively authored and decried dictatorship. The affairs of Africa or events occurring on the continent are not secrets as they are documented, televised, or shared on various social media sites. The end of the colonial era was expected to set the continent in motion to pursue peace, democracy, prosperity, fight diseases and poverty and generally empower the human population strapping across the continent. This vision was jilted. Instead of pursuing a vision that would have pulled the continent out of the challenges it faces in the modern world, leaders focused on self-enrichment. All these historical happenings are covered in the various books Senator Sani has authored.

Truly, a look at the life of Senator Sani divulges a character of a person that is a democrat. Since he captured the senatorial position after two failed attempts, his campaign for democracy, good leadership, and human rights has been noticeable. But still, he is not a celebrated national hero. That shows how myopic people are getting as a nation. This is a leader with a vision that is in good physical shape for restoring decelerating democracy in Nigeria. He is a leader and if supported fully by the citizenry, can bring meaningful change to the country. The mere unfortunate fact that he is not celebrated per se in the country is an indictment on how Nigerians are losing social power. It is incumbent upon citizens to rally behind leaders who are fighting for a genuine national cause such as democracy.

In spite of the unwillingness of leaders to observe the rule of law, Senator Sani has stood as a true campaigner of human rights. It is a job that he enjoys, and it feels like it is his call to serve people unconditionally. If a person does a job they cherish, they unreservedly pursue it with a focused mission to achieve positive results that bring meaningful change to society. Mr. Sani has demonstrated that he is a true human right and freedom defender, which has been the phenomenon that has just made him a true advocate of democracy.

Sani's human rights activism and outspokenness, a basis for Nigeria democracy

The democratic governments that exist today mostly came into power through activism. Activists have been at the center of campaigning for democracy, shaping public policy, piling pressure on dictators, and lobbying for government reforms. Though activists risk their lives particularly when dictatorial regimes feel threatened, activism is one central noble cause worth dying for, for the sake of the country. Senator Shehu Sani has refused to retreat or be cowed in the heat of crackdown on activists by the military generals. He forged forward as a hero to campaign for democracy through activism, a cornerstone of democracy. To reject the ludicrousness of fake democracy, activists have had to lead people to protest, picket and demonstrate. Activism continues to contribute significantly to the democratic gains Nigeria has made today. This is despite the constant rising wave of authoritarianism. Pro-democracy voices are becoming loud in Nigeria courtesy of unrelenting activists like Senator Sani.

Amid rising dictatorship and diminishing respect for human rights in Nigeria, Sani has stood steadfastly to oppose such moves. This is because he comprehends that when leaders respect the rights of people, democracy gets space to flourish. It is an absurdity to expect democracy to thrive in an environment where leaders explicitly do not respect your rights. As such, the distinguished senator has always been at the forefront to admonish the retrogression into a dictatorship of the military era. The courage exuded by Sani to call out current Nigerian leaders to protect human rights is laying a strong foundation for democracy. Shehu Sani, as part of his scheme, to continue with human rights activists, he sought a political office. It is sometimes a herculean task to protect and empower people that are out of the power equation. Maybe that is why Sani combined politics and activism to get a platform in the legislative body to drive home his ideas. Speaking from the authority bestowed upon him as a senator, Sani has been at the heart of empowering society. Through press conferences, on the floor of the senate and in other forums, his energy is frankly channeled to protect and advance democracy in Nigeria.

He became a political activist because he understands that the protection of human rights cannot be achieved without political goodwill. Politics is an integral part of human rights activism. After all, when an activist blames political leadership for being a hindrance to human rights, they pursue a political cause. Activists would have to marshal support from political actors that share similar ideals of democracy for civil liberties. Sani on that ground has been demanding that the leadership of the country upholds the constitution. He has been supportive and active in the Senate supporting motions aimed at empowering people. This bears a political outcome that keenly advocates for human rights.

Nevertheless, in modern societies, democracy is achieved when the civil and political rights of people are upheld. This stems from the fact that democracy is pegged on the rule of law that protects individual liberty and equality. Besides, democracy without universal human rights is amorphous and fake. It is an absurdity of the highest level to claim to protect democracy when human rights are trampled upon. For a nation to advance democratically, it has to constitutionally protect human rights. Equality for all people before the law must underpin all political decisions. But when politicians' interests override the basic human rights and leaders become drunk with power, democracy naturally fades away. This is the logic Senator Sani uses to foster human rights in Nigeria.

Nigeria is a country of great odds. Human rights are not fully respected by the political class. A contradiction to what democracy stands for, this is a country with significant diversity, insofar that can threaten democracy due to competing for political interests. Democracy is delicate in a diverse society where power struggle is do-or-die. With the tension and unpredictable future of Nigeria democracy, what is key here is empowering society to understand their human rights and protecting same. When society understands that their human rights supersede the political interests of the corrupt elite, they can stand against any divisive attempts. The divide and rule tactics are a cardinal principle that selfish leaders exploit to undermine human rights. Though, Mr. Sani, the human rights or political activist. Senator Sani trusts that as a society or government body, the major focus should be serving citizens democratically. That is something that any Nigerian that knows Senator Sani cannot object to. His utter support for the civil rights in all probability is something of hope for Nigerians. Senator Sani does not dine and wine with oppressors.

Given that in 2015 he won the election to represent the people of Kaduna Central Senatorial District under APC, one would have expected him to retreat on the defense of human rights. APC is the ruling party, and as far as human rights and democracy are concerned, the buck stops with it. His membership of APC, for his opponents, can be construed negatively. Those who oppose him would think that he has aligned and is dining with a repressive party. Lest we forget, that the victory of President Buhari in the 2015 General elections was on the grounds that Nigerians, including Senator Sani, believed he would speedily transform the country. President Buhari instilled hope and rode on a transformative agenda, which Sani himself saw as a good thing. But when the President fell short of his promises, Mr. Sani openly bolted out of the party. He did so not for personal interests, but to dissociate himself from leadership that became wide off the mark to what he believes in. This was a bold step that visibly projects him as a principled man with an unshakeable commitment to stand for the rule of law and rights and equality in his country. His defection to PRP (Peoples Redemption Party) was a reasoned-out decision. It is wise to ditch a party and its leadership if they do not share same ideologies with you.

Sadly though, to the APC members and leadership, Sani discovered that the party he once supported was for "the emperors and their lackeys." This indicated that party democracy had deteriorated. If that were the state of the party, it would have been immoral for the distinguished senator to be a member. His departure from the party is something to ponder about and as to understand the true character of Senator Sani as far as his activism and politics are concerned. To be objective and honest, a majority would agree that APC has failed to serve Nigerians and protect their rights. It would be a betrayal of democracy by Senator Sani to stay in the party doing what he is fighting against.

Sani condemned actions that were calculatingly designed to undermine people. Self-absorbed leaders tend to abuse power. Knowing that as an activist, he cannot support or tolerate high-handedness and bias. Mr. Sani locked horns with his Kaduna State Governor, El-Rufai whom he accused of dictatorial tendencies. This is a demonstration that for democracy to mature and leaders to shape up, people should not tolerate what they disagree to. Tolerating dictators or bad leaders has for long dented efforts to shield human rights in many countries.

Consider North Korea in the contemporary world, it is among the most oppressive states where political or civil liberties are controlled. People do not have freedoms of religion, assembly, association, and expression. There is no independent media or civil society at all. The country is in absolute control by the dictator Kim Jong-Un. Executions, torture, and arbitrary arrests are normal practices in this country. So unfortunate, even children or vulnerable people in society are not spared from human rights abuses. For this grotesque state of affairs not to happen in Nigeria, citizens should support activists, speak their minds, and viciously condemn leaders that want to erode the democratic gains made so far. That is the only way that will help a frail democracy from degenerating into dictatorship. For Nigeria to move forward and realize its dream to become a first-world nation with a strong democracy, high-handedness must be rejected strongly.

Rejection of despotism should cut across all levels of governments and institutions. It is on that very reason that Senator Sani admonished his governor. In this commitment, he rejects any form of despotic control. That is clear in the manner he encouraged people to speak the truth to the presidency. As a senator, Sani did not fear to call out leaders whose sole purpose is to stay in power, but not to serve people. It is common sense that the reason Africa is still lagging behind is because of leaders that do not care or leaders that do not listen to others. A leader that cares and listens knows that they have a responsibility towards the citizens who elected them. However, according to Sani, the current leadership does not like Truth-tellers. It does not like to be corrected or to be advised. It may be risky to speak the truth to the power that is not ready to listen. It is hazardous because it can fight back. Bad leaders always silence their critics through assassinations, which understandably have been skyrocketing in Nigeria. These assassinations or extrajudicial killings happen chiefly if the government wants to shut opponents up. Truth be told, the government cannot kill everyone. If they do so, who will they rule? Sani wants Nigerians not to fear but to reject bad leadership.

In one of his addresses, he fearlessly spoke about the situation of Northern Nigeria. He lamented that the region is under siege following insecurity and tolerated banditry. What is wrong to demand that the government addresses this? Is it criminal to ask the government to do what it is supposed to do? It is not criminal to ask the government to be accountable. Hence, what is deduced from the outspoken nature of Sani is that people should not fear to tell the truth. Truth ordinarily hurts autocratic leaders. Even if it hurts, Senator Sani wants citizens to continue saying it. It would be helpful and good for democracy when people say the truth unashamedly. Even though the government can use security or some officials to stop their critics, citizens should not concede defeat. Capitulating over fighting against dreadful leadership and apparent government failings are hazardous to democracy. To protect democracy, citizens must not capitulate. They should instead, hold their leaders accountable in whichever legal means they can. This is a spirit Senator Sani has instilled into his followers.

It is the sole responsibility of citizens to question their leaders. It is a civic duty of citizens to stand against leaders that are not serving them. This is what Nigerians have observed from this senator. For patriotism, Sani has been a voice for Nigerians who do not want to speak up or ask hard questions on major issues affecting them. Through him, a new generation of empowered people needs to get out of slumber and realize that the future of Nigeria is dependent on them. In young democracies like Nigeria, what citizens should do is press hard on the government. It would be self-betrayal to be quiet while leaders stay in power undermining fundamental human rights and freedoms.

Nonetheless, this is not to say that Nigeria has collapsed under APC and its entire leadership. There are positive things that this administration has done. Although as far as the country's democracy remains fragile and human rights are crushed, people should not tire to oppose repressive practices. The Senator declared that leaders without dedication to advance democracy and unite the country regardless of race, religious and ethnic biases, must be rejected. If despotic leaders or generally egoistic individuals are in power, human rights abuse can become the norm. In effect, the state of affairs can go downhill when religious or ethnic hatred escalates.

In an expedition to bring down corrupt leaders, Sani is firmly giving a voice to his followers and all citizens to not just sit and wait. His clarion call is simple: It is time for all Nigerians to put aside their ethnic and religious differences to demand their civil liberties. This will be a payback to activist Shehu Sani who has altruistically fought for human rights, freedoms, and democracy in this country. Given that it is this activism that pulled Nigeria out of military rule, Mr. Sani deserves praise and national recognition. However, he would feel more celebrated if Nigerians of every tribe unite and fight for the cause he believes in.

CHAPTER 7

BUBA GALADIMA

Well, probably it shocks you that Buba Galadima, a once-close ally of President Muhammadu Buhari broke ranks with him, politically. It is inconceivable that Galadima ended the romance he so cherished with Buhari. He has been an ardent supporter of Buhari before and after he became the President of the Federal Republic of Nigeria. Today, they do not see eye-to-eye. This emphasizes how things could turn out to be when people differ politically. However, the current turn of events reveals political deceit and mistrust in the country.

Galadima is that he has been in politics for a long time before the restoration of the fair democracy Nigerian boasts of today. For all that time, he has been in opposition parties. Usually, what edge him out to the opposition are disagreements with elected leaders. For him, when an elected leader fails to deliver as promised, the honorable thing to do is to walk out of that relationship. That is how he found himself out of the Buhari-led government.

In retrospect, this is a man with a perfect understanding of the murky waters of Nigerian politics. A sneak peek into his political history shows that he became a chieftain of ANPP (All Nigerian People's Party) in 1999. This was one of the major opposition parties in the country then. During President Olusegun Obasanjo's reign, he was a prominent critic. With his stinging criticism of the ruling class, he was arrested many times. Some arrests were construed as mere attempts to intimidate him into silence. Being a virtuous man with strong ideas and principles, the arrests only braced him up. In the early 2000s, he was apprehended for direct involvement in anti-government protests. Many of these politically motivated arrests did not lead to any serious prosecution. They were only threatening and Galadima appeared not to bother a lot about the arrest, knowing that no genuine charges could stand his way.

Mr. Galadima was appointed the National Secretary of CPC (Congress for Progressive Change) party. President Buhari was an influential party member and the party's presidential candidate. Through this party, he took a stab at the presidency but failed to clinch the seat. Afterward, Galadima played a crucial role that resulted in the formation of the current ruling party, APC. After differing with the party, he defected to PDP, the current leading opposition party, where he served as a spokesperson. He claimed on several occasions that President Buhari did not legitimately win the 2019 presidential election. The controversy of such an assertion did not come as a shocker, given that the general election was clouded with malpractices. The 2019 general election was an acid test for democracy in Nigeria and voter intimidation uncovered its fragility. Intimidating the electorate in the camp of opposition supporters is a common practice in countries with leaders determined to undermine voters' choice.

Nevertheless, Mr. Galadima is a party hopper, no doubt about that. He has been switching parties from the early 2000s. While looking for the reason/s that perhaps triggered Galadima to ditch the APC, I arrived at the conclusion that the ideology Galadima stands for underlines his party-switching behavior. He has been at the forefront of fighting the social injustice that permeate the Nigerian society. He has been locking horns with elected leaders who do not stick to their pre-election promises. Politicians have sweet tongue that generally persuades the public into supporting them. They entice people with several promises only to fail them when elected. This trend appears to disillusion Galadima to the core and leaves him with the only option of walking out to a party that is not people centered. When leaders he wholeheartedly supported turn out to be turncoats, the democratic decision is to bolt out of the party. Galadima was always persuaded to work with people that share the same ideology. This is indispensable in transforming Nigeria into a true democracy.

His apparent rebellion against President Buhari leaves tongues wagging considering the fact that he has supported Buhari since 2003. Let us look at this analytically. Going by the performance of Buhari as president - his lackluster approach to tackle problems facing Nigeria - you are likely to agree that Galadima is fighting for a national cause. He is not driven by self-interest but driven by the performance and development of Nigeria. He is a person who would stand for another who has the interest of the country at heart. Every President from 1999 to the present, have not performed outstandingly. These leaders promised a lot, but only to let the public down. Galadima, who became chairman of the ruling APC (All Progressive Congress), assailed President Buhari for disillusioning the public. He once stated that; "APC has run a rudderless, inept, and incompetent government that has failed to deliver good governance to the Nigerian people." From this claim, it is crystal-clear that Mr. Galadima saw that the APC and its leadership were no longer working for Nigerians. On that basis, Galadima was sensible to part ways with the party and work with like-minded people. As someone who is focused on seeing his country develop, it would be a betrayal of the public trust to continue working for APC. Even if some individuals view him as a "scavenger" or an "opportunist" who quit APC after getting a raw deal. He has a vision for this country that is pushing him to work with like-minded people and with a determination to lead and develop Nigeria.

Galadima - a fighter for people and democracy

We will all agree that Nigeria is a great country with great potential. It is a country that the whole world looks at with interest and admiration. Unluckily, the socio-economic inequality and poor leadership continue to pose a significant threat to its democracy. In every chapter, and perhaps paragraph, you must have come across the phrase "poor leadership." You would wonder why it is overly used in this book. That is the only problem we have in Nigeria, summarily. When leadership becomes good as everyone would wish, then major problems facing West Africa, and indeed African would be solved. But because the country is in the hands of politicians, whose personal interests regrettably supersede national ambitions, Nigeria continues to lag.

Year in and year out, the dreams of a developed society and economic empowerment are gradually fading. The dreams of an improved country can only be realized when there is good leadership. Lack of it is detrimental to democracy, justice, rule of law and economy. A society cannot be fair and just with poor leaders holding onto power without regard for citizens. Galadima, a former close ally of President Buhari, has seen it all and believes firmly that leadership is not about personality. It is about acceptance by people and working for people. This goes to the very essence of democracy itself – defined as *"government of the people by the people and for the people"*. Politicians are supposed to work for the nation altruistically. However, this is not happening as majority of leaders in Nigeria are turning their backs on the citizens they are expected to serve. This reflects how poorly the country is led. National issues that require urgent policy-guided actions are not prioritized; instead, politicians at the chagrin of their subjects are living ostentatiously.

Insecurity, corruption, poverty, ethnic cleansing, and authoritarianism are threatening Nigeria's democracy and ravaging every aspect of nationhood that this country has been fighting for so dearly. The senselessness with which the Nigerian leaders are running the country is a trend that has energized patriots like Galadima to go against the grain, a stormy wave that, if he does not tread carefully, can sweep him away - given that political differences in Nigeria can cost someone his life! Extra-judicial killings are not new in this country and those whom the government considers "saboteurs" have all the reasons to worry about their lives. After all, it is a basic truth that quitting the ruling party is not an easy decision especially for pawns. In Galadima's case – he is not a pushover at all, bravely ditched his long-time friend to pursue a cause that is of public interest. Considering that the government can be so ruthless on its vicious critics, in particular, those who at some point were in the inner circle of the President, it was a risky resolution by Galadima. Some privileges come with supporting the President for those who blow his trumpet even if he is the laziest or most inept leaders perhaps on earth. That did not persuade this brave man to stay in APC-led government that he is fully convinced has failed the citizens.

Nonetheless, for the sake of Nigeria and the desire to support a visionary leader that can save the country from endemic problems like corruption and poverty, Galadima had to walk out on Buhari. He did not ditch his friend just for the sake of doing so, but he took the step to fight for a better cause for this country. He had to defect to a party that he believes is ready and committed to serving Nigerians and that is observed in the way he supported, wholeheartedly, PDP's presidential candidate Atiku Abubakar. The country, in his view, needed fresh leadership which the former Vice President Atiku Abubakar would have offered. Ousting President Buhari could have been the beginning of a journey to reconstruct Nigeria both economically and democratically. That dream was cut short though, following the controversial re-election of Buhari. Perhaps, optimistically, the circumstances can change as Buhari still has room to correct his first-term failings. Although the rank and file of APC have been creating a narrative that Galadima's decision to leave the party was for his selfish interest, it is however firm on his mind that he quit because of the party's ineptness. APC and President Buhari sought a mandate in 2015 to serve people, but the public became a non-issue and were ignored after victory. The inability of President Buhari to transform Nigeria and pull people out of poverty as pledged is a failure of the entire party. Aggrieved and disillusioned by the leadership of President Buhari, Galadima opted to fight for justice, fairness, and rule of law. On Television interviews and public forums, this man boisterously and daringly spoke about the Nigerian Dream as he restated how he has been fighting for justice, rule of law and fairness since 1978. It is factual that Galadima has been fighting for what he says, and there is no denial about that, especially for honest students of history.

From a personal analysis of this daring politician, I have come to a reasonable conclusion that the betrayal of the APC government to the Nigerian people accounts for broadsides Galadima directed at Buhari. In one of the interviews on Garfield TV with Mercy Abang, which can be accessed online, Mr. Galadima insisted that he quit the party to protect personal integrity. This ethical man felt that supporting President Buhari further could have brought into question his integrity- a value that he has protected jealously for many years. Integrity to this man Galadima is paramount and he could not trade it for personal material gain. He is a unique leader who stands high on a moral pedestal, something that has been lacking in Nigerian leadership. To deepen democracy, integrity among leaders should be held highly and equally. This is critical for leadership. There is vast literature that argues that integrity is the core of leadership and it secures democracy. Integrity, not in a scholarly definition, refers to the consistency of principles, measures, values, methods, outcomes, and expectations. It is about committing to doing only the right things at all times. If a leader or any person upholds integrity, they cannot breach trust or be corrupt. With politicians like Galadima not compromising their integrity, there is hope that with time, we shall get ethical leaders back to the helms in this country.

As the spokesperson of the presidential candidate of Atiku Abubakar, Galadima also insisted on electoral integrity. In this, the focus was for Nigeria to conduct an election that is transparent and accountable. It would be a pipe dream for Nigeria to claim that it has made tremendous democratic progress if electoral integrity cannot be guaranteed. This is not a solitary call by Galadima, but it is for all people that care about this country to insist on fair elections to advance its democracy. It is a fortune to have a leader who can audaciously demand electoral integrity. An election is an essential element of democracy that gives people the right to elect individuals that will lead them democratically. The very moment the country allows politicians to undermine electoral integrity by rigging or intimidating voters, we destroy democracy. The 2019 general election, as I stated earlier, was a litmus test for Nigeria's democracy. It was marred with intimidation of voters and destruction of lives and property. I do not have evidence to prove malpractices in the 2019 presidential election, but I am particularly interested in the electoral integrity in Nigeria which Galadima is clamoring for. In Africa, leaders, especially the incumbents seeking re-election, deliberately weaken electoral integrity. If their re-election is not a sure deal, they retain power and rig themselves in. This is an affront to democracy that cannot be condoned if we are serious about free, fair, and transparent election that Galadima is fighting for.

Experience from Zimbabwe, Gambia, Uganda, and Kenya disclose the consequences of undercutting electoral integrity. Every election cycle in these countries has been characterized by bloodbath - when citizens display their displeasure in peaceful protests, incumbents use the police to teargas and even fire live ammunition on them. The results have been unwarranted deaths and destabilization of the social fabric of society and business activities. From this experience, we can understand where the reasoning of Galadima on why we should protect the integrity of every election comes from. The only means Nigeria can develop and reinforce its democracy is for the leaders to live with integrity. Similarly, they should insist that all processes such as an election are conducted with integrity. If truth be told, if leaders whether political, religious, or corporate can act with this value, it would be feasible to solve national problems like corruption, nepotism, and tribalism.

Scrutiny of the life of Galadima further indicates that he is a person who has always striven to do what is right for the country. His interests do not come first, but last, because of his commitment to improving Nigeria and calling for leaders to be responsible to the people who elected them. It is rare to get a person of such high caliber so interested in serving people rather than enriching himself. In spite of having served in public offices, it is no secret; he has not amassed wealth like the majority of Nigerian political leaders. This is an affirmation of a politician that is devoted to making Nigeria a society that works for all, instead of a select few who steal for self-enrichment.

Nonetheless, the issues this man stands for, confirms him as a national hero that we have continuously snubbed. We refuse to crown people like Galadima. We do not give them public support that would energize them to fight for reforms in this country. Justifiably, our lethargy has encouraged the elected and non-performing leaders to carry out national duties with impunity. In my personal observation, I have noted that the critical aspects of his argument are the brass tacks we need for our democracy. When a person of Galadima's stature raises concerns and criticizes the government, he wants the public to have a sense of what democracy is. It is not that he is fighting for personal interests, but for leaders to focus on service delivery and build institutions that democracy rely on. He speaks about issues such as transparency and accountability, human rights and freedom, good governance, electoral integrity, and fair treatment of people. When the government or, the Nigerian leaders observe strictly these essential issues, the country will be headed in the right direction.

Apart from that, he has also condemned human rights abuse in the country. If this is not heroism and dedication to fight for democracy, what else should we call it? This is a man who has been there before we even gained civilian rule. He has observed much and understands how governments brutalize citizens with the intent to silence them. Here, Galadima does not care about the likely viciousness he is to face from the government he was once part of. Threats to his life are not swaying him away from pursuing a cause that would guarantee the protection of every Nigerian's rights.

My mind remains clear that Buba Galadima is a straightforward politician whose fight for democracy deserves recognition. He may have flip-flopped here and there in the eyes and minds of the Low-Brows, but people should acknowledge that this is a man of the people. A man who stands for justice the Nigerian society is passionately looking for. The government should work for everyone and address speedily and effectively issues affecting the Nigerian society. This is a call that Galadima is making to the leadership of Nigeria. Nigerians should accord respect to and celebrate Galadima in whichever fashion they can for his continuous and consistent efforts to fight for democracy.

CHAPTER 8

KADARIA AHMED

Kadaria Ahmed is a Nigerian columnist, media business-person, and TV host. She began her profession at the BBC in London and has worked in print, radio, TV, and online platforms. As she clocked 50, she chose to offer back to the calling she is so passionate about by starting the "Daria Workshop Series" in three urban areas: Kano where she was educated, Uyo where she served and Lagos, the city she calls home. She launched a training, called Media Trust Limited in Abuja where numerous Daily Trust reporters were trained extensively for the purpose of being able to differentiate counterfeit news, embrace ethical standards. It was additionally meant to handle the most critical issues putting journalism in danger and preparing members on how to rehearse free, skilled, moral, and socially mindful journalism.

Sit down for a moment and reflect on the role of the media in society, governance, and democracy. In your reflection, you will appreciate the work journalists do in fighting for good governance, and democracy. The media is a mirror to society and in one fell swoop a bridge between society and government. It is through the media that people can understand their environment and society. It is the media that links the government and the people.

For Nigeria to fully democratize, respect human rights and empower her people, the media must continue to play a pivotal role in achieving such fundamental goals that seem farfetched in our country. The media is critical in the realization of Nigeria's democracy and the journalists sometimes are assailed for speaking the truth. Even in the face of intimidation, Nigerian journalists continue to put their lives to danger in pursuit of truth, democracy, and good governance. Sometimes, we may not agree with some journalists, and accuse them of bias and sycophancy, they still do a commendable job. I have witnessed or observed the journey of Kadaria Ahmed and cogently concluded that she is a campaigner of democracy- a voice for the voiceless. I do not think anyone needs to doubt that. Her work, experience, and record speak volumes about this exceptional journalist.

As I explained in the beginning of this chapter about Kadaria Ahmed's career, she is not a one-trick pony, but an outright all-rounder. She is a highly respected TV host and media entrepreneur who is using her position to speak truth to power. Her cultivated personality and fearlessness in reporting analytically make her stand out as a voice for the voiceless. Her career spans up to 20 years starting with the BBC as a senior producer working on award-winning programs that focused on Network Africa. In that capacity, she helped shape the news agenda for leading programs and reported from different parts of the world She has a degree from Bayero University, Kano (BUK) where she studied Mass Communication and then a master's degree in television documentary from Gold-smith College, University of London. This mother of two is an indigene of Zamfara State who worked as the editor of the now-defunct newspaper NEXT. She has moderated several events including the 2011 Presidential Debate. She is also a judge on the Wole Soyinka Centre for Investiga-tive Journalism and a member of the Nigerian Guild of Editors. She is presently hosting her show Straight Talk on Channels TV. She is the CEO Radio Now 95.3 a Lagos based radio station.

The anatomy of Zamfara problems
Ms. Ahmed dabbled into

Kadaria, as a citizen of Zamfara State, rose up to the plight of the Zanfarians at the time her people were going through tough and bitter experience of killings of innocent citi-zens. It was then she described the former Governor Yari of Zamfara State as "the most useless governor in Nigerian history" due to his inability to handle the troubling situ-ation. While addressing journalists during a protest over the killings in Zamfara, she decried the killings and kid-nappings in her state as abhorrent and called on the state governor to hang his boots. In her statement, she did not fear to call out leaders who only care about citizens when it comes to elections.

Kadaria Ahmed looked at the brewing crisis in Nigeria and that of Zamfara and recalled "Growing up in about 50 years ago in Nigeria's north-western Zamfara State, I would never have envisioned its fate of pounding destitution and heightening savagery as it is now. There was also a textile company; Sugar giant Tate and Lyle had its presence there then, an oil plant and a cotton plant. As children at the time, the most loved arena in Gusau was the sweet processing plant, which was run by a Lebanese family who was, in every practical sense, local people. There, we could fulfill our longings at no cost. A working rail line moved merchandise out and all over Nigeria and got passengers into the state, a significant number of who were attracted to the area's flourishing enterprises. In Gusau, there was ethnic diversity- Igbos from the south-east, the Yorubas from south-western Nigeria, Indian and Lebanese communities included. This cosmopolitanism completely fueled the area's aspiration for statehood. This was accomplished in 1996." This is a nostalgia that paints an exceptional and progressive journey of Zamfara state before it plunged into penury, despondency, and bleakness.

Kadaria, as a concerned citizen of Zamfara who persistently wants her state to turnaround for a better future lament the expanding destitution in her state. She notes that instead of using the natural resources that God provided for the region, especially Zamfara, to educate and support citizens, the northern political class has looted from their people for self-aggrandizement. The Oxford University Human Development Index once indicated that Zamfara State's poverty rate was about 92%. While the economy declined, ultra-conservatism shot up. In 2000,

Sharia was introduced in Zamfara State by the past governor, Ahmad Yakima, which genuinely undermined the multicultural thought of the state.

Only a weak and uninformed leader forces religion on his people. When they want to manipulate and rob their citizens dry, they exploit religion to intimidate others, just to send a caveat to the opposition, when they themselves are scoundrels. Introduction of Sharia laws was a sideshow and apparent disregard to critical issues that required secular approach. In Kadaria's mind, the governor and other leaders should have focused on pertinent issues such as cattle rustling rather than using religion to cudgel dissenting voices. If you remember, when cattle rustling became a thorny issue in Zamfara, Governor Abdulaziz Yari created a local vigilante organization to battle with the thieves in 2013. Was that a right decision? That is something that, in Kadaria's line of thinking was wrong since this seemed to be a strategy that was doomed to fail. Reading her mind, which ostensibly some may consider a misreading, Yari was not a strategic decision maker in that case. Good leaders strategise on how to solve problems, but in this case undoubtedly, Governor Yari was in a knee jerk reaction. Kadaria's fight for justice and security, indeed, is a genuine one, considering the events witnessed in her Zamfara State.

Fighting for a secure state for her people and holding leaders in power to account in all possibility affirmed Kadaria's commitment to encourage her fellow citizens to ask for what is essential for their living. About 28 people were butchered on 28 March 2019, by the obscure shooters who operated on motorbikes in the town of Bawar Daji, which was some 90km (55 miles) from Gusau. Those killed were at a funeral service for the people killed during past and agonizingly comparative assault. For quite a while, the kidnappings, killings, and ambushes were simply occurring in almost all the nooks and crannies of Zamfara state. It was underreported and those killed at a funeral lived on the edges of national awareness. They were poor, provincial individuals, who only squeezed out a living as peasants and herders in a zone that is geologically expelled from the point of convergence of the state administration.

The killings did not fit the parallel revealing that the Nigerian media find enchanting. Since the situation at hand did not look like the Hausa-Fulani against different other groups nor Christians against Muslims or North versus the South, which the media preferred. It cannot be accounted for as proof of the already broken Nigeria along religious and ethnic lines. The reckless and unstoppable killings disclosed a more extensive, national concern of the country's failing State that cannot satisfy its most essential central role of ensuring quality security for its citizens. Thus, the individuals of Zamfara are left only with their destiny.

Across Nigeria, there is a lot of ungoverned space that lends itself to disorder without a utilitarian state security apparatus. Rugu forest in the north-west cuts over various locales including Zamfara, which borders Niger. That forest has been compared with the Sambisa forest in Borno State, which has become an alcove for Boko Haram as of late. Chris Ngwodo, who is a specialist in the region, stated: "the circumstance in Zamfara is compared to where Borno State was in 2009-2010 when Boko Haram propelled its bloody uprising.

The banditry killings in Zamfara are deteriorating every day. There's a great concern in northern Nigeria over the degree of banditry and abductions in the territory of Zamfara". Ms. Kadaria Ahmed lashed out at the Zamfara government over what she termed "a flood of killings". "Consistently we buried between 30, 40 and 50 individuals," she said in a video, on TV and afterward broadly shared via web-based networking media. She stated that there were a bigger number of killings occurring in Zamfara than in Adamawa, Borno and Yobe states, and other regions of north-eastern Nigeria, which was influenced by the Islamist aggressors, Boko Haram.

Zamfara has long been faced with some problems of kidnapping for ransom, armed bandits, cattle rustling, and attacking communities which incited some local individuals to organize vigilante gangs. Recently, there has been development in casual mining at the mineral-rich state, which has pulled in non-indigenes to the state, further fueling influx and exacerbated the precarious situation. Toward the start of April 2019, the new governor for the state, Dr. Matawalle reacted to worries over the expanding levels of viciousness and used the opportunity to suspend all the mining exercises in the state, and also sent extra troops to the zone. The Nigeria Security Tracker, delivered by Washington concerning Foreign Relations (CFR), featured a huge upsurge in the killings as indicated by the following figures. In 2017, 52 deaths; 2018, 288 deaths; 2019, 262 deaths. The CFR information additionally demonstrates a sharp rise in the killings of individuals from armed groups, which would incorporate the vigilantes, bandits, and others that engaged in criminal activities. These senseless killings not only exasperate Kadaria, but also a majority of Nigerians. It is intolerable and unacceptable to continue losing such important lives. It is shameful to expect to be called an Honorable, a Governor or a leader, at a time killings and murders are becoming so common in Zamfara.

When leaders fail, the best thing to do is to take to the streets and call them out. Leaders have the power and mandate to protect people, and in case of failure, they should be admonished. In her effort to bring to the street the horrendous situations in Zamfara, the citizens of the state joined hands with Kadaria and used the opportunity to demand for the resignation of Governor Yari. However, Ms. Ahmed's action received back-to-back stinging criticism from some quarters. The Coalition of National Democratic Watchdog of Nigeria after a review of the killings in Zamfara condemned Kadaria Ahmed for a sustained attack on governor Yari. The coalition cunningly exonerated the Governor from noticeable failure in protecting his state. The reaction of The Coalition of National Democratic Watchdog of Nigeria on Ms. Kadaria in the way she handled the protest against the killings in Zamfara state was appalling to me. Shockingly, a coalition will go on defending a sitting government of the state where such terrible killings happened. The terrible situation that even the non-residents of Zamfara and the whole world saw and may likely come up with the same conclusions that the governor was indeed not capable of leading the state. As long as someone is the Governor of a State, "the good, the bad and the ugly" of that State are attributed to him, same applies to the President of our nation – where the buck stops.

We all know that President Buhari is good and God-fearing as an individual. However, as the intellectual apparatus, both at home and abroad diagnosed his system of governance, it concluded that his government performed below par because of the obsequious people he surrounds himself with as advisers. Remember, he chose them; hence, he must take those failures as his responsibility. The same applies to governor Yari; we do not care if the system goes this way or that, all we know is that he was the governor of Zamfara state as at the time those inhumane killings happened. He once raised his hand to an oath that, he will defend and protect the state citizens. So, the accusation by Ms. Ahmed at that terrible time is spot on. That is my personal conclusion on the matter.

It must also be understood that Kadaria is a citizen and one of the mothers of that state. The death of one person in that state or the entire country is like her own! Is it not written in the Quran that; the killing of one person is the killing of everyone in that nation! According to the analysis of the coalition, the actual operations of each state of the federation are in the hands of the Governor. So, the coalition is telling Kadaria or the entire nation that governor Yari should not be blamed for any wrongdoing, but president Buhari should be blamed. That is fine, and I think President Buhari is hearing or reading this. However, the main representative of President Buhari when those evil occurrences were going on in Zamfara was Governor Yari and whatever actions or names that the Zamfara citizen called him, he deserved. Let critics understand this very well: as long as Nigeria decided to be democratically governed, such reaction by Ms. Kadaria is inevitable. In modern constitutional states, freedom of expression, including freedom of speech and freedom of the press is recognized.

Abysmal state of affairs in Zamfara state and media role
Does "The Coalition of National Democratic Watchdog of Nigeria" understand that, in 2018, only 28 pupils registered for the common entrance exam in a state with a population of almost 4 million? Around the same time, the Senior School Certificate Exam NECO that was written in November/December of the same year, only 186 students from Zamfara took it. The pass rate was horrendous, which was at 13 percent. This indicated that just 24 students measured up. Also, the outcomes for the last West African school certificate were no better either. Out of the 36 States in Nigeria, including the Federal Capital Territory, Zamfara came last. The indicators used to quantify development were likewise appalling. The Oxford Poverty and Human Development Index made it known that, in Zamfara, 92 percent of the state's population, 9 out of 10 individuals live in destitution.

With the above statistics, I do not think any reasonable and reputable organization should have the guts to accuse Ms. Kadaria of any wrongdoing. Zamfara is a state with worse poverty level than a state like Borno. Borno State has been in the heart of insurgency for around 7 years, with criminals and stronghold cattle rustlers rampaging unchecked. The degree of instability in the state was nearly as high as that found in some of the country's combat areas. Tremendous swathes of this state are adequately ungovernable and constrained by scoundrels and rustlers, basically putting a stop to agriculture, which is one of the main backbones of the state. The consequence of this is a society that barely ekes out a living and which is additionally left to fight with several maladies like cholera and meningitis. These are diseases that have been a situation of the past in many areas of the country. The Nigerian Medical Association, Zamfara chapter depicted the wellbeing of the state as poor. They said the offices are 'lacking' and in a 'sorry state' with inadequate health workers. The World Health Organization has depicted the meningitis episode which kills hundreds yearly as avoidable if a great leader comes out to help.

All things considered, as can be concluded, Zamfara suffers from only one problem: Bad administration, ill-equipped leaders. Each issue that affects the state and its populace can be attributed to the scourge of having successive governments that intentionally 'administered' for themselves as opposed to serving the all-inclusive community. The decision of Zamfara striving for statehood was partly fueled by the centrality of Gusau, which eventually became the capital city of the state due to its relative affluence. It should be understood that agriculture shaped the bedrock of the enterprises that fueled this success. These enterprises incorporated an oil mill, some ginneries, a sugar manufacturing plant, a textile company, and a tannery whose raw materials are traded in the area. The tannery by John Holt, a British company, processed hides, and skins for export to Europe. Gusau had a pluralistic populace, where most of its people had jobs that enabled them to look after their families and live-in dignified ways. The outcome was a dynamic, flourishing community whose future was bright.

Remembering the yesteryear blessings and the good images of Zamfara, Ms. Ahmed used what she has and what she is good at to help her people. She is a Journalist, celebrity, and an activist in her capacity. Having this uniqueness is a plus for the actions she took to salvage her state from the hand of the enemies at the time. In line with the good use of media to influence situations in our society, celebrity activism has an exceptionally constructive outcome on society too. Celebrity activism usually draws attention to every kind of diverse issues, just as the terrible conditions in Zamfara. Therefore, more celebrities ought to move toward becoming activists. What is more, celebrity activism offers famous people like Kadaria a chance to utilize their riches to benefit an option that is more prominent than themselves. Celebrity activism truly assists the less fortunate and offers back to the community. As obvious throughout the world, celebrity activism ought to be praised as it invigorates mindfulness and stands out to every single distinctive sort of purpose.

Besides, celebrity activism helps bring issues to light for a wide range of causes. Kadaria as a celebrity activist pays attention to political and social issues which are especially important to every nation. In conclusion, activism enables celebrities to get included and work for something that has effect on other people. By combining her profession as a journalist, using mass communication to bring to light the ugliness that befell Zamfara State at the time, was a thing many of my colleagues here abroad applauded her for. Therefore, mass media influences contemporary societies.

The influence of mass media is certainly vast. Media can be used for good or bad outcomes. Media can be used to manipulate the public, bad for the government when it is used for the benefits of the masses and good for the government when it is used to benefit them when the rigging of election is for their good. Hence, the neutrality of the media must be sacrosanct.

Neutrality is fairly easy to define when; for instance, it is a question of apportioning the use of the media for political propaganda at election time in a democracy. I believe that, in this situation, neutrality is not possible, and that, if it were possible, it would not be right. To try to be neutral between what one deems to be right and what one deems to be wrong is tantamount to taking sides with what one deems to be wrong, since this would be a breach of one's moral duty to take sides with what one deems to be right. Therefore, on moral matters, neutrality is impossible between issues of right and wrong. However, I insist that the neutrality of the mass media is essential. As a guideline for defining this kind of practical neutrality, I might offer this suggestion. The mass media must consistently protect the right of the people and deliver their news from the viewpoint of respect for life and to this end; Ms. Kadaria Ahmed took the side of the masses and must not be accused by any coalition whatsoever but applauded for a job well-done.

Let us not forget, leadership is a struggle. In any endeavor in life, taking the initiative is most important. Ekiti people have a saying: "Seize the initiative and you will win". Failing to take the initiative at the right moment can lead to defeat. Seizing the initiative is the sure way to victory. Give full attention to even the smallest matter. Always take the appropriate measure in any situation promptly. Each sensitive and earnest action taken for the sake of our people, for Zanfarians and the country's happiness and the success of our struggles spread joy. Standing up by a leader like Kadaria gains momentum through the passion, encouragement, and swift responses of the populace that came out with her in the struggle. In any undertaking, victory goes to those who are firmly determined to win. That is why it is important to focus our minds on winning. If we pray with this kind of resolve, then, courage and wisdom will well forth from within us. Our lives will shine brightly and vibrantly. Only by refuting error can the truth be established. It is crucial that the Nigerian populace blaze with the dauntless spirit of "refuting the erroneous and revealing the truth", just like Ms. Kadaria Ahmed did. Truth is strength. We must courageously demonstrate that strength, letting it resonate as a powerful conviction in our words. As my father used to say: "Advance with courage and confidence!"

Thus, being gentle to those who are suffering, let us be resolute in our opposition to corruption and wrongdoing with the same spirit as the saints. When we act for the sake of good in this way, we will gain benefits without fail. We use our voice to refute the erroneous and reveal the truth. When we speak in earnest, we can vanquish devilish functions. Our vibrant, invigorating voices can completely change other's hearts. The important thing is for us to share our convictions with honesty and courage. The voice of truth is the spark that awakens others.

The Nigerian youth have a special mission in this regard. Having seen what a leader like Ms. Kadaria Ahmed has done as regards the freedom of Zamfara from the hands of those brute leaders of yesteryears, they should summon up the courage of a lion king and never succumb to threats from anyone. The lion king is known to fears no other beast, so also its cubs. Oh yes, there will be slanderers, but they should also remember that slanderers are like barking foxes, and that Ms. Ahmed's followers are like roaring lions. She is calling on you all to speak up with the same spirit as she did. The united declarations of mentor and disciples are the roar of lions.

The dividend of her struggle produced the Zamfara-like-paradise we are seeing today. Zamfara of today looks as if there was no killing and the shedding of innocent blood as it was in the yesteryears. Thank you Dr. Matawalle, the current Governor of the state. Even our noble's past is thanking you, you have done great. You did not let the sweat of people like Ms. Kadaria Ahmed go dry before you turned what seemed like a brute society into something like paradise as it is now. I have said so much about Governor Matawalle in the pages dedicated to him, I will not go further.

You see, a leader is another name for one who strives with courage. A dynamic spiritual current flows through such an individual that makes him shine. Their powerful commitment draws others to them like a magnet and inspires those people to stand and act. They can unite people's hearts. It is not about strategies or methods. When you strive in faith, earnestly determined to take full responsibility, boundless wisdom will well up from within you. So, being appointed or elected a leader for a group or society and working hard to actively support his fellow citizens will enable him to be a great leader throughout the three existences of past, present, and the future. This is surely the law of Cause and Effect that is bound in us all. Thank you, Ms. Kadaria Ahmed, you are a true lead.

⊷⊶

CHAPTER 9

DR. PETER AYODELE FAYOSE

The majority of the country will be wondering what exactly someone has to celebrate with the leadership of Peter Ayodele Fayose. I think leaders who have previously held political offices and failed (according to some people's insinuations) at their obligations may likely have a hard time to clean their images or justify their performance. You may argue that Fayose held a public office and did not perform superbly; hence he lacks temerity to accuse others of being total failures or qualities that justify him as a campaigner of democracy. But his first and second election into governorship underlines his good leadership provided that his electoral victory was fair and just. He led Ekiti State twice and I may not right pass judgment on his performance. However, you can hold an opinion that may differ from mine completely based on your

informed assessment of what changed or did not change in Ekiti State during governor Fayose's reign. Even if we differ, I will ask you to look at this former governor from a different angle to get a sense of his love for his state and country at large. He is a person of unwavering dedication to change Nigeria for the better, based on his utterances, beliefs, principles, vision, and support he enjoys.

But before delving into why I deem ex-governor Fayose a great leader whose contributions to our democracy deserve commendation, I would state that his two terms in office point to a man who is dedicated to serving humanity. In retrospect, his election in 2003 as a governor in Ekiti State left the then incumbent's mouth agape because it was an unfathomable defeat to him. Before completing his term - unluckily, he was impeached in 2006, a jinxed occurrence that left him a wounded lion whose dreams had come to a halt unexpectedly. With his hopes high though, he later jumped into the gubernatorial race to become governor again in Ekiti State and floored another incumbent, winning a coveted seat for the second time in spite of a dark history of impeachment. An impeachment that spelled doom on his political future-ostensibly, he was left a fractured man whose aspirations became oblique going into the future. Regardless of a political tumbling following undesirable impeachment, his unexpected governorship victory in the 2014 election in Ekiti State proved that he is still a voice for the voiceless. It is a rare re-election, but since he won in his second run for the governorship, we cannot doubt that his ideas are welcome by his base and other Nigerians. You cannot call his re-election after an impeachment a big mistake given that people in

Ekiti State are educated in spite of being in an anecdotally poor state. Trust, this PDP ex-governor has ideas that are critical to better our democracy once all leaders commit to walking the talk-something that is lacking in our budding democracy.

It is important to note as well that Fayose declared his interest to run for president in 2019 on a PDP ticket. However, the party did not buy into his quest. He did not capture the PDP presidential ticket, but clearly, there was a group of people who believed that he was up to the task to steer the country in the right direction. A person that people trust to have the ability to run not just a state, but the entire country is one that cannot be rubbished. I am a believer in his philosophy of what the Nigerian democracy should be. He is a politician that believes that we should redefine our democracy from the Nigerian perspective, not from the western world standpoint. Not that he has issues with the West, but his understanding of democracy is always based on context. In the context of Nigeria, democracy is about leaders lifting the downtrodden in society, empowering, protecting and leading them most humanely. When leaders work tirelessly and in a non-discriminatory fashion to foster justice and improve lives, they are rooting for democracy. I may mention this again; modern democracy is not an arranged script where leaders refer to check if they are governing democratically.

Although I reiterated the tenets of democracy, my message is that Nigeria's democracy is different based on the perspective of Fayose. His understanding of democracy is basic, but appropriate in our society: serve the people, keep them safe, foster peace between and among the communities and treat them fairly. The simplicity of this view on what democracy in Nigeria should be, however, does not complicate the general view we have about democracy. Fayose is just a confident person that believes we should treat people fairly, unite communities and empower them so that they can focus diligently on nation-building. Is it such a hard task? It is simple and democracy in the literal sense is easy and easily implementable if leaders view themselves as servants to the people. We sometimes complicate democracy when it is the simplest thing to implement. Dictatorship is expensive to sustain while democracy is easily sustained if leaders govern within the edicts of the constitution or according to the will of the people. If corruption is what is weakening democracy in Nigeria, leaders across the political divide ought not to antagonize, but instead, unite against the bane. As I write this book, I am aware of the latest happenings in Africa. See what is happening in Kenya. President Uhuru Kenyatta and opposition leader Raila Odinga put aside their political differences for the sake of democracy, the economy, and the people. In their unity of purpose, high ranking government officials such as a minister for the country's National Treasury were prosecuted for corruption. For your understanding, the man that was charged in the court of law in Kenya held an office like that of Nigeria's Minister for Finance. It is not a trouble-free decision to charge a person of such ranking. But it was the right thing to do for the sake of democracy, and responsible management of public resources and office.

While this may not be sufficient in eradicating graft in East Africa's largest economy, it went a long way to show that something can be done to cut the appetite of corruption in the continent. The African continent can say no to cross-border corruption where leaders plunder their country and stash their wealth in other corrupt countries. In our own country, Nigeria, corruption has been the primary impediment to our economy, democracy, and unity. This means that it is a national disaster that will require everyone to rise to fight. If for instance, it takes the opposition leadership and the ruling leadership to pull together to fight what is ailing in Kenya, why should we not do a similar thing in Nigeria? This kind of cooperation between rival political parties or personalities is already happening on the continent. In Nigeria, the same needs to happen for the country to have leaders that can fight vices like corruption. It is unfortunate to mention, that the ruling leaders in the APC, would consistently see PDP as enemies rather than individuals that also mean good for the people.

Leadership requires that you and I stand for the people and fight for what is right in our country. Sometimes we have to compromise not to rile each other for the sake of Nigeria and her people. That is how Fayose thinks our democracy should be and work. Political parties are simply vehicles that we use to race in a political contest. Though the sole purpose of every political party is about serving the people and governing the country accountably, Fayose feels that the failure of leaders to cooperate to fight vices undermining our democracy is what is preventing us from realizing a dream of a free, just, and fair society. Our political philosophy has to change for us to realize true democracy, a strong economy, and a peaceful and united nation. The politics of the North and South of the country is a negotiated democracy that should not be allowed to tear the country into two halves if indeed there is genuineness to democratize Nigeria and make it a society that works for everyone while protecting their rights and freedoms. In particular, I am going to argue how vital the beliefs and philosophy of ex-governor Fayose are fundamental to democracy in Nigeria.

Fayose views security as essential for a democratic and peaceful Nigeria

Every Nigerian understands that the security situation of our country is tearing down our peaceful coexistence. The Northern states, Middle Belt, and the South-west, plus the Southeast regions of the country are slowly becoming perilous due to numerous killings, kidnappings, and crimes that continue unabated and uncontrolled by security apparatus. The herdsmen, who I may be crucified for calling them by their tribe, are making it hard to achieve a serene environment for Nigerians and foreigners. In major parts of the country, security is no longer guaranteed as a killer celebrates a field day of butchering innocent people. The gunmen and evil-minded herdsmen are endangering the lives and properties of Nigerians. The vocal people who are supposed to speak for the voiceless in demanding the government to swing into action by securing our nation are going silent. For Fayose, silence is not his portion. He has been addressing the media and calling security officers and the top leadership to restore sanity by dealing accordingly with security threats. Fayose has been at the forefront to speak about our security without fear. As leaders who are supposed to help salvage the country from killers went silent amid continued butchering of innocent civilians, this has not been the position of governor Fayose. Fayose insists that, for a prosperous and democratic Nigeria, we must address insecurity. It is an impediment to unity, democracy, and a prosperous economy. Some people may see this as nothing to do with a push for democracy. Such people forget something so fundamental: that democracy cannot thrive in a volatile environment. Insecurity endangers the lives of many, and it does not add up for you to think that we can still become a democratic nation with the terrible killings that are happening everywhere and every day.

A democratic society is supposed to be peaceful, and people are guaranteed security. Even if we celebrate Democracy Day every year, we cannot realize democracy if we cannot fix our security. We would be just basking in the air. It gets unreasonable when leaders think that democracy is about voting only. The individuals running Nigeria praise and talk so much fairly about our democracy and if asked what makes them think we are a strong democratic nation; they would base their argument on the election. It gets on the nerves of any smart person for someone to premise our democracy only on voting. Yet even this voting process has been plagued with killing and maiming throughout the elections. The mere fact that the government of the day has failed to improve the security situation of our country is a justification of how our democracy is diminishing. Look at the United State of America, the United Kingdom, and other mature democracies. Security is given a lot of attention because that is the only way to secure democracy. I do not mean that these countries do not experience security lapses, but my position is that you cannot claim to run a country democratically if it is insecure. You must first improve security and ensure that the communities are happily coexisting. This is why I consider the call of Fayose to the federal government to improve security as a call of a great leader. With beefed up security, lives and property would be protected.

Notably, the right to life is a universal right that is highly protected in any established democracy. If this right is breached, it would be irrational to assert that our democracy is stable. Let us get our thoughts together to understand where my argument roots from. As someone with Masters in Counter Terrorism and Homeland Security, I see national security as a fundamental phenomenon that if not handled properly, can degenerate a country into a dictatorship. Since that is not our goal, we must appreciate the courage of Fayose to call out security agencies and unhinged leadership of President Buhari to rescue the country from the arrow and gun-wielding criminals taking over our nation. The killings, kidnappings, and the destroying of the farmers' means of daily livelihood still go on, unabated, and unchecked by security apparatus and there is no genuine commitment of the country's leadership to address the situation. What we would expect as patriots, is for the President and every leader stand up against criminals taking over our country. We cannot lose national sovereignty to a few criminals. It is the duty especially of the President to bring people regardless of their political affiliations together to get a solution to the current security problem in the country. This is a national problem that transcends party membership. And every leader should know that if indeed we are committed to democratization, we must work as a team to solve national problems.

What annoys, however, is the laxity with which the security concerns in some regions are handled. There is no quick response to deal with security threats and concurrently the country lacks the will from the government to put aside our political posturing for the sake of the country. That is why leaders like Fayose are left to single-handedly become "security activists"; if indeed there is a categorization of activism in that line. It is not that I am insensitive to what President Buhari is doing to deal with terrorists and other lawbreakers. But I feel that he is doing little and does not seem to budge when leaders from the opposition seek his collaboration with them for peace in their regions.

We are aware that Fayose has been accused not once, but numerously. This is different from the other Southwest region governors who were reluctant to hold the federal government accountable for insecurity in their zones, maybe because they belong to the ruling party. Though it is his own opinion, he argued that some governors in the region were protecting their relationship with the powerful figures in the ruling class. Those governors want to be in the good books with the leaders of their party who have openly failed in their duties. For sure, if that is the case, then we are in a serious problem because of leaders who want to maintain good relationships with those in the corridors of power at the detriment of people they are leading. You do not deserve to be a leader if you can callously value a political relationship with the few elite in power at the expense of masses- in their millions - you are supposed to protect. This is the kind of sycophancy that is truly undermining our democracy by all accounts.

My reasoning informs me that constructive criticism is healthy for any democracy while sycophancy makes leadership bad and insensitive. I have previously reiterated that it is better we call a spade a spade, which would be the only way we can go to tackle the security challenges facing us head-on. If leaders gloss over important issues such as security, the people who suffer are the penurious individuals. In my understanding or perception, perhaps, Fayose wanted governors with affected regions to put aside their political differences in other to get a solution to the insecurity ravaging their region and the country. In any case, if governors from the insecure or criminal infested regions bring together resources for a cause that benefits every Nigerian and paves way for peaceful coexistence, we will have a better tomorrow. Aside from urging governors to secure the safety of their followers as well as accusing them of sycophancy and laxity, Fayose was seen meeting with police authorities particularly in Ekiti State. The meetings signaled a committed governor that wanted his people to live peacefully and harmoniously. It was also tactical in his approach where, instead of just castigating the police, he opted to collaborate with them. This kind of cooperation in all probability strengthened efforts to deal with criminals accordingly. As we saw in governor Fayose's move, it was no longer time to accuse the police of incompetence and ineptness. Rather, it was time to pool resources together to secure Ekiti State, the whole western Nigeria, and its environs.

The meeting with police authorities and other stakeholders focused on coming up with proactive measures that helped the police prevent unbridled scathing attacks on civilians. This was a good move by the governor because, rather than staying comfortably in his air-conditioned offices and lamenting that the police are doing nothing to restore peace and sanity, he was at the roundtable proposing solutions to the problem. A democratic leader takes the problems of their followers as their own; they do not just complain but are out there seeking solutions to the problems they may be facing. It is against that backdrop that I argue that Fayose is a leader who thinks that we do not need to act grudgingly, but cooperate where necessary, provided such cooperation is for the good of the people. When the security situation is left to worsen, nobody will be left unhurt. For instance, we have heard cases where police, soldiers and national youth service corps lose their lives in their line of duty. In addition, nurses and local administrators in Ado local government reportedly lost their lives following raids by suspected robbers and kidnappers. Now, in this case, it is not just a common man staying home that risk losing their lives to attackers, but also civil servants. The insecurity Fayose was lamenting about could not spare anyone unless you are their sponsor. With that in mind, Fayose worked with rank and file of society to reinstate security for his state and the country at large, so as to be secure and favorable for the economy and democracy.

At public forums, Fayose was heard loud and clear, appealing to Nigerians to be concerned about their national security. It was not just a challenge for a particular region. This shows a man with the interest of the entire country to be safe. In his warning to Nigerians against worsening insecurity, he sought to bring the attention of everyone to this national disaster. The safety of everyone is what the good ex-governor sought. It is unpatriotic for those who are safe to sit pretty well at their homes, offices, or hotels when kidnappers, gun-wielding men or criminals wreak havoc on others. Democracy asks us to be concerned about everyone, and it makes us to see some problems that may be affecting us all. That is why democrats like Mr. Fayose continue putting more effort into living a legacy of a leader that dedicates himself wholeheartedly to fight for national security, an essential ingredient for our democracy. Taiwo Lakanu, an Ekiti State commissioner of police was pleased with the swiftness and willingness of Fayose to work with them. They acknowledged his efforts to bring the security chiefs together to bring back unity, peace, and harmony to his region. Governor Fayose equally commended the police for their great work on fighting for the sake of security in the state, even when he believes that there are still some security lapses in the states. But what was important was to improve the security situation of the state and the country at large.

Fast forward, if leaders can collaborate and put aside their differences in order to have a moment of brainstorming over problems facing states or the entire republic, Nigeria would be headed in the right direction. The federal government under any president, not just President Buhari, can forget any party differences and collaborate and welcome even dissenters or their fierce critics to the roundtable for the sole goal of addressing national issues. Nigeria will be the one to benefit from such, which would easily bring more maturity to the country's democracy. While you think this is wishful thinking, I would urge that politicians across the political aisle see this as an approach to strengthen our democracy. We hold different opinions, but that should not block us from engaging each other on central issues that can help us forge forward as one united country. Regardless of the power your office wields, it is critical that leaders enthusiastically work together for the sake of the country. In mature democracies, leaders may hold sharply contrasting opinions, but when it comes to vital issues, they have to sit down and propose resolutions.

Idealistically, the type of security that Mr. Fayose has been advocating for in the country has a direct impact on how, going forward, we can strengthen our democracy by paying more attention to it. By guaranteeing people's safety, you create a favorable environment for them to participate democratically in nation-building. In fact, in my conviction, if we can guarantee people's security, we can equally have the moral authority to nurture our democracy. In another way, I believe that fostering the safety of Nigerians is one step forward in growing our democracy. That is why I applaud Mr. Fayose as a figure of democracy who walked out of his office to seek solutions to the insecurity that to date remains a blockage to our democracy. He has done his part and I wish that other leaders press hard on the President and security apparatus to indefatigably continue providing adequate security for all Nigerians.

Defeat of incumbents by Fayose-a proof of electoral democracy

Aside from security, the politics of Ekiti State is intricate. It may require further study to understand how Fayose defeated the then incumbent governors. This is a state that is populated by well-educated citizens and a majority of its residents are civil servants. However, the citizens of the state are poor, though, are not supposed to be if not that they had forgotten the children of whom they are. Ladies and gentlemen, Ekiti is an Agrarian state, so also are its people. The day we lost this important aspect of us, the day we were nicknamed "stomach infrastructure people." What ludicrousness? Ekiti! Wow! The poverty in the state is a subject for another day. But going forward, the state requires creativity, high capital investment, and innovation to turn around its fortunes. The high poverty level in the state has precipitated Ekiti state into the politics of stomach infrastructure, a pointer of lack of rational appeal among voters. This is a debatable subject that I may not want to dwell on to analyze the ramifications of defeating incumbents. Mr. Fayose is not the only one who has defeated an incumbent; we witnessed the same in the 2015 presidential race where President Muhammadu Buhari floored his predecessor, Jonathan Goodluck. However, I am still gravitating to opine that Fayose's defeat of incumbent governors twice calls on us to protect our electoral democracy. As leaders, we should not compromise the electoral infrastructure to protect the seat when it is possible to retain or lose it as democracy dictates. It is paramount that we protect every aspect of our electoral system.

History of governorship elections in Ekiti State informs us that Fayose, a man who has mastered grassroots politics, marshalled political support that then necessitated the defeat of the then incumbent governor Chief Niyi Adebayo. The same repeated in 2014 when Fayose sought the governorship office after being out of it following the unprecedented impeachment in the state. He unseated the then governor Kayode Fayemi, who later again became governor in the 2018 gubernatorial election in the state. This is intriguing considering that power is now rotating among the minority elite. Leaders are being recycled, but that is not my point of interest as far as my discussion of Fayose's personality is concerned. The election of Fayose into office in 2014 reinforces the need to protect our electoral democracy as I earlier said. Elections should be free, fair, and just and that is the sine qua non of democracy. When we allow the electoral agency to run the elections fairly, we lean towards accepting the results of an election. When the impeachment knocked at the doors of Fayose, he did not use his powers to stop it but waited for about 10 years to seek re-election. In 2014, like any other candidate, organized his campaigns and later won the election transparently.

As a man of honor, Dr. Fayemi conceded defeat as well and perhaps because he believes in democracy as well. By accepting defeat, Fayose's incumbent also appeared to support democracy in the sense that he did not interfere with the decision of the Independent National Electoral Commission (INEC) to denying him victory. This does not mean that the electoral agency should not be called out if they conduct an election in a non-transparent manner. Though Fayemi had issues with the conduct of INEC then, which I think is usually normal for losers, the pain that comes with losing an election may likely cause jitters and sometimes false accusations. This situation was also repeated by Dr. Fayose when the same Dr. Fayemi had a landslide win in 2018. I love these two brothers, indeed.

Without losing focus, what I think about the unseating of Dr. Fayemi by Fayose is that electoral democracy in some Nigerian States is maturing. This is good for the country, with a decentralized system of governance. More states should follow suit. If the incumbents and influential politicians can conduct themselves with decorum, it would be easier for Nigeria to strengthen its electoral democracy not just at the State level, but at the federal level as well. To demonstrate that, Fayose is concerned about electoral democracy, he did not interfere with the 2018 gubernatorial election in his state where he was the outgoing governor with the ability to influence the outcome in favor of his candidate of choice, who was his vice. He supported the PDP candidate who contested against APC's Fayemi. As honorable as he is, Fayose campaigned though not so much on the policy-based platform for the PDP nominee who served as his deputy governor. The candidate he supported to take over Ekiti State governorship lost to Dr. Fayemi. It was a bitter pie for him to swallow. But the fact that he did not get in the way with the election, gives us an idea that he roots for electoral integrity. He wanted the next governor to win on merit but not through rigging which in essence curtails electoral integrity.

Even though the socio-political undercurrents in Ekiti State are of interest to political researchers, policymakers, and observers, the state has been on the right path to achieve electoral democracy. Although this is not purely an achievement for Fayose, his contribution cannot be snubbed. He is at the epicenter of the State's politics. To reinforce his support for electoral democracy, Fayose has always been castigating electoral malpractices under President Buhari's reign. Ordinarily, as a person that believes in a fair electoral process, this underpins democracy. You cannot be silent when powerful individuals try to dent what is for the good of all. Nonetheless, the fact that candidates can unseat sitting leaders should motivate us going into the future as a country to reinforce electoral democracy in the country. As we urge the government to respect our human rights and freedoms, we should not be tired to continue demanding for free and fair elections at whatever level of governance. That will help us buttress and develop our democracy.

In the United States, we have been following investigations into President Donald Trump's alleged collusion with the Russians in their interference to weaken the country's electoral democracy. The vigor which the investigators probed the collusion should inspire the Nigerian authorities and the electoral body in a way of conducting our elections transparently in the future. Failing to protect the integrity of our election will be the beginning of the end of our democracy because leaders who are fat cats and influential will corrupt their way into the office. While in office, they will subjugate democratic institutions and use all means to finally install autocracy.

In a nutshell, Ayodele Fayose is a leader whose advocacy for security and electoral democracy we should appreciate. These are critical elements that define and strengthen our democracy going forward. When he assumed office, he immediately stepped up to help restore the runaway security in his state and by extension the federation. He has also been vocal about and still focused on pushing for electoral integrity; even as an ex-governor. He does so because he believes that it is the only way we can strengthen democracy. Due to that, I have always thought that he is a leader that means good for Nigeria in spite of his apparent failings in some areas of his leadership when he was in the office. Again, you will allow me to state that, as human, he is not like cotton - he is not a saint too, but we should appreciate his determination to make Nigeria a strong democracy. In Africa, we are tackling challenges like national security which in all probability is bringing to a standstill, the democratization of a nation. Fayose's move can be replicated by all leaders on the continent.

◄══╬ ╬══►

CHAPTER 10

PASTOR ISA EL-BUBA

I n 1982, Prophet Isa El-Buba, an Islamic occultist, converted into Christianity. The conversion from Islamic occultism to Christianity changed his life forever by the power of the Almighty God and since then became the General Overseer of Evangelical Bible Outreach Ministries International (EBOMI) afterward. Through EBOMI, God has been using him mightily to reach millions of souls to bring them to the kingdom and at the same time using evangelism to address fundamental issues in the Nigerian society. Issues such as corruption, poverty, and terrorism, have been dragging the country behind for some time now. He is one of the few religious leaders who believe that their service to humanity is not merely to be confined to evangelism alone. Hence, the cleric has been making some concerted attacks on political leaders who, instead of working for Nigerians for good governance

and tackling the challenges facing society, pursue their personal or selfish interests. His attacks on the evil politicians in the country have been enchanting many other religious leaders too, as they are also standing up to put those corrupt politicians in difficult circumstances where their political survival is threatened. With figures like Prophet El-Buba, religious leaders are no longer watching on the fringes, but are painstakingly engaging in transforming Nigeria for better. It has reached a stage that the influential and good-meaning religious leaders cannot keep quiet any further.

To have a sustainable and enduring democracy or to turn Nigeria to a great nation as it should be, they believe that the country needs good leadership which has to be fought for since such does not come on a silver platter. However, the lack of good leadership has prompted Prophet Isa El-Buba to jump into the murky political waters to save the country from drowning. Bad leadership, not just at the top, but across all levels of the government is an ailment that we must fight against. It must be public knowledge that we live in a nation where many politicians who are supposed to fight for the masses are focusing on retaining power and enriching themselves. All is not lost though; if people like El-Buba and other devoted leaders continue to pull together to ask for transformational leadership that Nigeria is visibly hungry for now, things will soon change for good. As an Afro-optimist, I remain steadfast and optimistic that things would come to perfection one day, as a matter of fact, very soon. As long as we continue holding accountable our political leaders by reminding them what they should be doing correctly to build a better country, we will get there.

El-Buba's influence transcends the religious circles and that is why his political statements should be taken seriously. While studying him, I learned that he is a good religious leader concerned about his people and country. During electioneering for the 2019 general elections, he adamantly wished for the downfall of President Buhari. At some point, he predicted as a prophet that the President would lose the election, only to be disapproved when Buhari was re-elected under contentious circumstances. Importantly, if we intently listened to him, he never literally wished Buhari to fail out of abhorrence. He aimed to see President Buhari replaced with another person who would possibly lead the country with a superior vision since he and the majority in the country believe that the last four years of the President's leadership was a failure. In El-Buba's belief, Atiku Abubakar, the PDP candidate was best placed to replace President Buhari on account of his accomplishments, not only as a former Vice President of the country but as a businessman. He was so determined that Nigeria was ripe for great visionary leaders because the current President and his cabinet lack great strategies to take the country forward. His choice of Atiku Abubakar may not inspire those who are allied to neither PDP nor APC. However, his choice should be respected, though he is neither a PDP nor APC member. After all, Mr. Atiku was the main challenger to the incumbent, based on the opinion polls at the time. In a democracy where two dominant political parties contest for an election, chances of small parties winning are perpetually slim.

In respect to El-Buba's influence, I dedicate this chapter to him to discuss how critical he has been not only in giving a voice to the voiceless, but also inspiring us to think about how we can make Nigeria a great nation again. He is instrumental at informing the public about the change we should strive to achieve even as visionless leaders stay put in office. His stinging attacks on President Buhari at some point risked putting him at crossroads with the police. The government through the police once laid a dragnet for him to have him arrested and charged, but today, he is still a free man, championing altruistically for the rights and freedoms of his compatriots - thanks to his church members' support and prayers. Thus, my point of argument and defense of El-Buba as a figure of democracy fighting for the disadvantaged people of Nigerian stems from his recent advocacy for a leadership change that can make Nigeria a great nation.

El-Buba: Nigeria's greatness is dependent on good leadership

Looking at Nigeria's situation right now, some might be content with the present status. Some are driving top range cars, some fly private jets and choppers, while on the flip side; some can hardly afford one daily meal. This captures the widening gap between the rich and the poor in this Africa's most populous nation; a trend that should concern every people-centered leader. With almost half of our population plunged into extreme poverty, a good leadership should have been focused mainly on how to grow our economy.

Unfortunately, even those who are business magnates or those well-off in the society are not sure of what may happen to their country tomorrow as our economy stares at a downturn in the near future. The current leadership seems to be blind and unable to come up with any good ideas on how the economy should be developed. We live worrying about tomorrow because of the visionless and self-seeking leaders we have condoned for so long. These leaders seem not to think about the people they are leading and are only concerned about acquiring wealth against the poor they are supposed to empower. However, the future of Nigeria is to get those terrible leaders out of the way by replacing them with those who know what to do about the economy. The direction our nation is headed is candidly a wrong one as observed by prophet El-Buba, who concluded that it only requires good leadership to have a strong democracy to weave together a great nation.

I will not sound repetitive here on account that the subject of bad leadership has been previously discussed. But for us, the topic of Good Governance cannot be overemphasized. I insist that El-Buba considers President Buhari as one of the many leaders who have killed the Nigerian dream. His presidency is a catastrophe according to El Buba's analysis, a claim that I cannot deny because, we are presently in the worst-case scenario in Nigeria. The leadership challenge we are facing presently is indisputably due to the policies of Buhari administration and negative energies in his government. I do not want to paint Buhari's government as a complete failure, but what is happening in the country right now makes the prophet El-Buba to think that way. Before the general election, there was one decisive statement made by Prophet El-Buba while addressing the media in Jos. As a person who believes in the will of the people, he insisted that Nigerian people are resilient and strong- sufficiently to resist bad leadership. He seemed to think that President Buhari was unlikely to relinquish power even if he lost but was sure that Nigerians would not allow that. He also added that Nigerians would have to protect the integrity of the 2019 general election under suspicion that the incumbent would rig it.

I have been able to abstract two fundamental points from one of Prophet El-Buba's press conferences. The issues he was addressing were electoral integrity, transfer of power and our future as a nation. Some incumbents do not believe in democracy even when they overtly fail to serve people. All they do is rig themselves into power by all possible means. This has far-reaching consequences in a frail democracy such as ours. Although rigging is common in most African nations, it is a phenomenon that must stop if we want to move forward. More importantly, prophet El-Buba's main aim is fighting for good leadership which he is firmly convinced president Buhari cannot offer. He wants Nigeria to be a great and free nation where every dream is valid, unlike what we currently have.

El-Buba's criticism of president Buhari emanates from the dream of wanting to live in a GREAT nation - a status which by nature and by now Nigeria should have attained. What the Nigerians have been longing for since independence is good leadership. If that is the case, I think we need to understand what makes a country great. Let us take the United States of America where I am sojourning right now as an example. Its history absorbed me to think that the U.S. offers an olive branch, and a template of what an underdeveloped or developing country can emulate to become a great nation. As far as its history is concerned, it was once a developing nation, but it moved forward to become the largest economic power in the world and a benchmark for development and democracy for all nations. In my informed analysis of literature on this great nation, I have arrived at a simple definition that it is a country that keeps its economy stable, supports democracy, and respects the rights and liberties of its people while allowing them to pursue happiness. Do not get me wrong, the USA in all candors as a great nation, still encounters numerous challenges like gun violence and racism, but she consistently seeks solutions to her problems to prosper. Despite America's challenges, it is driving factor to prosperity stands tall. Democratic nations have their challenges too, but with great leaders and visions, the countries solve their challenges as quickly as possible as this explains how the economy of the United States has transformed in a phenomenal fashion.

What I am driving home here is that the history of America informs us of how a country can journey from a "developing" to a Great nation. You have seen that America protects the rights and liberties of its people, while in Nigeria, the freedoms we achieved during the inception of the civilian government are being taken away day in day out. Optimistically, Nigeria can follow suit to become a great nation like America if it wishes so. And if we get the right leadership that is utterly missing, according to prophet El-Buba, we will excel. This can only happen when we have good leaders in power. But with bigoted individuals in power, such would only be a pipe dream.

In the United States of America; the South and the North were once separated, but with good leadership, the two regions reunited to build a superpower nation. The American people throughout time have gained their liberties by respecting the laws, upholding tenets of democracy, such as transparency and accountability in all its democratic processes.

When it comes to Nigeria, there is a disconnect between the North and the South which Prophet El-Buba thinks should be fixed before the country can move forward to become a great nation. It would be the delight of everyone to see Nigeria rise in Africa and be a model of democracy and development for which countries across the world can yardstick. In its journey to becoming a great nation, the United States at the time of the Civil War, was majorly agriculturally based. As time progressed, America experienced rapid industrial development as a result of creating a political and capitalist economic system that fueled money flow among its citizens. Money flow lowered prices of products which allowed more Americans to have disposable income. Progressivism also played an imperative role in the economy as it distributed wealth from the wealthy to the middle class. This was a fundamental move that spread out wealth across America allowing everyone to be happy.

Now, look at Nigeria, you would see the disconnection between the so-called rich and the poor. This is because instead of spreading the wealth to pull out the poor from paucity, their leaders are pushing them down into abject poverty every day. This is what El-Buba has been fighting against; it is heartrending to see wealth concentrated in those minority leaders that are callous enough to snub the cries of the poor. When leadership is good, spreading wealth from the wealthy to the middle class and thus trickling down to the poor is possible. This is what needs to happen in Nigeria if indeed we are keen on becoming a great nation.

Take it into account this scenario; corporatism economy which arose in America created higher wages for its people who invested the same in businesses or economy. The rise in wages enabled people to purchase vehicles for faster transportation of their products and facilitated their movements. In effect, products were ferried faster to markets and ideas were spread. When the Great Depression hit America, there was a new solution which was the New Deal that restored the economy. The deal established policies that offered Americans bank security, consequently speeding up economic growth. The New Deal also took America off the gold standard which allowed the United States to spend more. What sparked the economy was World War II, which triggered increased production and creation of millions of jobs for the unemployed. America's economy, though facing hardships at times, has been stable and continued to grow from the Civil War to date. Is this not what prophet El-Buba is calling our leaders to emulate?

The kind of government established in America is the fairest and powerful in the world. The time after the Civil War, the federal government worked with the state governments to balance power. As America became more industrialized, the government also started to change. The Populist Party had ideas that William Jennings Bryan proposed to the Americans which eventually made some impact in their lives. It raised tariffs and created a graduated income tax which raised money. America started becoming a world power when Manifest Destiny started becoming a reality as the country annexed multiple countries. This allowed the country to acquire ideas from other countries to help it develop. This is not to state that Nigeria should equally be go-ahead to annex its neighboring nations; rather the focal point is to illustrate how the United States of America through good and visionary leadership made tremendous progress that made it a great nation today.

The New Deal created by Franklin Delano Roosevelt made the government stronger and it gave the people of America and around the world confidence in the democratic government. When World War II began, it tested the American government. It was the war for democracy that the country fought and came out on top of it by using its strong military. This made the United States a "superpower" till today. American government having gained strength by defending itself and gaining respect around the world made it a great nation. Furthermore, respect for liberty which comes from the checks and balances system of the government makes America a great nation. It gives people importance in society. After the Civil War, liberty was given to the people, particularly African Americans through the ratification of the 13th, 14th, and 15th amendments, which abolished slavery, gave them citizenship and the right to vote. Black delegates made their presence felt concerning that. The Freedman's Bureau was also put in place to provide education to the freed slaves. Free education also is liberty that helped in making the population so educated. The right to protest is liberty in which they utilized during World War I. Corporatism gave Americans a new life by providing better working conditions, shorter work hours, and higher wages. In that, Americans' ideas are now protected through patents.

In the entire struggle, being able to pursue happiness is a characteristic that defines a great nation. Everyone wants to be happy and if you do not want to be happy there is something wrong with you. America positioned itself to be a country in which everyone can strive to become happy if they work hard. The American Dream is real. I think Herbert Hoover, America's 31st President epitomized how a great nation-the USA- guarantees happiness. Mr. Hoover had everything going wrong for him. Both of his parents passed on when he was a child and lived his teenage years in an orphanage. He turned his life around by going to college, getting a job and eventually became rich. Americans have the opportunities to be happy all around them. Having eight hours of work daily, which allows them to spend time on themselves and acquire hobbies that keep them happy. Higher wages give them more money to spend on activities and on certain things that make their day jolly. No tool could be used to measure the happiness of Americans other than the commitment of their leaders to develop the country up to its present position in the world.

Now, let us go back to Nigeria where hard work by the poor is no guarantee for success. There are millions of graduates who worked industriously during their school years but now wallow in poverty because of bad leadership – with many being jobless. The leadership we are having presently is not distressed by the high unemployment rate in Nigeria. This is why Prophet El-Buba is angry at the bad leadership that is depriving the poor of employment and other economic generating activities. The present state of

Nigeria does not offer the young people great opportunities to pursue happiness on account of bad leadership that is disinterested in rebuilding the economy for the benefit of everyone. Statistics show that more than half of the world's population is less than 30 years of age. These young people are concerned about what the future holds for them. Their concerns are mostly on climate change, environmental sustainability, tribalism, corruption, nepotism, government accountability, unemployment, and lack of economic opportunity among other issues. One would expect a serious leader to stand up and engage in projects that will empower these young people.

A decent and others-centered leader ought to put resources into development projects because the eventual fate of young people requests them to do so. As innovation advances at a fast rate, we realize that the eventual fate of tasks will appear to be different from the types that we are instructing our kids at the present moment. Schools all over the world are effectively educating students on what is to come in the future as they focus to fight poverty and contribute to economic development. At the end of the day, students are not simply being shown the realities of things but are learning the best way to think and prosper very well in this intricate and interconnected world. If we have to truly catalyze a transition to future-arranged teaching, a good leader or perhaps President ought to create a favorable environment that will allow these young people to prosper after school by tapping into their talents and capacities.

Besides, a good leader should work tirelessly with everyone to alleviate poverty while promoting a free society. He should be able to encourage all citizens to work hard to stimulate economic growth, environmental sustainability, and social security. A good leader will uphold a bold and great program that should guarantee each family food on their table as need be. Resultantly, this would pull every family out of their abject poverty and present Nigeria as a great nation like the United States of America, UK, and Canada among other developed countries.

In essence, the kind of history presented here has clearly shown that America's rise to prosperity was based on creating opportunities and guaranteeing everyone's liberties through the well-focused and visionary leaders. When the government insistently commits efforts to serve its people, the public would be inspired to work diligently with hope and will then be able to contribute to the economic development of such a nation. But because of the kind of bad leadership in Nigeria presently, that is no longer the case. That is why people like Prophet El-Buba have come out to criticize President Buhari several times. Not that he hates him, after all, El Buba is a servant of God, he must have inherited the non-hatred spirit of Christ, not only as a prophet but as a genuine Christian with a tenet to never hate anybody but love them all. However, there is nowhere in the Bible where it says citizens should be stupid and silent when a bad leader is in the helm of affairs.

With all that said, Prophet Isa El-Buba is a voice of the voiceless that is determined like any other forthright leader to prosper Nigeria, first through good leadership which will create a favorable environment for economic empowerment, democracy, security, and liberties. As a consequence, the current leaders should not be left to abuse power and run the country to ruins. Instead, citizens should fearlessly fight for good leadership that would allow them perhaps, to develop like the United States of America whose greatness historically is pegged on democratic leadership. Thus far, his criticism of President Buhari is because of his betrayal of the people who elected him first in 2015. As things are, the country is governed poorly and therefore El-Buba's clarion call for good leadership is healthy for Nigeria's democracy.

⟮⟫

CHAPTER 11

SENATOR ISAH HAMMA MISAU

Nigeria is a frail democracy. All sensitive and patriotic Nigerians would expect leaders across the political divide to unite to strengthen democracy. It benefits the entire society when the rights and freedoms of people are respected and protected. Such anticipation remains a hope that is slowly diminishing in a continent that oscillates between democracy and authoritarianism. With the current leadership, Nigeria is pragmatically and gradually retreating to tyranny. The rule of law which is supreme in any free society is being obliterated openly.

Senator Isah Hamma Misau now fully understands that it requires sacrifices for his country to achieve true democracy or perhaps rescue it from a looming fall. Mr. Misau, born in Bauchi Nigeria in 1970 during the dark years, undoubtedly experienced the brutal rule of the military. He luckily witnessed the historic transition to a democratically elected government. With hopes high, he once believed his country was headed in the right direction. It was not easy for the military to hand over power to civilian rule. But because the country was super ready for democracy, it had to happen. With the country's fledgling democracy, Mr. Misau joined the Nigerian Police Force. Later, in 2015, he quit the force to run for the senate to represent Bauchi Central Senatorial District. He won and became the chairman of the House Committee on Navy- a committee related to his security background. He took his position as senator sincerely and considered it as a great opportunity to fight for democracy. Mr. Misau understood that there was injustice in the police force which in his mind, he thought he would resolve as a senator.

With a bang, it dawned on him that politics as well perpetuate the same injustices he observed in the police. The police force is as good and as bad as the government. When the incumbent government is bad and roots for injustices, the police observably would be unjust. With power bestowed upon him as a senator, Mr. Misau spoke against injustices, constructively criticized the Buhari administration and warned Nigerians about the speedily waning democracy. Now that he is out of the senate, a few would commend him for his devoted fight against injustices; others will not give a hoot.

I have an exceptional opinion about Mr. Misau. He is among the African leaders who deserve praise for being vocal defending democracy. It is life-threatening to lambast a sitting government in Africa. I am not a naysayer or bad-mouthing Africa. Truly, in many nations on the continent, the critics are invariably viewed as detractors even though they raise issues for the progress of society. The level of tolerance for critics in Africa is frankly low. Knowing how murky Nigerian politics are becoming lately, he spoke daringly and selflessly. When allegations and harassment from the police came his way, he was not surprised. Under President Buhari, critics hardly have a peaceful time. The government is using police to shut up perceived opponents, instead of rationally listening to critical issues they are raising. Democracy says aloud that even those we do not agree, should be allowed to raise their concerns. In some situations, even if politicians disagree on policies, morally, they are obligated to cooperate in political decision-making for the sake of the country. Truth be told, political behaviors in Nigeria, is far from this. The political climate is getting so unfavorable for democracy. APC, the ruling party under President Muhammadu Buhari, feels harassing the opposition members under PDP is one of its mandates. It is on that account that opposition members like Senator Misau have not been spared by a government that is so obsessed with shutting up opponents at the expense of service delivery and rule of law.

Having brought forward the personality of Senator Isah Misau, this chapter will critically analyze his struggle for democracy, liberty, and rule of law in Nigeria. A democratic Nigeria is healthy for the entire African continent. A dream of democracy that Mr. Misau holds for Nigeria can trickle down to other nations on the continent. Although some people may not identify him as a campaigner of democracy, he selflessly fights for democracy in his Nigeria. He was not cowed but he assailed the government forthrightly for intimidating good-meaning leaders and silencing legislators, pinpointing corruption and injustices perpetrated. For true democracy to be achieved not only in Nigeria but around the world, the Legislature, or all arms of government - must work autonomously. Evidently, that is something the Buhari administration has tenaciously been trying to undermine. Senator Misau knowingly stood his ground to defend the independence of the senate and castigated attempts to use police to weaken lawmakers through intimidation, inhumane arrests, and harassment.

Senator Misau wrangles with the police; key to democratic reforms in the force

Senator Isah Misau is a leader that believes that strong democratic institutions are critical for Nigeria's democracy. Within his four-year tenure as a senator, he took the police boss head-on for presiding over corruption and illegal promotions. This was an accusation that had a heavy weight on how the police, going forward, would operate in Nigeria. Aside from alleging that there is corruption in the police force, he also dressed them down for harassment, especially on the legislators. From where I sit, Senator Misau understood that it was worthy for the police to reinforce their independence on account that they are an essential pillar of democracy.

Powerful and influential state officers have the propensity of using police to harass their opponents. However, this is an exception for nations where the rule of law is not supreme. An independent police force or service regardless of how it should be called is not subject to manipulation and misuse by the government officials. As emphasized earlier, police are important for growing democracy and it would be dangerous for society to tolerate the political elite abusing them.

Senator Misau has been audacious enough to accuse the police of partiality and abuse. This is a guy who condemned the police on the manhandling of other senators like Dino Melaye. Although many did not agree with him, his criticism of the police is undoubtedly good for democracy. Being a former police officer, Senator Misau was an authority to point out police abuse. He was not criticizing for the sake of political relevance. He does not dislike the Nigerian police given that he is a former police boss, but he dearly likes and respects them. Nonetheless, he knows that there are people who do not like to see independent police execute its mandate autonomously. The police are a mainstay of democracy that cannot be allowed to be used wrongly by political leaders or their seniors to settle scores. The civil liberties, human freedoms, civil rights, and due process are ingrained in policing. The moment police abuse becomes a norm in society, it is in that instant that democracy fades away.

By extension, if the police can harass the perceived enemies of the government like the senate president and truth-telling senators, the public perception is that they are being misused. When a colleague in the senate, Mr. Dino Melaye, was admitted to hospital following his apprehension and torture by police, Senator Misau was denied passageway to see him. He claimed that the hospital management and even the police asserted there was an "order from above." This, in essence, affirms efforts by the ruling elite to manipulate and control the police to their advantage. It is something that the senator decried and wondered why nearly 20 years after democratic rule, there are still "orders from above." These "orders from above" destabilize the independence of the police as well as their role to move democracy forward. It is an authoritarian practice that should be rejected by all means in the spirit of securing democracy. Some politicians have been asking for "*mano dura.*" In other words, those who have been keen on police brutality or abuse must have heard the phrase "*Los Que piden la mano dura.*" That is Spanish. What this loosely translates into in English is "iron fist way of fighting crime or even "detractors." Cases of police abuse in Taiwan and Argentina, before becoming democratic, should jog your memory how significant it is to have effective and human-rights-defending police. When police use force or fight crime ruthlessly, democracy in every aspect loses its democratic character.

Thus far, the Nigerian police have not been atrocious as such. However, utterances like "orders from above" must be resisted. In the spirit of resisting return to police abuse, Senator Misau insisted that they should follow "due process". In the same breath, they should not accept to be manipulated; instead, they should strive to enforce the rule of law. The police should also not be perceived as simply enforcers of the laws. They have a greater role than that. As important actors, they can define how a government runs its affairs and reaches society. Police power is not something to disparage, but it can influence society.

With this in mind, it is the obligation of those in power to call out rogue police. Speak about the injustices they perpetuate. This was visible in Senator Misau. His accusation of senior police officers for corruption may be false or true, but it should be appreciated. In developing democracies, it is common knowledge that police are corrupt. Lamentably, in some worst-case scenarios, junior officers bribe senior police officers to be extended favors like promotion and transfers to "money-spinning" posts. That is not to mean that it is happening in Nigeria, but it is common practice in many developing countries.

Senator Isah Misau alleged that Nigeria's Inspector General of police (without stating the name) was paid billions (in local currency) for providing special security services to VIPs and corporate organizations. It was an allegation which I cannot dwell on. But if in any way such magnitude of corruption happened in the police, it is an undesirable, immoral and unethical act that chips away at our democracy. In the corruption proceeds, there were other beneficiaries. The accusation notably was from Misau, an ex-Deputy Superintendent of Police. It would have been erroneous to rubbish such a claim; given that this was a high-ranking police officer.

In any case, Senator Misau should be regarded as a whistle-blower. To achieve democratic police which intrinsically is a pillar of democracy, this senator should be praised rather than demonized. Some people would think he was deliberately admonishing or tarnishing the image of the Nigerian police, but that is superficial. It is the responsibility of a leader with interest to democratize his country to expose dubious dealings. Many Nigerian policemen and women do a good job. However, there is a group of people in the rank and file of this esteemed force that is rotten. Perhaps it is the reason that Mr. Misau took upon himself to whistle-blow for the sake of a better police force that is paramount in democratization efforts in Nigeria.

The police are a sub-system in the criminal justice system that must undertake reforms within its circle. Corruption in the police may not entirely be blamed on the Federal government, but leaders managing the department. With the intent to reform the police, Senator Misau was focused on having right-minded and duty-oriented individuals to lead them. If morally upright people run the police force, they can facilitate reforms. When reforms are carried out, the police can regain independence and embrace democracy. That is the dream Mr. Misau has for the police and for Nigerians.

Policing in a democratic society is exceptionally different than in dictatorial states. Now that Nigerians desire nothing less than democracy, Senator Misau should be praised for his courage to raise important issues. It takes patriotism for a genuine leader to criticize top-ranking officials in the police undermining efforts to positively transform policing in the country. These are powerful people. Without bravery and self-sacrifice, it is tricky to accuse them of corruption because they can in return, fight back so viciously. "Fighting back" is a common practice in skewed leadership that can put a critic's life in danger. And many times, corruption unites to fight back, sometimes silencing critics through death and injury.

Some people might have generally perceived Mr. Misau as a mere "loose mouth." But the truth is that this is a person determined to expose the rot that will clean our police. The consequence of his accusation would be restoring democracy within the police whilst edging out nepotism and discrimination that confront the effectiveness of the police force. It was not just a mere accusation, and if it were so, it will noticeably be in some way impact the operations of the police. Now that he divulged perhaps what is happening in the Police, there is a possibility that heads will roll. Corrupt police officers hypothetically will have fears of being exposed for corruption. By and large, the exposure of corruption, skewed promotion, and transfers in the police will one day bear hawk-eyed scrutiny which will push out all corrupt cops.

As Senator Misau leaves the senate after being floored in his second bid for the senatorial race, his attempt to take a graft purge to the police is a display of strength and altruism. He is a citizen that is determined to see Nigeria grow democratically. Nigeria's development and commitment to steer the African continent to prosperity is hinged on reforms and democratic institutions like the police. This is a country with potential and all institutions should be strong and must resist political manipulation for the sake of democracy.

Senator Misau's dream for an effective and efficient government

We cannot deny as a continent that a majority of African leaders are preoccupied with how to deal with opponents, winning the next election and becoming strongmen. There is not much effort dedicated to development. What many leaders do in this part of the world is usually paying lip service. That is not to say they do not have good ideas. Some leaders have ideas, but they like sideshows and normally power blindfolds them. In Nigeria, development is slow but tough talk without action dominates the national platform.

In 2015, the election of President Muhammadu Buhari inspired and gave hope to many. The smooth transfer of power to him by President Jonathan Goodluck was an event the world watched with excitement. It was a positive turn for Nigeria. At present, the hope for an effective and people-oriented government is diminishing if the present wave of criticism against this administration is anything to go by. Senator Misau is among Nigerians who are disgruntled at bad leadership and lack of tangible development in the country. There is a strong and irrefutable connection between democracy and economy. The below-par development by President Buhari has dealt a fresh blow to democracy. Since his performance record is not something to celebrate, he has been pushed to a defensive position. Such defense has resulted in a crackdown on critics. Commonly, when you feel defeated you would try to clutch at straws. Perhaps by fighting enemies or using sycophants around you to fight your battle against unrelenting critics.

Senator Misau, having observed that President Buhari failed to deliver; he publicly wondered why he sought re-election in 2019. Did Nigerians, and the compact majority, wonder about the same? Conceivably not - because President Buhari was vividly re-elected to Aso-Rock. It is good to be pragmatic. If a leader fails to perform in his first term, should he be re-elected? It is something to ponder on. In my view, African electorate rarely gets it right when it comes to electing good presidents. Nobody bothers to look at issues. The electorate does not care about policies, development, and service delivery. Rather than voting non-performers out of government, they whine, they complain, and blame them, but, somehow, during another election cycle, they vote them back. Sometimes it gets tribal and that is why elections are habitually along ethnic lines. This trend is what is killing accountability and responsibility not only in Nigeria but also in other African nations. Many electorates fall into the blindfolds of politicians who make them believe that the misfortunes in the society are an act of God; not a creation of failed leadership. They have therefore, neglected to perceive the immediate connection between a capable administration and a superior society.

Mr. Misau viciously opposed the decision of President Buhari to seek re-election for predictable reasons. In the run-up to the 2019 general election, Nigerian economic outlook showed the country's economy was growing at 1.9 percent. With a slowly growing economy, declining democracy, and rising insecurity, it was implausible to re-elect this government. This is a sentiment that Senator Misau shared. If Nigerians care about their country, they would rally behind such a senator. It is not a lecture to Nigerians or a rebuke for re-electing Mr. Buhari. The opposition to Buhari was something independent-minded and patriotic people wishing their country prosperity would not reject.

Naturally, of course, power is what a majority of leaders find hard to let go, especially in Africa. But when you consider the position of the senator, it was plausible for a leader to step down if they cannot get things done as they promised. Having a person with such temerity speak objectively on public platforms against a leader people believe is doing them a disservice is good for democracy, economy, and development. Misau envisions a situation where leaders step down if they cannot deliver as they promised.

In developed nations, in June 2019, the United Kingdom's Prime Minister Theresa May resigned. The reason for the resignation was comprehensible to everyone. She was unable to deliver Brexit as promised to her compatriots. The Brexit deadlock in her belief, it was time someone else took over. Perhaps her successor would get Brexit negotiations done swiftly and successfully. This was bold. Stepping down from the Prime Minister office for someone better positioned to handle the UK's post-Brexit vote was an excellent decision. This is a kind of leadership Mr. Misau expects in Nigeria. If a leader finds it hard to perform optimally, they should let power go. That is heroism and maturity. Admitting failure is not a weakness but strength.

Senator Misau pointed a finger at supporters of President Buhari. Even though this was their democratic right, democracy does not authorize people to make uninformed decisions. Democracy requires citizens to make right choices. It was genuinely the obligation of Misau to call out voters who are supporting a wrong cause. It is painful not only to Senator Misau but to all people wanting their country to democratize and develop, to observe the electorate make wrong decisions. The tirade and anger channeled to the supporters of President Buhari is disillusionment.

This is a senator that believes that Nigerians must be empowered to avoid wrong decision-making at the ballot. Voters should always support a cause, but not to vote emotionally. When people give reason and priority over tribe and emotions, right choices can be made. Lack of reason is what makes voters exercise the right to vote along ethnic lines. For positive change to be achieved, voters must always reason alongside issues such as social amenities, infrastructure, good economy, rights, and freedoms. By doing this, bad leadership will be totally removed from power. It would be a wise choice to have good leaders steer the country forward.

Nevertheless, Senator Misau decried the rampant corruption in the executive. That is not to say it is only the executive that is corrupt. Corruption has been rampant in Nigeria and as a leader; he has to speak against it. Fighting corruption is not solely the responsibility of one leader but requires concerted efforts. The National Assembly within the constitutional edicts is mandated to expose corruption. It should equally approve nominations of people with high integrity that would be the beginning of a transformed Nigeria.

He was not re-elected as a senator. But his commitment to calling out corrupt leaders was an absolute display of determination to fight for a democratic Nigeria. He does not hold a personal vendetta against President Buhari or any other leader. What Mr. Misau was simply asking for is good leadership, a leadership that fights corruption creates employment, tackles insecurity, and develops the economy. All these can only be achieved if the leadership in the executive is solely committed to following the constitution and checks its government. Government officials should not be given space to steal, weaken the constitution, and abuse offices.

CHAPTER 12

GOVERNOR BELMAT BELLO MATAWALLE

S ome leaders in Nigeria continue to inspire even as the country faces numerous challenges from corruption to insecurity. Governor Belmat Matawalle has epitomized good leadership since he took over the leadership of Zamfara state. He recently became governor, but what he has achieved is no mean feat particularly when compared to the abysmal performance of his predecessor. He came with determination to positively transform his state and serve the constituents. This has persuaded me to see him as a leader that champions democracy, good leadership, and unity.

Governor Matawalle was born on December 12, 1969, at Maradun Local Government Area of Zamfara State in the family of Muhammadu Sharu. He confidently made his first attempt of becoming governor in 2019 general elections and won at the Supreme Court (SC) after contesting against the APC candidate who had been declared winner of the election in controversial circumstances. The decision of the Supreme Court to overturn the APC candidate's victory was a Victory for Zamfara state dwellers because they had for long wished to genuinely have their will prevail at the ballot. Their will indeed prevailed, and a leader of their choice was declared winner of the gubernatorial race where APC was resolute in capturing a win, not based on service delivery, but party supremacy.

Matawalle is an experienced person who has previously served in the country in other key areas. He was the ad hoc committee chairman, house committee on marine security and safety commission (NSA Office) from 2007 to 2011. He was also the chairman of the House committee on security, intelligence, and public safety from 2011 to 2015. He doubled as a member of the amnesty committee on Boko Haram between 2012 and 2014. These many positions that he held proved him as an appealing and hardworking leader, which in the history of the state, makes him one of the longest-serving legislators today. At the moment, he has a record that his opponents' envy because he has achieved what they failed to do in the many years they held public office.

The secret behind the success of His Excellency, Bello Matawalle, first and foremost, is the desire for good leadership in his state. He is exceptional at implementing policies aimed at eradicating poverty, fostering unity, and improving security. Governors in the northern part of the country are implementing some of his policies to foster peace in their various states. Peace has been elusive in northern Nigeria and it takes good leadership to restore it.

When he assumed office, he directed his energy towards fighting poverty which was the paramount cause of the numerous ills and lack of progress in his state. His philosophy of leadership is one to reckon with; he is focused on tackling problems that directly affect Zanfarians. He has always believed that by stamping out poverty, you empower people to be independent and hardworking.

Governor Matawalle: epitome of good leadership

My choice to feature Governor Matawalle as a voice of the voiceless stems from the recent reforms he has made in Zamfara state. As a leader, he has concentrated on restoring unity and peace through cultural festivals which are so significant in our social fabric. In the recent past, he restored the forgotten cultural festival of *Sharu*, leading to its celebration on 13th August 2019. This festival had been moribund for more than a decade in Zamfara but Matawalle is unwavering in reviving the degenerating bond of unity and friendship that existed between the two traditional neighbors: Hausas and Fulanis. The onerous effort to bond the two communities will surely relax the lurking and prevailing tension generated by the violent crisis in the state. The governor used the impact of Sharu festival to restore the frosty relationship between Hausa-Fulani.

There have been many years of bad relations between these two ethnic groups, both in religion and culture. As known for centuries, the Hausa are farmers while the Fulani are nomads and the symbiotic relationship ought to be cordial to avoid re-ignition of ethnic strife. Though many clashes have happened between these communities before due to land disputes- commonly regarded as *Burtali* -their conflicts have been resolved through successful and peaceful dialogue. I believe Bello Matawalle was able to trace the root cause of the animosity accurately and proceeded to seek a resolution through dialogue.

In pursuit of harmony between communities, he has also been keen on observing religious celebrations to foster peace and unity. A few days after his swearing-in as governor on May 3, 2019, the Muslims in the country celebrated Eid-el Fitri. During these celebrations, the governor opted to share his love with orphans, something that showed that he is a leader committed to service to all and sundry. His philanthropic and loving nature are connected to his humanitarian attitude since he projects himself as a naturally born philanthropist, friendly, polite, devoted, dedicated, and pitiful leader. He is a leader that considers orphans and less privileged as important people that he should use any opportunity God has given him to serve them industriously. As a democratic leader, he brings himself closer to the people to the extent that he interacts by shaking hands with them, not minding their status. The proven attitude of the governor can be seen when he was interacting with some children in society as he considered himself as their father. These children indeed feel happy and proud of him. A citizen of the state once said that his advocacy for peace, love, and unity justify him as a good leader with the interests of Nigerians at heart.

Today, Zamfarians believe that their governor is not on the throne to enrich himself. Instead, he is focused on transforming his state and serving people who for long have been stuck in poverty without hope of a better future. The people are convinced that he aims to resurrect Zamfara and lead it to prosperity. He is different from the past leaders who only sat in their offices with no clear policies and vision on how to transform the state.

We can view Bello Matawalle as a leader that is ready to emancipate Zamfara from the politics of anarchy and strife to politics of democracy, peace, and development. His mission and vision are to use the natural resources available in the state and create a favorable business environment that can spur economic development in Zamfara. He sets his eyes on creating jobs, boost farming activities and enhancing education in the state. Although in his manifesto security is the priority, he has gone beyond that to iron out other fundamental issues of dire concern among his people. In his determination to revive the economy of the state, first and foremost, he elected to provide electricity which obviously will breathe a new life into the collapsed companies and industries. Solar energy plants in Gusau and hydro plants at Bakalori Dam Talata Marafa will soon be established according to him. Still, on reviving the economy, the governor is set to pave the way for the development of cargo airports to promote international business between his state and other countries.

Another interesting development is that while in Abuja, the governor met with one charity organization from Qatar where they promised to construct 15 mosques across the state, 15 hand pumps and 20 motorized boreholes. Moreover, another achievement made in Matawalle's journey to Abuja after his inauguration was that he met with the Managing Director of the Bank of Africa with its headquarters in Egypt. The Bank Manager was in Abuja purposely to meet with the governor. The Bank promised to invest One million dollars in the state to revive Zamfara textile, *Generis* and some allied industries that have been shut down for years. Also, Bakalori Dam will be used to construct a hydropower plant that can provide the state with constant power supply.

Gusau, the capital city of the state is an industrial center. It was observed that most of the industries were shutting down during the last administration, perhaps due to economic reasons or for non-supply of constant power supply to the industries. However, within his few months in the office, governor Matawalle has liaised with the Power holding Company of Nigeria to improve the power supply in the state. This gives him the confidence to call on the owners of companies to reopen their companies to create jobs for the people of the state. These good stories in Zamfara state are not fabricated. It was said the governor was overheard saying in the media that peace is not possible with the men in the bush through dialogue but through military action. The irony behind this is that the trouble happened in the state because somebody who was once in charge of the state failed to do his job and is now attacking somebody who is doing it.

It is a pitiable situation for those people who criticize governor Matawalle for their selfish reason. They have nothing worthwhile to tell but just to express their anger in frustration. But their negative utterances cannot and will never pay them any good dividends, instead will terminate their future hopes. They ruled through their wishes and not the wishes of people in the state. Their agonies are Matawalle's success. In less than three months in office, we are seeing fruits of good leadership. People have confidence in the style of Matawalle's leadership; that is why many communities in the state embarked on special prayers for the governor to succeed. The former governor of Zamfara failed to accept fate as the frame of life. He has forgotten how he was before he became a governor; he is an opportunist because he did not work for his success, but somebody did it for him. He came to power through the popularity of his master and not his own popularity. He failed to establish human relationship but feels too big and boastful. Where is he today after his unceremonious exit? He is only trying to create a new identity by attacking the government in power.

I agree with the governor, His Excellency Bello Matawalle as he cautioned those who are trying to sabotage his effort to bring peace into Zamfara state. His promise to deal with anybody who attempts to destroy the peace process he is embarking upon will not be accepted by Zamfarians. He remained committed to jettisoning his comfort for the sake of his people. As the Chief Security Officer of the state, he portrayed his leadership qualities, to rescue people from captivity and their family will never forget the effort. He had met with President Buhari where he showed his delight over the development of state security. The President equally assisted the state with 140,000 bags of fertilizer to be distributed to the farmers, especially those that were affected by insecurity. He also met with two service chiefs- Chief of Army Staff and Chief of Air Staff - and proceeded to the office of Inspector General of police, all for the sake of state security.

The number of people rescued from captivity by Governor Bello Matawalle in less than two months of his administration was about 147. These rescued Zamfarians were captured during the tenure of the former Governor. They were the people criticizing the peace accord between the government and the bandits because they saw many flaws in the process and mostly on how it was handled. For example, the former regime believed that military action was the best in restoring peace instead of striking a peace deal with the bandits. More than four thousand people were killed and the then governor neither sympathized with the people nor assisted the families of those killed or injured. The former regime claimed that they spent billions of naira on security in the state without any positive results. Governor Matawalle conversely is resolute on championing his people's rights and foster peace while implementing constructive policies that will spur development.

For sure, the greatest desire of Zamfara state in the past eight years has been peace. At the time when some leaders failed to establish egalitarian settlements, people got a great leader, who fears God. Since he became governor, Bello Matawalle has been determined to stick to his peoples' demands and strive best to make it possible. Just see how good leadership can turnaround a situation positively. Motorcyclists who could not operate at night as a result of the curfew placed by the government became vigilantes who protected their town and villages at night. Now that the former regime is gone forever, people in the rural areas are happy for the return of peace. They now move freely to their farms and do all their businesses conveniently. They have forgotten the last time they had a mass burial in their settlements. Many that fled from their homes have returned and have continued with their normal lives. People now travel at night within the state boundaries without any fear. When last did you hear about kidnapping and cattle rustling in Zamfara in the media?

Matawalle has set a genuine model for others to pursue. His dedication, enthusiasm, compassion, trustworthiness, and honesty have become an integral factor. His good interpersonal abilities and basic leadership capabilities are going to benefit Zamfara. I believe he is not resting on his oars on the success recorded but putting more effort to keep the success growing. What he needs as a leader is the support and cooperation of Zamfarians.

For the few months he has been in power, I have come to appreciate what good leadership can do to Nigeria. When we get leaders that are problem-solvers, it becomes easier for us as people and our country to make tremendous progress. In my observation, Governor Matawalle knew the radical surgery his state needed, and he has striven to solve the problems that he thought undermined peace and democracy within his state. This is what makes him a voice of the voiceless that Nigeria should be proud of in the 21st century. He is a harbinger of hope that a better country is possible through focused and purposeful leadership.

⊷ ⊶

CHAPTER 13

HER EXCELLENCY, DR. ERELU BISI ADELEYE-FAYEMI

I am fond of the sentiment of the eminent Russian author, Leo Tolstoy who said that: "to polish oneself is more important than any other goal in life." Erelu Bisi Fayemi, one of the daughters of Ekiti, shines as an exemplar of such development; she works for her community indefatigably. A few days ago, a luminous full moon adorned the sky of Ekiti as the clock of night descended. The moon's bright light reminded me of the smiling face of one of the daughters of the *Obirinkete*, loosely translated as "the mothers of Ekiti." It was an inexpressibly beautiful daughter, the one that never forgets her roots. Who exactly am I talking about here? It is HE (Dr) Erelu Bisi Adeleye-Fayemi - Ekiti State First Lady. She is a British-Nigerian writer, policy advocate,

social entrepreneur, gender specialist, and feminist activist.

She is inspired to serve the Nigerian community, particularly by giving women a voice. For me, "Obirinkete of Ekiti" is an epic journey of women's movement by Erelu Bisi Fayemi that is fundamentally enlightening women in Ekiti, Nigeria and by extension Africa. Worrywarts may not appreciate her work. They may criticize her and fail to appreciate the lofty endeavor by Mrs. Fayemi to empower women. I have observed and read about her, how she is championing the rights and freedoms of women with gusto. Her noble struggle to enlighten women is what determines the future of humankind. Yet, her critics themselves are not lifting a finger to benefit others or build a better world and as such, they never run the risk of incurring the inevitable derision that hounds those who champion good for women.

To my observation, the Obirinkete of Ekiti is a great movement dedicated to creating an era where all people win, where everyone can fully take pleasure in peace and happiness. That is the meaning of this "women movement." Erelu Bisi Fayemi is a Noble daughter of Ekiti Kete. In the rain; she walks through the muddy, desolate streets to encourage sisters, mothers, and friends to spread the meaning and benefits for the women empowerment in the society. She believes in egalitarianism, which for many years has been elusive in the state and Nigeria at large. The valiant wife of Governor Kayode Fayemi - also, one of the mothers of Ekiti Kete, in the sun, sets off into the scorching, energy-sapping heat to reach women and empower them. She embodies the quintessence of humanity and fully dedicates herself to helping people find real and solid happiness.

How wonderful is the sight of our daughter, sister, wife, and mother, Dr. Bisi Fayemi, walking hand in hand with other women as she advances happily along the path of her mission? A female leader who tenaciously presses onward, bathed in sweat as she carries such a great mission on her back. Her efforts are for the sake of others' happiness, and a better Nigeria. Mrs. Fayemi admirably exerts herself in society, where darkness and uncertainty reigns, she illuminates all with the light of her compassion. She possesses a heart of gold, with no thought of seeking personal recognition; as she has given herself today and again tomorrow to encourage those who are weighed down by heavy tear and wear. She is helping our society realize a state of happiness, equality, and social justice.

In 2001, she helped set up the African Women's Development Fund (AWDF), which was a fundamental Pan-African initiative towards empowering women. She also served the country by representing Nigeria as a Senior Advisor for the "UN Women Forum." She was also named as a Visiting Senior Research Fellow at King's College, the University of London in 2017. When her husband, Dr. Kayode Fayemi became the Governor of Ekiti State recently, she effectively advocated for social inclusion programs and grassroots empowerment programs in her State. She led the campaign to institute a Gender-Based Violence Prohibition Law, HIV Anti-Stigma Bill, and an Equal Opportunities Bill. She has served at the Executive Board of the Global Fund and African Women's Development Fund. She once chaired the Advisory Council of the Nigerian Women's Trust Fund and also served on the Governing Council of Elizade University in Nigeria. Mrs. Fayemi is a symbol of women's empowerment and the epitome of positive change. In her efforts to build a society with empowered women - this has earned her a prestigious Zik leadership award. She is an uncommon blessing to Ekiti State, Nigeria, and the world at large. As a feminist activist and social Entrepreneur, Mrs. Fayemi has dedicated her time, ability, and assets to protect the rights of women and girls.

It is generally known worldwide that, women and young girls bear enormous hardship during and after humanitarian crises, especially during armed conflicts. They generally have less acces to health, property ownership, education, and employment. They are far more uncertain than men to be politically dynamic and undeniably bound to be casualties of abusive behavior at home. Gender fairness infers a society where women and men appreciate comparative outcomes, rights, opportunities, and responsibilities in all circles of life. Nigeria today is on the cusp of a worldview change in its development and improvement and its position on the planet. The two people (men and women) must act unequivocally to catch this opportunity. We need to get ready for a noteworthy future and scale up rapidly in every district, be it in Agriculture, education, industry, economic-related services, infrastructure, or equality of the two genders.

In an earlier time, most women were confined to their homes. As in Nigeria and other African countries, men have consistently gone about as the ace of the scene and they have been making policies impacting women. With female leaders like Dr. Erelu Bisi, women are being increasingly empowered to fight for their position in society, a phenomenon that some conservative men are not comfortable with. To help and lift women in Ekiti and Nigeria to leadership and socio-economic activities they need to be empowered.

When it comes to the issues that concern women, Erelu Bisi Fayemi always comes in. She is a leader of vast and varied experiences, who is determined to show other women the way to freedom. Therefore, her stand, and I concur that the empowerment of women of Ekiti Kete is the prerequisite to transform a state and transform Nigeria. Empowerment has multiple, interrelated, and interdependent dimensions on economic, social, cultural, and political sectors. It can be understood in relation to resources, perceptions, relationships, and power. Educational accomplishment and economic interest are the key constituents in guaranteeing the empowerment of women. Educational accomplishment is fundamental in empowering women in all circles of society. Erelu Bisi Fayemi has placed herself at the nerve center of women empowerment because she sees it as an opportunity to develop her society.

Sometime ago, Mrs. Fayemi's entourage on Women Empowerment Program, went to Ikole Ekiti, for the Community Engagement and Advocacy tour in the state as part of her local commitment and support for the 16 local government zones of the state. All the while, she gave some edification campaigns against genital mutilation; sexual orientation and sex maltreatment. She additionally said the state government is resolved to step up its war against Female Genital Mutilation

(FGM), sex assault, children servitude and open defecation which is a disgrace to the state. She was more concerned with female genital mutilation problem and open defecations, which in all candors, we must all stand against.

In her effort to eliminate the uncouth practice, a few women who were professionals and practitioners of FGM turned out and renounced the practice. They additionally gave the paraphernalia for performing genital mutilation to Erelu Fayemi, who then got them enrolled for government empowerment programs. She demanded that the attackers and those obstructing justice in the trials of sex offenders should be confronted with the fury of the law under the Governor Kayode Fayemi-led regime. She emphasized and repeated it that, "It is a dishonorable thing for Ekiti state to be positioned third in female genital mutilation and first in the open defecation in Nigeria. This is unsuitable and unacceptable to us, she said. Let us stop the practice since this jeopardizes our lives."

Should the severe trial of life simply be accepted as destiny? No. Our goal as human beings should be to transform our destiny, to eradicate misery from our lives and to accomplish our human revolution so that we can savor lasting joy, happiness, and abundant good fortune. Within this frame, Erelu Bisi Fayemi has continued to empower women, put up a fight against archaic and dehumanizing practices that endanger the lives of women. She believes that she can lead in the front and deliver women to freedom, and independence. She has dedicatedly continued to fight for women's rights because she perceives this as a way of changing society positively

He Erelu Bisi Fayemi cornered in the FUOYE Melee

In her commitment to empowering women, Erelu Fayemi has faced some difficulties that seek to discourage her from rebuilding her society. One of the worst experiences was the one at the Federal University of Oye (FUOYE) where two students were unfortunately killed during a violent protest by FUOYE students, leading to an attack on the convoy of Mrs. Fayemi while touring the 16 Local governments for empowerment program. The regrettable and saddening incident touched my heart and I am still very disturbed. However, a lot has been said by various segments of the public, particularly on social media. Some are worth reading while some are to be trashed into the ocean of misfortune. In all, nonetheless, it will be highly suicidal to overlook any of the comments particularly as it affects Erelu Bisi Fayemi.

Sometimes, I wondered why many people judge others from a point that is most convenient for them without piecing it all together. I then realized that it is easy to be filled with sentiments than being objective. In the past days, many people have trampled on the dignity of our humanity using the unfortunate death of bright young students to advance causes that are inimical to our existence and prosperity, as a group of people. For me as a father, and a crusader of peace and happiness, I was dismayed at the way people have since upturned this tragedy for personal gains and instigated institutions against one another, in what I have seen to be a fruitless adventure. The public, in my opinion, has passed their judgments on who is at fault in the handling of the violent protests by FUOYE students.

The most painful part of this crisis was the unfortunate loss of lives. When an ugly event like this happens, it becomes impressively difficult to know whose account to believe or reject as evident from the arrays of social media comments over the past few days. However, I might not be personally present at the venue of the crisis at Oye, but I have read some reliable accounts. Also, the most painful and unfortunate comment on this whole matter was to believe that Erelu could have ordered the security men to shoot at the protesting students. This was a point where we all seem to surrender to the enemy forces. A point where I believed those who are planning to make cheap political blackmail against the government of Dr. John Kayode Fayemi rested their cases.

Erelu is a social crusader and woman activist, it is a well-known fact that she believes so much in genuine protest against any form of social injustice or ill-treatment. It will, therefore, be out of place to assume or believe that the wife of the governor ordered the shooting of the protesting students. I was told by a reliable source that, there was an interview that was conducted by the leader of a reliable group. In the whole interview, there was nowhere the leader of that group ever implicated Dr. Bisi Fayemi. It was also believed that in the said interview, the leader of the group agreed with the position of Dr. Bisi Fayemi that, the protest had already happened by the time Erelu came in for her program in Oye Ekiti that fateful day. So, where is the evidence to nail this gentle and easy-going woman in the entire Brouhaha and Imbroglio?

With all I have read about her, Erelu is a woman of peace who will never allow anything to cause harm or injury to anyone, not to talk of openly asking his security details to shoot at anyone. Erelu is more passionate about her philanthropic work than to be distraught or distracted by anything. She is a focused and caring mother and her objective is never to see anyone suffering. We all pray every day never to play into the hands of our enemies. The enemies are haters of good gestures and most evocative detractors. Erelu's good gestures happen every day, and that was the idea behind her *Obinrin Ekiti Kete* tour to all the 16 Local Government Areas of the State. She was on that tour to touch lives and never to maim or kill anyone. To be frank, I was terrified by the violence and deaths that resulted from the Oye protest. It is in this vein that I decided to include this potion in this book and sound it to the hearing of the public that Erelu is a genuine mother - caring and conscientious.

Erelu is someone who cares for all and sundry and would always come to the rescue of those in a difficulty. For example, Mrs. Bisi Fayemi once read about a story of Mrs. Sade Ojo who gave birth to a set of twins in the social media on Sunday, the 1st of September 2019. The twins' mother was stranded at the Ekiti State University Teaching Hospital, Ado Ekiti, since August, due to her inability to pay the hospital bill. The actual bill rose to N80,750 following some complications she went through in the process of delivering the twins. Accordingly, Mrs. Fayemi immediately dispatched an official, Mr. Dauda Lawal, to the hospital to verify the claim. The woman and her surviving babies were rescued as the said amount was paid by Mrs. Fayemi through Mr. Dauda Lawal. Though, Mrs. Sade Ojo was already discharged on August 31st without paying the amount she owed. The nursing mother and her family, mostly the husband valued the gesture as they thanked the governor's wife for her prompt intervention.

She also picked the medical bills of seven postnatal patients recently. These mothers had been stranded at the Ekiti State University Teaching Hospital, Ado Ekiti, since September 2019, following their inability to pay their respective medical bills. The seven patients owed N682,300, which was paid. Also, social media is awash with other philanthropic gestures linked with Erelu Bisi Fayemi. She once single-handedly paid the bill of a medical student at Ekiti State University to aid him complete his medical program and has now graduated. The Governor, Dr. Kayode Fayemi who is the husband of Erelu also offered all the 43 graduates of the Ekiti State University College of Medicine automatic jobs. One wonders how a family with a propensity for such kind-heartedness could suddenly turn around and sponsor violence or attack against Nigeria's future leaders. Look at this caring leader, as she was put in the angelic errand of rescuing a terrible situation that the Ojo's family and those helped students were finding themselves at a particular time and never know how to get out of such. Then, the first lady, Erelu Fayemi jumped into the situation and did the needful. Is this not what humanity (Christ) requests of us by saying: "I was in need you came to my aid!"

I was told that Erelu is popularly known as "Mother General." If this is true, then I concur that she is surely a Mother General because she has led many away from ruins into greatness and has ensured that they found their way back into bliss. She remains a genuine social crusader who has and continues to run programs that help to improve the lives of boys, girls, men, women and the aged. Her tour, which is another testimonial of her genuine efforts to make life better for everyone is another evident to all her goodness. I want us all to depart from where we politicize a matter that should make us all sober and mourn the great souls who have departed our midst untimely. As a father and one concerned in the Ekiti project, I urge the youths, the future of this great country, to shun violence. Nothing good can come out of violence – it only begets more violence and fatalities. They should embrace dialogue and consultations while airing their grievances. This nation needs her youth if she would reach the Promised Land.

In all, we may call a stone a jewel, that will not make it a jewel. We may likewise call a jewel a stone; this will not affect the nature of the jewel. Whatever others may say to the contrary, the truth is the truth and what's right is right. The important thing is to speak out loud and clear, without being afraid. Just as one of the ancient Roman philosophers, Seneca asserts, "What madness it is to be afraid of disrepute, in the judgment of the disreputable"! In any event, truly deep and lasting human ties are not created by the coercion of authority; they are forged through personal courage, wisdom, and integrity. Our mothers, the *Obinrinkete* members are the lofty emissaries of happiness, peace, and justice in the arena of grass-roots diplomacy, surpassing all others.

My father once said that, just hearing the word mother produced a feeling of peace, happiness, and comfort with a warming heart and that if people gave more thought to mothers, there would be no war. I heard this profoundly moving statement as a youth, and I have never forgotten it. That is why the Russian writer, Vladimir Korolenko (1853-1921) wrote that "human beings exist to be happy just as birds exist to fly". These are words worth pondering deeply upon. Human beings or birds, we each are here to fulfill our potential, thanks in large part to our mothers who gave us life. That is why we must strive to build an age in which mothers' faces can beam with smiles of unsurpassed happiness and peace. Is that not what Erelu is doing right now!

Though, your attires may be simple and modest, you wear in your heart a treasure that surpasses those of the wealthiest millionaire, your life radiating with an inexpressible vibrant, golden brilliance. You are never defeated. You are never beaten by ridicule or venomous attack. Never being defeated is itself victory; it means you have already won. One who lives life in such a way is a true victor. I doff my cap for our mothers.

I will conclude this with the words of one of American poets, Joaquin Miller (1837-1913) in a poem titled "The Bravest Battle," which contains these lines that have always stayed with me;

"the bravest battle ever was fought; ....
shall I tell you where and when?
on the maps of the world, you will find it not;
It was fought by the mothers of men"

CHAPTER 14

REV. BISHOP MATTHEW HASSAN KUKAH

Religion, politics and legislative issues, a capricious blend in numerous countries. Strict activism is a developing power for change. Clergymen of numerous influences utilize their lecterns as sounding board for sincere, yet regularly conflicting calls for sweeping new social orders and invigorating contemporary discussions over the detachment among church and state. Generally, the public authority's profound and good components have been a wellspring of motivation for those looking for equity and opportunity. In any case, they have additionally prompted sacred wars and psychological warfare. Today, notwithstanding, the genuine inquiry is not whether religion ought to be ensnared with worldwide legislative issues, as contends by most church and mainstream pioneers, the issue currently is how much inclusion the administrative ought to have with the non-administrative and what structures it should take. On this, there is a touch of meeting of the personalities.

In the West, especially the United States, the church and state division are a protected command. However, recent years have brought the warmed discussion over the height of the alleged mass of division and whether this hindrance ought to be sufficiently permeable to permit such practices as school prayers, supplication, and public guide to parochial organizations to see through. In different part of the world, there is no such administrative government division. There, the superb issue is the congregation's part in keeping up patriotism and the conventions of the past or in affecting social and political change. Some demand that the congregation and its church should hold themselves above explicit plans and hardliner positions. Love for God and man in a worldwide society, they say, are the legitimate religious objectives. Others would put churchmen dirt in the government seat, battling for profound beliefs in an exceptionally political manner. Some even legitimize the utilization of brutality to accomplish "strict" ends. Maybe the new embracing of "freedom philosophy" in Latin America and the Philippines best outlines one significant part of the debate. For instance, the Roman Catholic Church's job in removing Philippine President Ferdinand Marcos is presently under investigation by the two scholars and government authorities. These priests named the contested presidential elections of Feb. 7 "unmatched in their direct deceitfulness." The pastorate's podium and in-the-positions uphold for challenger and now President Corazon Aquino were noticeable.

Be that as it may, a few spectators do not see a critical distinction between the church's situation in the Philippines and Roman Catholic pastors' political activism in Nicaragua, where Rome has banished a group of four clerics in the left-wing Sandinista government from practicing sacral capacities. The contention is not probably going to be settled soon. The political contribution of the church has profound verifiable roots. It goes back to the seventh century when the Prophet Muhammad joined political and strict position. From the Protestant Reformation and Counter-Reformation to current occasions, the clerical authority has then gained appreciated, noticeable quality as well as been dispatched to a mediocre situation in the West. Today, the job of religion on the worldwide scene keeps on introducing a progression of mysteries. At times, the congregation centers basically around man's profound necessities. In others, its essential job is in pushing innovation and underscoring material advancement.

In specific cases, religion calls for harmony and cultural solidarity. In others, it is a wellspring of contention and brutality. Furthermore, certain parts of coordinated religion receive liberal political and social plans. Others embrace customary traditionalist if not traditionalist fundamentals. Notwithstanding, these contentions, researchers and administrative pioneers will in general concur that churches and strict ideas are progressively impacting public and worldwide legislative issues.

Regardless of a solidly established obligation to the partition of church and state, hardly can any see the simple communication of the administrative and non-administrative as a danger to a country. "Blending governmental issues and religion are just about as old as a fruit dessert." "Jesus of Nazareth expressed the perpetual inquiry: Render hence unto Caesar the things which are Caesar's and unto God the things that are of God." But he gave no exact recipe for tackling explicit issues. Some experts on the part of religion in defining government strategy, says that, from one viewpoint, a free society ought to properly have philosophical underpinnings. Be that as it may, they likewise caution about the "threats of conjuring heavenly authorization for specific situations on open issues."

Of late, despite sharp analysis, both the strict religious left and right in America have advanced toward politically dynamic positions which expert says are foundations for concern. For instance, different liberal church gatherings, including the National Council of Churches, US Catholic Bishops, and other reformist Protestant and Jewish associations censured the weapons contest and atomic war, advocate financial change, back asylum in the US for unlawful refugees from Central America, and restrict government interest in bigoted South Africa, all for the sake of religion. Then again, strict preservationists keep on campaigning for enactment of restricting abortion, re-establishing endorsed school petition prayer, and managing the cost of public guide to private schooling. Overall, "genuine religion should remain over the fight," "and judge the abundance, everything being equal".

Similarly, as I counted over, a free society ought to appropriately have religious underpinnings. This is the place where, out of numerous clergies, I picked one in this book. Somebody like Reverend Bishop Matthew Hassan Kukah is known to take care of the business of solidarity. A religious leader fighting for justice and respect for human rights. He tells it as it is without mincing his words. He wants an equal Nigerian society with a perfect union in the country. The categorization of the country as Northern and Southern is no long a matter of Geography, but political regionalization. Bishop Kukah is clear on his mind that the Buhari administration is installing northern hegemony, instead of directing efforts to save the country from terrorism, banditry, corruption, and all other social evils.

Kukah presently serves as the Bishop of the Roman Catholic Diocese of Sokoto. The diocese is in North-western Nigeria. He has held some positions such Vicar General of the Archdiocese of Kaduna, and Secretary General of the Catholic Bishops' Conference of Nigeria. The Rev. Bishop Kukah has been involved in some presidential initiatives to address electoral justice, and abuse of human rights. He has sat on the Human Rights Violation Investigation commission. He was also a member of the National Political conference and the Electoral Reform Committee.

As a presidential facilitator, he brokered truce between the Ogoni residents and Shell Petroleum Development Company. He has been involved in assessing the crisis and damage caused by Boko Haram in the north. The Bishop has been an active religious leader who has gone beyond teaching the word of God, to serving and brokering peace deals in the country. In 1980, he acquired a master's degree in Peace Studies at the University of Bradford. He has a background in Public policy, and this explains why he is involved in shaping governance in the country. With his Kukah Centre, Public Policy Think tank, it has been possible for him to address public policy and religious issues.

Kukah, a key player in northern Nigeria's state of affairs
Bishop Kukah is an influential religious leader in the country's north. In a Muslim dominated region, the Bishop has continued to serve people regardless of their faith. He is a genuine servant that is committed to ensuring that Nigerians coexist peacefully not considering their religious or political persuasions. He has witnessed Nigerians being battered, maimed, and tortured by Boko Haram. The insecurity in the northern part of the country has been an issue of concern to him.

Being a catholic in northern Nigeria comes with a lot of challenges. Bishop Kukah has seen it all, and notes that Christians in the northern part of the country face constant threats from Boko Haram militants. As a bishop serving the minority-Christians, it is a difficult task. Christians in this part of the country live under Islamic laws. This is a sad situation, in a country that is determined to foster religious liberty. There is nothing to celebrate when Christians are forced to live under Sharia laws. Both Muslims and Christians are supposed to coexist peacefully and respect each other. This is not the case though. The Muslim majority are in control of the northern region.

However, Bishop Kukah has been pushing for the restoration of security and tolerance in the north. As the Most Rev. Bishop, Kukah believes in religious liberty. He wants Muslims and Christians to have a dialogue that will ensure peaceful coexistence. If the people in the north put their religious differences aside, it becomes a less difficult task for the government. Right now, as the government fights the Boko Haram insurgents, there is also less trust between Muslims and Christians. The two factions need to pursue unity and put aside their religious differences and cooperate with the government in fighting the terrorists.

Bishop Kukah has been vocal on Christian-Muslim dialogue to end animosity between the two sides. This loathing will make it hard to restore security in the region. Some time back, Bishop Kukah spoke in the U.S. about the state of affairs in northern Nigeria. While raising awareness about what was happening in the north, the bishop noted that the Christian communities were the target of the insurgents. He talked about the religious conflicts and their effects on peace and unity in the north. The church feels weak in the region because Christians are the minority. However, he noted that ending ill feeling between Christians and Muslims will be a considerable move toward a better Nigeria.

The Boko Haram militants exploit the differences between Christians and Muslims. They will target churches to stoke the religious feuds. The persistent attack on the church somewhat leads to hatred for Muslims. But Bishop Kukah wants this to come to an end. He is encouraging religious tolerance for the prosperity of the region. Ending conflicts between these factions is a key interest to this Bishop. He feels the urgency for these two religions to see each other beyond their beliefs for the sake of their country. He does not see the need for Christians to hate Muslims or vice versa. He basically wants unity and broadmindedness that will help these communities coexist and win against the insurgents.

Bishop Kukah understands the challenges that the church is facing in the north. In his own diocese in Sokoto, building more churches and schools has been challenging.

The local conflicts and religious animosity are stopping all the expansion plans, which are geared towards building more schools and churches. Building more of this infrastructure will open up the north and allow religious freedom. More schools will attract many children to the institutions for learning and knowledge acquisition. When there is access to land, it is possible for the church to expand and build more schools to attract more children to school.

Kukah is a mediator who wants the best for everyone. He does not see Muslims as a problem. Neither does he see Christians as such. He considers the religious split as something that can be resolved through dialogue. Dialogue is one-way effective way of resolving conflicts. And as graduate with Peace Studies, the Bishop is applying the knowledge he has acquired to rescue society from conflicts. It is not easy for him to unite these people, but encouraging dialogue is the basis under which a solution can be found. His mediation skills are top-notch and that underscores why he has been involved in many commissions and committees to push for peace. He has undertaken several presidential initiatives to address peace and reconciliation, particularly in the north. Peace is essential especially in the north; otherwise, it will be difficult for it to realize any significant development. People should live tolerantly for them to get the peace of mind to work diligently. The Bishop will continue mediating and preaching unity and harmony as his resolve to improve the state of affairs in the north.

His mediation acumen is central in the realization of a better Nigeria. He is speaking to all and sundry that people can disagree but should not result in enmity. When people can disagree in such a manner, it is a demonstration of maturity and willingness to rebuild Nigeria. People must be listening to the bishop, and there is hope that in his capacity he will continue to play a principal role in uniting people. A people united can never be defeated. In the best-case scenario, if Nigeria unites and stops bigotry or anything that distorts their thinking, it is feasible to make sound decisions on the ballot.

Unity brings a sense of sound judgment in every decision that people make. There is a persuasion that in disunity, political cons wiggle themselves into power. Politicians are crafty, and sometimes they sow seeds of disunity so that they get into power. Disharmony makes people illogical and completely unreasonable when voting. They will consider their tribesmen or religion. A Christian will not elect a Muslim to be president or vice versa. This can be on the basis of disunity. However, if people can see beyond their religious differences, and consider the ability and genuineness of a leader to deliver, then Nigeria will elect caring and performing leaders.

In Africa, leaders have mastered the art of divide and rule. They coalesce into tribal cocoons and whip emotions so that it becomes a political battle of "Us versus Them." In this context, Muslims will go the ballot thinking that it is a contest between Christians and them. It is a sad truth, but that is our voting pattern. This has to stop when unity is fostered. Let everyone see a Nigerian as their peaceful compatriot, and fight for a common good. The common denominator here should be good leadership. The persuasion should be about good leadership, not religion. In

Bishop Kukah's mediation role, he is clear on pushing for unity. He understands that the moment we realize that it is not long an issue of Muslims and Christians, then it makes us better understand that it is a matter of good leadership that the country is missing. Nigerians want to be secure. They want jobs, which can only be created when the economy is booming.

However, this is becoming a pipe dream because of the naïve and self-centered leadership in our country. It is notable that this Bishop will not stop mediating and promote religious tolerance in the country. Such tolerance is handy and can push us towards meaningful development and democracy.

Bishop Kukah on security and good governance

Bishop Kukah has been advocating for a better country. He has rubbed shoulders with the most powerful because of his strong belief in social justice, equity, and equality. He is a straight talker. He has been telling the Buhari administration that it is its role and responsibility to keep the country secure. As a watchdog of the government, he has to speak out on the rot and failure of this government to secure the north and other parties of the country.

What the security challenges in Northern Nigeria is facing is a failure of the government. The government needs to act more swiftly to respond to the needs of people. First, the government has ignored how religious differences were fueling insecurity and mistrust in the region. A genuine and well-meaning government will dig into the root cause of insecurities of the North. Insecurity in this part of this country goes beyond terrorism, but other underlying issues such as religion. The government has been out of touch with reality, due to incompetence and corruption. Those in power are focused on mass accumulation of wealth through corruption because that is where their interests rest on.

As a human rights activist, Bishop Kukah is talking tough and critically so that the government can fix the situation in the country. Nonetheless, he understands that resolving security challenges in the country is not a one-day effort. It is about public policy and looking for avenues that shall bring all leaders together to face every national security threat with concerted efforts. This would be the only way to restore Nigeria to the positive trajectory. Religious leaders are watchmen. They try to protect society from evil, but the government with all the apparatus, intelligence and resources need to do its job. The job of securing the country is the job of the federal government, which Bishop Kukah seems to be failing. It is against that backdrop that the good Bishop insists that he will keep on telling the government of its failures. He urges Nigerians to reject bad governance that is hell-bent on corruption, nepotism, and sectarianism, instead of uniting the country.

The Bishop insists, "the duty and responsibility of government is the security and welfare of its citizens". This is a strong message and reminder to Nigerians to hold the government to account. This is how a leader who is a voice for the voiceless lets out their inner feelings and beliefs. The government has to play its role and stop taking people for a ride for so long. Besides, in most of summonses, the bishop has been taking swipes at the government and points out its weaknesses. He urges his congregation to reject corruption and bad governance. The bishop sees himself as a watchman, whose role is raising an alarm in case of danger. Since he has witnessed danger lurking in every part of the country, he has to speak his mind and let the world know that the federal government is letting the country into a free fall. This is the courage that Nigerians want from those who have voices to speak out.

Nevertheless, the Bishop has been pushing for electoral reforms in the country. He believes that a fair and just electoral body is all that Nigeria needs for its democracy to have a room for development. The good bishop is well-meaning. He is using his platform to transform Nigeria. He does not hide from the truth but emerges as a truth-teller. Bishop Kukah is not playing politics, but he is saying what he sees. He is not running for or interested in a political seat. Instead, he just wants a government that is caring and serving all Nigerians. It will be hypocrisy for him to sit and watch when his followers are hopeless due to bad governance, corruption, and all other politically instigated problems. He is the voice that Nigeria wants at the moment to end corruption, bad governance, electoral fraud, and insecurity that are order of the day in Nigeria, today!

⇥ ⇤

CHAPTER 15

PASTOR SARAH OMAKWU

A s posited severally, fighting for change and a better society does not necessarily need a person to hold a political position. You can defend and advocate for democracy at whatever level. Pastor Sarah Omakwu is one brave religious leader that has mastered that art. She has many followers that she ministers to and in the same way she has to be concerned about their welfare. She is obliged to address issues such as corruption, insecurity, human rights, and freedoms. The position she holds as a Christian leader gives her authority to voice her position on a raft of issues affecting Nigerians.

Sarah Omakwu was born on 31 July 1962. She is a prominent Christian speaker and Nigerian pastor. She is the Senior Minister at the Family Worship Centre in Abuja. Her evangelism is no longer local, but international. This is a positive trajectory asserting the influence of Pastor

Omakwu in Nigeria and beyond. To add, she has been running a radio program dubbed "Moving Forward with Pastor Sarah." In her resolve to change lives and improve her society, Pastor Omakwu, through the church she leads, supports operations of mission agencies and missionaries in Nigeria.

Her teachings aim at reaching every Nigerian, with their religion or ethnicity notwithstanding. This evidences her determination to advance her country to equality which today is a chief obstacle to democratization in Nigeria. For a country to democratize, leaders have to embrace equality and bring both the majority and minority communities to the roundtable. When leaders from all communities feel they are one and united for a common goal, a country can swiftly progress. But with the current state where leaders are wrangling and the top leadership is not much absorbed in building an all-inclusive government, it would observably be difficult to have an equal society. What is paramount is to fight for positive change. That is the best approach to use to achieve a fair and just society. Pastor Omakwu always aspires to live in that. As a Nigerian citizen and parent, she has dedicated her life not only to spiritual issues, but also to social and leadership affairs. She knows that her freedom of worship can as well be curtailed if people of her standing do not speak against misrule. Certainly, this is a religious leader that wishes her country to become fair and just for everyone.

I find something intriguing about Sarah Omakwu. Her inspirational stories about her private life and journey to higher social standing instill hope and to underscore what is commonplace to everyone. President Barrack Obama spoke about hope and was able to win the U.S. presidency. In the Nigerian context, hope is still key to everything, because it inspires people to campaign for change. When one campaigns for change, which straddles the line between the rule of law and the people to elect as to foster democracy, a country can achieve regime change. Regime change, not in the sense of overthrowing a government, but from the lens of failed leaders resigning and giving people back their power to elect good leaders, leaders that will run a republic justly and democratically.

The candid cleric, interestingly, has not been shied to assail President Muhammadu Buhari for failing to tackle the ills that are facing her country. It would be a betrayal to followers and Nigerians to have individuals occupying influential positions go silent on political leaders running the country downhill. Mrs. Omakwu considers her position as vital in speaking the truth to the political and corporate circles. This is healthy for holding leaders accountable. Reprimanding and piling pressure on irresponsible leaders is vital in shaping the leadership of a country. That explains why Pastor Omakwu is vocal on slapping leaders on the wrist and at the same time urging them to work for people rather than amass wealth at the expense of poor masses as it is in the present-day Nigeria.

She intelligently blends evangelism and politics in a highly commendable way. Her perspective on the present leadership and blatant criticism of the unhinged government has the potential to sway how her followers will exercise social power. The influence of religion and its leaders in society is paramount. Religion builds a sense of community which can excite members to pursue change not considering the price they will have to pay. To be clear, that is not to indicate that religion advocates for violence. What this simply implies is that religion can unite people as one community against evils perpetrated by the ruling class. When a community unites and feels it shares a similar vision, people can inevitably rise against vices like nepotism, tribalism, and discrimination. People can feel the need to defend themselves against the domineering government by fighting the aforementioned challenges.

This sounds hypothetical to some extent, but do not close the eyes to the influence Pastor Omakwu and her followers have. They hold social power, which if properly exercised can trigger a wave against leaders who for long perceive public offices as personal property. It is not that I advocate for revolt against the present political leaders. Also, it is not that I view the church and followers of pastor Omakwu as possible rebels. While some may take it as so but downgrading the power this cleric and her followers have is perilous.

To this point, there is no open resistance against the government. That should not be considered as a weakness and powerlessness. The quest for employment, better lives, development, security, peace, and democracy can trigger civil disobedience. Nigeria is not in the worst state of affairs in the world, but people should not be tired to ask the government for better. Religion, especially Christianity, is a voluntary belief and it stands for trust and integrity. As voluntary as it is, its followers have the right to protect these fundamental values in society. It gets to a point where people would have to arise against leaders washing down these values. As a Christian, Pastor Omakwu stands against the corrupt and dishonest leaders who masquerade as good and kind people. Such dreadful leaders would want to make lofty contributions at church, as a way of "cleaning" their stolen money. In response to that, Omakwu has on several occasions warned leaders against bringing "dirty" offerings to the church.

Incidence of the political class using the church as a place to dump dirty money to earn loyalty is a growing concern in Africa; and a high risk to democracy as well as Christianity. Such cases have also been reported in countries such as Kenya where many politicians use religious platforms and misfortunes such as funerals to sell themselves as generous and compassionate in the eyes of the public. This is done at the expense of meaningful development.

To my mind, it is clear that once other religious leaders like Pastor Omakwu speak against evils such as corruption, nepotism, murders, and tribalism, religion would have a significant effect on Nigerian democracy. While it may take time for all religious leaders in Nigeria to speak in one voice, things may change in the future. Probably it will get to a point when religious differences will be shunned for citizens to unite for a common cause, a cause that will possibly bring sanity, development, democracy, and unity to Nigeria.

It is not that I am a naysayer. As someone that believes in a true democracy and a dream of a first-world nation in Africa, the way Nigeria is led, honestly needs to change. This is the reason the evangelical works of Pastor Sarah Omakwu is of great interest to me. Though some people may pay no heed to her and fall short of recognizing her devotion to support a transition to true democracy, Omakwu's dream remains steadily focused on good leadership.

Pastor Sarah Omakwu address on national issues

I find the work, actions, and teachings of pastor Omakwu very inspiring and important to nurturing Nigerian democracy. She is adamant, crystal clear and courageous in all that she says. The authority with which she addresses national issues is splendid. No doubt about that. Although she did not directly speak about democracy, she addressed critical issues that if not resolved, can encumber democracy. To bring out how she fought for democracy, I will build an argument that links every issue to democracy. Let me narrow this down to what in theory and practice undermines efforts to achieve democracy in Africa's most populous and largest economy, Nigeria.

Indisputably, corruption which I have extensively mentioned in the previous chapters is a major obstacle to the realization of the Nigerian Dream and democracy. If you keenly read the earlier chapters, you came across the description of corruption as a monster. It is a monster that must be slain lest Nigeria collapses. Religious, political, and corporate leaders must address this national disaster. Transparency International – an NGO combating corruption globally claims that there is a connection between this vice and democracy. The 2019 Corruption Perceptions Index claimed that the failure to curb this problem of graft that has contributed to a crisis of democracy across the globe will bring doom to Africa and humanity.

In support of this claim, Transparency International has based its case on corrupt leaders fearing condemnation and heavy punishment for perpetrating corruption. To walk scot-free, these corrupt leaders thwart democratic checks and balances on their alleged involvement in corruption. There is truth in this assertion. Countries like Nigeria that rank high in corruption are finding it hard to strengthen the democratic system or institutions. This is on account that the corrupt leaders who hold power feel secure in a corrupt system. Instead of growing a strong democratic system they will weaken them and botch up any corruption investigations against them. Such powerful dishonest figures go the extra mile to manipulate and compromise corruption busters.

This claim is logical. When corrupt people dominate the government, they cannot set up strong institutions that can prosecute corrupt leaders. Rather, they weaken them by all means. In the end, a country will have weak institutions that cannot challenge authoritarians and sway the leadership of a country. In equal measure, Nigeria has not established strong and effective anti-corruption and integrity mechanisms. This is a challenge that is affecting the majority of countries that have recently achieved democratic governance. Now, the democratic institutions are not empowered to independently tackle and prosecute high-profile corrupt leaders. Despondently, even leaders who gained power by promising to combat corruption have destabilized the democratic institutions which legitimately require political goodwill to slay corruption.

President Buhari was a populist leader as can be seen in 2015 as he got overwhelming support from across the diverse society of Nigeria because he promised to run a sustained and productive graft purge. On the obverse, he has failed to strengthen democratic institutions and anti-corruption mechanisms which stand a great chance to maintain the fight against corruption. The relevancy of this is so clear: corruption is still rampant in Nigeria. The corrupt are still thriving and the war on corruption has been politicized. It is now used as a bludgeon against political opponents where false allegations are heaped on opposition leaders to shut them up. From this brief analysis, it is evident that corruption weakens democracy or even destroys it. Since the perpetrators and beneficiaries are within the government, they will do whatever it is within their means to cover up corruption. They will destroy evidence and suppress voices that unwaveringly support the purge.

On a positive trajectory, prominent individuals are stepping up the fight against corruption in social institutions like churches. Pastor Omakwu is one of those individuals. She has taken the fight to churches where corruption proceeds are given as offerings and tithes. Corrupt leaders are cunning and real schemers. To calm and weaken the influence of religious institutions, they use stolen money to attract support. You cannot doubt the fact that money buys undeserved loyalty. It is unmerited in the sense that it is bought. To defeat the attempts by politicians to offer corrupt money, Omakwu has been warning politicians not to offer their corruption proceeds, mostly in her church. In her preaching and addresses at several conferences, cleric Omakwu has not shied away from talking about graft. Theft of public resources in Nigeria is no secret. The callousness of leaders and their get-rich-quick mindset can push the country to the brink of collapse. In reaction to the ongoing stealing of public resources, Omakwu has taken her time to take head-on corruption within her church. She is not dilly-dallying on condemning and fighting graft. She sees

and places the church as an important and critical partner in the fight against corruption. She has openly warned
looters not to offer their ill-gotten money to churches.

Sarah Omakwu, the Senior Pastor at Family Worship
Centre is insisting that civil servants should not tithe their
loot. She is on record maintaining that the congregation
should not offer to her church money they cannot explain
their source. In her argument, she said that they rather
not offer than give stolen money, because to her, a hand
that gives ill-gotten fortunes will not be blessed. Instead, it
would be cursed. The major point Pastor Omakwu drives
are that the church should fight corruption. It should not
be a conduit for cleaning stolen money. It is a common
practice for politicians to hide in the church. If you have
been observant enough, there has been an ongoing assault
on politicians in the East African nation, Kenya, perceived
to be donating millions of monies in local currency to
churches. Though the politicians are defending themselves. The clergy in some churches still accept donations
from leaders. Corruption still stands as a major challenge
in the country. Similarly, in Nigeria, there is an attempt
by the political class to flood the churches with sums of
money that are from questionable sources.

Kenya, in this case, is used to illustrating how the
churches in many African states are used to "sanitize"
looted money through donations, tithes, and offerings.
Religious institutions should speak against politicians and
civil servants bringing their loot to church. No religion
supports theft and to avoid being accomplices, the church
must reject the attempts by civil servants and politicians to
offer stolen loot or money from undefined sources. Prob-

ably Pastor Omakwu has discovered that it is time for the church to get involved in this fight. It would be a betrayal of society for the church to continue abetting corruption by accepting looted money. Rather, it should intensify calls by Omakwu not to be recipients of corrupt money or beneficiaries of graft. This is a decisive action that portrays Omakwu as someone devoted to fighting corruption that is collapsing the democratic institutions in the country. She deserves praise for combating corruption right in the church. To intensify this fight, more religious institutions should come into the fold to condemn and reject proceeds obtained corruptly.

Aside from corruption, Omakwu has complained about insecurity in the country. She valiantly criticizes President Buhari for inaction to restore order in the country. Nigeria needs peace to democratize. The rising insecurity in the Northern and recently, the Southern parts of the country is a major threat to peace and democracy. It is time to call the president into action to save the Northern part of Nigeria and pacify the region. Omakwu is not the only one demanding action that will bring harmony to war-torn areas. She shares the same sentiment with other critics of the President, not because she hates Buhari, but because she wants the best for her nation. This can only be realized if there is a commitment by the government to end violence and restore unity and peace. Where there is no peace, democracy fades away. Within that logic, Omakwu continues to hold the president accountable for the deteriorating peace. In the 21st century, herdsmen killing innocent civilians cannot be accepted. In this new century, it is wrong and backward to allow bandits to destabilize peace in the country. At a time when people are expected to be innovators and change-makers in society, some are still stuck in banditry. Think through this, people!

Nobody should be allowed to mete out mayhem on others. When an attack happens, the President should not be silent. He should speak and direct security officers to swiftly respond to the situation and bring to book all people that are threats of national security. This is something that everyone would expect a democratic leader to do. Unfortunately, as witnessed, the President has not been decisive enough to tackle such unending attacks on civilians in the country. It angers Omakwu to see her country regressing to the Dark Ages at a time everyone expects it to be the beacon of hope in Africa. The myopic top leadership of the country is making it hard for it to realize real democracy. As long as leaders like Omakwu speaks, it would be difficult for the President to happily enjoy his presidency when religious and ethnic divisions are gaining momentum in the country.

It is upon the president to unite the country by, among other things, ironing out divisive issues mushrooming from diverse religions and ethnicity. As a secular nation, where freedom of worship is guaranteed, it would be calamitous to pit Muslims against Christians or any other religion. What is expected is that all Nigerians should live harmoniously. That is how we should live. In a democracy or a country that is determined to be democratic, the President should protect fundamental rights like life. It is a betrayal to allow people to render the country insecure by murdering others; whether they are herdsmen or professionals in any field. Mrs. Omakwu has exclusively spoken about the issue of security in the country. She sees it as a humongous impediment to democratization. To pursue and cultivate democracy, such obstacles should not be allowed to become perpetual. They must be stopped by all means. Pastor Omakwu is perfectly championing for a safe country that guarantees prosperity, democracy, unity, and cooperation among all members of society regardless of its heterogeneous makeup. A Muslim should live happily and freely within a predominantly Christian community. In the same vein, a Christian should not feel threatened or insecure in a Muslim-dominated community or neighborhood. That is the dream Omakwu has for Nigeria.

About Northern Nigeria, Mrs. Omakwu has been angry at how politicians take citizens for a ride. She has been critical not of the President alone, but all politicians. When politicians and policymakers deprive a region of development and access to basic social amenities, they engage in crime. It is as simple as that. They can take part in the destruction. Omakwu has decried the poor leadership in Northern Nigeria so vehemently. Politicians in this region do not have time to improve social amenities in the region. According to Omakwu, lack of social amenities and poverty is rampant in the region if compared with other regions in the country. However, even the South is not rich per se.

The moral points the cleric is raising is that politicians are failing to offer good leadership that is hinged on development in Nigeria. Politicians are stealing from these extremely poor masses. The resources meant for development are directed to benefit a few individuals. Consequently, the poor are left without something to depend on and this could be the reason why insecurity is doubling in the region. It is despicable. Or deplorable, whichever adjective you can use to describe the callous actions of the politicians to display opulence while the majority is left wallowing in abject poverty. It is not acceptable to allow this to go on. It is unhealthy for democracy that guarantees equal opportunities and dignity for all.

By impoverishing people and turning them to mere voters, a country cannot make headway like that. Elected leaders should dedicate their services to serve people selflessly and distribute development across the country. It will be a wise decision that will solve the current problems of insecurity. Poverty brews anger that fosters animosity against each other. The reverse is true. If all people feel they have equal opportunities and can get what they need to live better lives, they cannot fight or murder each other.

The dream and vision of pastor Omakwu for her country should get people to action to fight for their human rights and freedoms, development, and security. If followers, politicians, citizens, and everyone can listen to her message, it will be at that juncture in which Nigerians can have a rational and national debate on how to prop up democracy and develop. The national dialogue should focus on key issues such as evenly distributed development, improved security, zero corruption, and high moral values. These are the building blocks of democracy.

If as a country, the government can fight and win the war on corruption, politicians, among other leaders, will collaborate to address security concerns and restore a value system that dignifies every human being. In this case, it will be possible to address all other issues like electoral reforms and voters' empowerment that matter to democracy. Empowered voters would elect good leaders and they will be the final decision-makers of who will rule them.

Pastor Sarah Omakwu is one religious leader that should always be commended and motivated to continue advocating for reforms. It is time her contribution to the national dialogue on significant issues that we must tackle is recognized. She should not just be seen as a critic, but as someone who has the interest of the nation at heart. She should not be underrated because her influence is growing, and her followers will one day does not allow the country to run to the dogs.

What is crucial is that other religious leaders should pull up their socks and speak about the problems threatening to block democracy and take the country in the wrong direction. It is too late to be quiet or complacent. It is time to offer public support to democratic institutions and speak truth to leaders. Keeping silent is ignorance which can destroy a country. Silence can energize thieves and enhance impunity. As long as Nigerians will speak like Pastor Omakwu, this country will head in the right direction and the leadership will naturally have to transform.

⊰⊱

CHAPTER 16

SENATOR ENYINNAYA ABARIBE

M any Nigerians who followed the more recent outburst of Eyinnaya Abaribe over official handling of security in the country might not remember that the parliamentarian was not new to controversy. In fact, he adorned controversial garb almost all through his 21-year career as a politician and public office holder. His often calculated and decisive stance on sensitive issues over that period, along with his background as a scholar, adequately prepared him for the task of giving voice to the voiceless in society; and speaking truth to power fearlessly.

It is on record that Abaribe, as Deputy Governor of Imo State between 1999 and 2003 survived three impeachment attempts. It was not by chance. He doggedly addressed the subject underlying his proposed impeachments and took relevant actions to defeat them. In the first attempt, in August 1999, he responded well to the charges leveled against him by the House which then let him go. The genesis of his problem had to do with his irreconcilable differences with his principal, former Governor Orji Uzor Kalu of Imo State. Unknown to many, Abaribe was fighting for the rectification of some anomalies, which could negatively affect public interest. He was prepared to step on powerful toes to protect the people's interests. It is instructive that Abaribe, as a typical politician, said much later that he had since reconciled with his former principal.

In the second attempt to impeach him mid-2000, the House of Assembly levelled charges on him but did not wait for the statutory 14 days' period to obtain his reply. Rather, the House asked the Chief Judge to set up a panel in pursuit of the impeachment. He consequently sued, challenging the process, but the court ruled against him for lack of jurisdiction to intervene in legislative affairs. The Court of Appeal upheld the High Court's position. Abaribe nevertheless survived the second attempt by a marginal vote.

At the end, he resigned honorably in 2003, having seen the handwriting on the wall about the irreversible decision of the State House of Assembly to impeach him for the third time. Even his resignation mode was controversial, as he decided to resign by transmitting a letter to that effect to the House through a courier service, so that the record of his letter would be public and undeniable. The House still went on to declare him as impeached, an action Abaribe subsequently described as "medicine after death." Those incidents marked the beginning of focus on him as a promising and courageous leader willing and able to challenge the authorities with the aim of taking society to a level that would resonate with the average person. So,

Abaribe flashing the spirit of courage in criticizing the President is not his first time to push for reforms in the country. His political activism can be traced back to his relationship with Orji. He was instrumental to the dismantling of "mamacracy in Abia".

He was to intervene in 2007, along with other members of South East Senators, in the arrest and detention of Ralph Uwazuruike, leader of the Movement for the Actualization of the Sovereign State of Biafra (MASSOB). They met the president at the time, Umaru Musa Yar'Adua to plead for Uwazuruike's release. The late president heeded their plea and ensured that he was released almost unconditionally. Much later following the arrest, detention, and prosecution of Nnamdi Kanu, leader of Independent People of Biafra (IPOB) for treason, Abaribe led the caucus of South East Senators to the presidency for his release and two other colleagues. The court granted the accused persons bail in the sum of N100m surety each. Abaribe stood surety for him and somehow managed to perfect the bail condition even for the two other detainees. Kanu was to jump bail and escape from prosecution, prompting security agency, Directorate of State Service (DSS) to go after Abaribe, arrested and detained him for some time; and searched his house. Abaribe did not allow that episode to deter him from pursuing what he believes was in the public interest, not minding the powerful opposition that he was up against.

Till today, the presidency never missed a chance to castigate him for failing to produce the accused person. Although the development directly pitched him against the federal government, especially the Presidency, it rather made him stronger and more popular. It endeared him to the people who now see him as their mouthpiece in times of critical assessment of public affairs. As was seen, the Presidency was more vehement in criticizing him after he demanded the resignation of the President for failing to do enough to secure Nigerians. By calling on President Muhammadu Buhari to resign for his failure to secure the lives and property of the average Nigerians, Abaribe stirred the hornet's nest. Beyond that, he succeeded in beaming a heavy touch light on an issue that touches Nigerians perhaps more than any other matter. The reactions that his contribution on the floor of the Senate generated, coupled with the potentially far-reaching measures adopted by the upper legislative chamber are clear testimonies to the weight of his statement, as well as to the concern of Nigerians

Ordinarily, calling a President to resign consequent upon relative lack of success in controlling crime or even any other matter of public interest is deemed in many parts of Africa, including Nigeria, as an excessive or outlandish request. This has to do firstly with the fact that Nigeria is afflicted with so many ills. And her diversity in culture, language, tribe, religion, and orientation more often than not, complicate debates and suggested solutions to a nagging problem. Therefore, the official thinking is that, why go to the extreme of calling for the President's resignation, when the problem had existed long before the President was elected; and the past Presidents during whose tenure the same problem either originated or festered were not asked to resign? In other words, the official tendency is to waive such calls as that made by Abaribe and rather, see it as mere politicking by the opposition party seeking relevance. The reaction of the Presidency to Abaribe's call highlights this official notion. In a typical fashion, the Presidency's spokesman, Garba Shehu described Abaribe's call as "foolish", adding: "If a leader like President Buhari needs to resign, there are millions of other Nigerians who need to resign; including Senator Abaribe who unlocked the door to enable the escape of traitorous and treasonable suspect." This was a clear reference to Nnamdi Kanu.

But Abaribe certainly achieved an objective of directing the attention of Nigerians to the sore issue of insecurity pervading the land. More than 26,000 tweets were reportedly tailored towards Abaribe's call with many rallying behind him for his courage, while others point accusing fingers to President Buhari over security condition of the country. Some people advised Garba to listen to the message rather than attack the messenger. Mr. Dalhatu Musa Ezekiel; the leader of the FCT indigenes warned both the Nigeria leaders and the populace at large about the impending dangers that are coming to the country, saying: "What the Nigerian Army is doing is recycling insurgency, they are simply recycling insurgency, and my worries and pains for Nigerian people are that we have docile leaders from different sections of this country, from different ethnic nationalities. Leaders that have chosen to be docile, that have chosen to deliberately remain dumb and stooge and walking sticks in the hands of the youths."

I totally agree with Ezekiel's posit because we have prominent leaders from the South-East, South-West, from South-South, from Middle-belt, who are witnessing this carnage but have chosen to be dumb simply because they erroneously believe that they are protected with the retinue of security details around them. But I assure them that in no distance time, they will be affected. There is no champion forever. They will not remain in power forever. And the evil that befalls Nigeria people today will catch up with them tomorrow. So, it is time they spoke up to this unprofessional military conduct. There is danger ahead

I am a trained forensic psychologist. It is easier to rehabilitate a mentally retarded individual as a result of drugs or any other factors, redefine his mindset and integrate him or her back into society in society than an insurgent who is an extremist. An extremist can sacrifice even his or her life because he/she has been indoctrinated into believing that what he is doing is to the glory of God Almighty. A few years ago, we had OPC militant in this country whose excesses "terrorized" the South-West and the Government had no choice than to disband them. They were never seen as potential to be re-engaged into the Nigeria Army. There was also the Bakasi militants. I am sure you still remember the Niger Delta militants, The Avengers etc. They were all disbanded but the Nigerian military could not find prospects in them by absorbing them. IPOB was dislodged, proscribed, and even prosecuted by the Nigerian government. I am aware that most of them are still in detention. This group of persons were not seen as potentials to be rehabilitated and engaged in the Nigeria military. But a terrorist group Boko Haram who perceives the Nigerian military as their number one enemy, come out headlong to confront the Nigeria Army, killing them and other innocent people, including kidnapping of innocent minors, are being treated with kid gloves. Because they claim to have surrendered, the next thing is for the Nigerian Government to spend taxpayers' money to not just rehabilitate, but also to engage same into the military, rather than prosecute them in line with the act of terrorism and murder, and completely take them off. No doubt, there is serious danger. If our docile leaders from the different nationalities do not speak up about this impending danger that will befall us in the nearer future, then something is wrong with them.

It must be remembered that some of us have sacrificed our lives to say and put truths on the table to help us and our future. I see myself as a leader in the nearer future and will not be leading a country that is in total chaos. America, as powerful as it is, has never engaged a terrorist group or member into their military, it is not done. America military instead infiltrates the ISIS to get intelligent reports and then nip it in the bud on whatever situation to curtail their excesses. But in the case of Nigeria, you are now seeing Boko Haram infiltrating the Nigerian military, and that is to tell you the danger that lies ahead of us. In the next 10 to 20 years, we will have thousands of Boko Haram terrorist in our Nigerian military, recycling insurgency. Meanwhile, we have vibrant, able-bodied, committed but jobless Nigerian youths who are ready to join the Nigerian military but were not allowed. A worst-case scenario would have been debriefed, sensitized, rehabilitate, and engage them into what is called civilian JTF. What is so important that qualifies them as officers of the Nigerian military? The multiplier effect is unimaginable!

The flurry of activities churned out of government, including the National Assembly, following Abaribe's call is a testimony of the impact of his outburst. For instance, the Senate after the heated debate resolved that the security architecture had failed; that the President should declare a national emergency on security and relieve the Service Chiefs of their jobs. The day after, the House of Representatives called for the resignation of the Service Chiefs and infusion into the system of people with fresh ideas on how to tackle insecurity. Almost simultaneously, President Buhari summoned a meeting of military commanders and other heads of security agencies in the country. If the meeting were coincidental, it shows at least that government could not ignore the fact that security deserved to be on the front burner in the country. The President was to say later that he was surprised at the growing insecurity, promising that his government would act against bandits.

Abaribe was not done on what he considered to be anomalous in the polity. On January 31, 2020, he, and Chairman of the Peoples' Democratic Party (PDP) Prince Uche Secondus led a protest to the embassies of the United Kingdom and United States against the judgment of the Supreme Court removing the party's candidate, Emeka Ihedioha, as governor of Imo State and replacing him with Hope Uzodinma, the candidate of the ruling All Progressives Congress (APC). He was to justify his action later by observing that what the court did was contrary to the precedents it had laid down in other election cases, and that such was not proper for the well-being of the country. That he went to such length to register his disapproval for a judgment that has turned out to be one of the most controversial in recent times is a pointer to his willingness to give voice to the voiceless.

Abaribe's emergence as a force in parliament

At President Muhammadu Buhari's second coming in 2019, many keen observers of Nigeria's political landscape cast a critical glance at the constitution of the National Assembly and dubbed it a "Rubber stamp" of the Presidency. This fear has not been allayed by the utterances and actions emanating from the National Assembly vis-a-vis the body language of the Presidency. Indeed, not too long ago, Senate President Ahmad Lawan and his deputy, Senator Ovie Omo-Agege, had shocked stakeholders with their unpretentious disposition to please President Muhammadu Buhari, claiming that, "Buhari always knows what is good for Nigeria".

To a large extent, the country had since been run in a ding-dong manner. In many sectors, it has been a spiraling, agonizing downward trend, particularly in terms of security. In recent times, virtually on a daily basis, Nigerians are robbed, kidnapped, killed on the highways, on their farms, in their homes. Things are indeed "falling apart" in the words of the world acclaimed writer, Chinua Achebe. In all these, it has been a conspicuous silence in the National Assembly 's "wilderness".

Curiously, as insecurity escalates, government made a lot of hype on its activities to stem it. A Senator lamented that the N4.5 trillion given the military between 2012 and 2014 to fight insurgency appeared to have no impact. What is very annoying to the public is President Buhari's implicit faith in his Service Chiefs, appointed since 2015. To many, the men are tired and no longer endowed with the necessary idea to get rid of criminal surges across the country. But the President ignored calls that they should be changed. Bihari was later forced in January 2021 to replace them when the call became too deafening.

Yet, no fewer than 20,000 people have died, and more than two million have been rendered homeless as a result of insecurity. This has provoked public debates on the desirability or otherwise of state police, lack of proper coordination among security agencies, lack of political will, as well as expiration and tenure of Service Chiefs. But now, a strident voice of one legislator has been heard in the wilderness! Crying: *Enough is enough!* The voice is that of Senator Enyinnaya Abaribe.

Senator Abaribe could no longer maintain his silence in the midst of the harrowing ordeal of Nigerians. He rose to his feet on the floor of the Senate and declared that in the midst of the deplorable security situation in the country and the obvious inability of President Buhari to control the situation, the president should resign. One of the media organizations carried the story thus:

Uproar in senate as Abaribe calls for Buhari's resignation
"The call by the Minority Leader of the Senate, Enyinnaya Abaribe, on the President, Major General Muhammadu Buhari to resign immediately based on Buhari's inability to curtail the alarming security challenges in the country caused a stir on the floor of the red chamber on Wednesday.

Abaribe spoke after the Senate Leader, Yahaya Abdullahi, presented his motion on rising security challenges in the country. Abaribe said the attitude of the president to insecurity in the country, surprised him. He said those who live by propaganda will die by propaganda. Abaribe said he was building up to the fact that they said Boko Haram has been defeated. He said the hard work that was supposed to be done to secure the country was not done because of the propaganda.

He said excuses for non-performance is now staring them in the face. He said Niger and Jos killings by Boko Haram terrorists indicated that the insurgency war was far from over. He said the opposition members in the National Assembly are of the opinion that Buhari should resign from office. He said, "Nigerians will go to the government and ask the government to resign because they are the ones, they elected to office - they did not elect the chief of staff, the police IG, service chiefs and others."

The security challenge

This was Abaribe's contribution to the debate on the motion tabled by the Senate majority leader, Senator Yahaya Abdullahi. It was on the 29th of January 2020, barely 24 hours after the Senators resumed from the Christmas and New Year break; they decided to spend the entire day of the plenary session to brainstorm on the very burning issue of security challenges confronting the country. For six hours, the Senators were at the hallowed Chamber deliberating; there was tension, uproar, sharp disagreement, but at the end of the day, they landed on the same page. They resolved that for the very fact that the security infrastructure has failed in the country, President Muhammadu Buhari should as a matter of urgency declare a National Security Emergency.

The Senators also asked President Buhari to walk the talk and if he would achieve this, he must as a matter of urgency, sack the Service Chiefs who they said were no longer fit and had ran out of ideas to tackle the myriad of security problems where Nigerians are maimed, killed, raped, kidnapped daily and property destroyed. The lawmakers told Buhari that the time has come for Chief of Defense Staff, General Abayomi Olonisakin; National Security Adviser, NSA, Major- General Mohammed Babagana Monguno; Chief of Army Staff, General Tukur Yusuf Buratai; Chief of Air Staff, Air Marshal Sadique Abubakar and Chief of Naval Staff, Vice Marshal Ibok-Ete Ibas to go and allow new persons who will put in fresh vigor to take over.

The Senate Majority leader, Senator Yahaya Abdullahi, All Progressives Congress, APC, Kebbi North came up with the motion, titled, "Security Challenges: Urgent need to restructure, review and reorganize the current security architecture." The motion was co- sponsored by 105 Senators. Presenting the motion, the Senate Leader said that the Senate: "Notes the recent upsurge of security related challenges and the devastating loss of lives, limbs and properties that it unleashed on the nation; Further notes the comprehensive new national security strategy that the government unfolded in December, with its very clear statement of goals, objectives and challenges that faced the nation particularly those challenges whose recent upsurge have a direct and devastating impact on the lives and safety of the people. This include:- Terrorism and violent extremism; Armed banditry, kidnapping, militancy and separatist agitation; Pastoralist /farmer clashes and Cattle Rustling; Organized crime; Piracy and sea robbery; and cross border crimes of smuggling and illegal drugs and fire arms trafficking; Appreciative of the recent effort to redefine our approaches to the security challenges, it is our view that implementation strategy must be operationalized in a manner that takes a critical and intrusive review of the nature, structure and disposition of the security institutions, particularly the Police, Civil Defense, Intelligence, Customs, Immigrations, etc." He further notes the various local, state, and regional responses to these security challenges by way of self-help initiative such as Civilian JTF, *Hisbah, Yausakai, Yanbanga* and more recently *Amotekun* which are mainly expression of peoples' desperation and disappointment with the failure of the state security architecture to protect them.

It was a landmark decision by the Senate. But it was the radical call made by Abaribe for the President's resignation that caused the uproar and added impetus to the debate. This call by Senator Abaribe singles him out as a courageous and patriotic citizen. The consequent barrage of attacks from the Presidency, from the ruling party and some lovers of the government is not unexpected. In what is seen as a "moderate" reaction from a member of the Buhari administration, Festus Keyamo has said that Abaribe's call was "unnecessary and uncalled for." Keyamo, the Minister of State for Labor and Employment, in a tweet posted on his Twitter page added that the hullaballoo that greeted Abaribe's comment needed not to have arisen. The human rights lawyer said it is usual in any democratic setting all over the world that the opposition parties would also find something to discredit the government in power. Keyamo, however, said that the government understands that the opposition was telling the All-Progressives Congress (APC)-led government to do more for the citizenry by their call for President Buhari to resign. He also added that the Federal Government should also see the call as a wake-up call to do more for Nigerians.

But more support came for Abaribe from other quarters. The Human Rights Writers Association of Nigeria, (HURIWA) backed his call for the resignation of President Muhammadu Buhari. According to HURIWA: "We, the members of the foremost civil Rights advocacy group, Human Rights Writers Association of Nigeria have watched with a great deal of consternation and unfathomable disappointment, the unconstitutional and malicious reactions from the desk of the media adviser to President Muhammadu Buhari to Distinguished Senator Enyinnaya Abaribe (PDP) a ranking, reputable Legislator of global acclaim and the Senate Minority Leader, over his legislative assertion that President Muhammadu Buhari should quit for failing spectacularly to rein in the ever expanding frontiers of grave threats to Nigeria's national security over the last five years. We condemn the malicious dimension that Shehu Garba, the Senior Special Assistant on Media and Publicity to The President took in his reaction to the statesmanly call by the Senator."

My take here as the author of this book is that the call by many Nigerians like our representatives that the Service Chiefs be laid off is a bipartisan call indeed. It is presumably the principal topic by which the individuals from our two main political parties concur. Obviously, we are tired of the ceaseless insurrection whose collateral damage is colossal. Yet, while we do not question the prevalence of the call, I am worried that nobody has given believable proof that the removal of the Service Chiefs would take care of the current negative issue in the country. We need to understand that if care is not taken, Nigeria may once again manage the symptom as opposed to the cause for our concern.

Let us put it in another way, if the new Service Chiefs that will eventually replace the old ones operate in the current tangled condition, the necessary changes expected would barely come. Therefore, the question is why is it that the Service Chiefs are the main ones to go? Shouldn't something be said or done about our Minister of Defense? For what reason is it that nobody is saying anything about the National Security Adviser? Does it mean he has no hands in our present security problems? For those who are uninformed, it must be known that the Service Chiefs report to the Chief of Defense Staff (CDS).

If that is the case, it seems legitimate to first remove the CDS before expelling the Service Chiefs or to remove all of them altogether. Else, removing the Service Chiefs alone will be tantamount to failure. If our agony is that the war against the dreaded insurgents has been ineffectively prosecuted, we cannot blame only the Service Chiefs and leave their bosses untouched, they all have to go. The government itself must take an enormous lump of the fault.

Indeed, even the call by Senator Abaribe for the government to leave or resign is not new; it has been like common song in our society. What those individuals who countered Senator Abaribe neglected to acknowledge is that Senator Abaribe's call was a concern to the lawmaking body too because it is a part of the government in question. Is anyone of us in doubt that the insurgents find it simple and easy to recruit its followers from a large number of jobless young people in the nation? It is not just that some vacancies of jobs are not there in the government arenas of the country, but the few opening are filled through the back relations and companions of the individuals in the administration, including Senators and other top political office holders, without a mind for the quality of their certification. Meanwhile, the qualified but jobless Nigerians are left in limbo, and would have no choice than to do anything to eke a living. Therefore, if Nigerians want an end to the present insurgency, then the war on it must be extensive; it must be drawn from all approaches as was done with the Ebola cataclysm a few years ago. It must start with all the positions in the present government that seem to be occupied only by the Hausa-Fulanis in the country. What happens to the other tribes; the Ibos, the Yorubas, and the others?

My advice is to implore the presidency to stop insulting our sensibilities, especially the Middle Belters and the Southern Nigerian people, in the eyes of the world. We are already in hell in this country. According to Malcolm X: Hell is defined by a lack of freedom among other values challenged by vice. Hell is when you are dumb; Hell is when you are a slave; Hell is when you do not have the freedom and when you do not have justice. And when you do not have equality, that's hell...And the Devil is the one who deprives you of justice, equality, civil rights. The devil is the one who robs you of your right to be a human being. I do not have to tell you who the devil is right now in the country. You know who the devil is in Nigeria already.

Abaribe as a statesman

Abaribe is a true dyed-in-the-wool Democrat and a staunch advocate of the rule of law. Like a visionary, he had warned that Nigeria will be isolated by the international community if the Federal Government continues to disregard court orders. He spoke shortly after the release of Omoyele Sowore, the pro-democracy activist, and Sambo Dasuki, former National Security Adviser (NSA). Abaribe described the development as "encouraging", but he asked the government to free other detainees in compliance with court orders. "The presidency must seize the momentum and release the rest. FG must not be seen to be selective or acting on impulse. Again, the Federal Government must now respect and adhere to the rule of law at all times," Abaribe said, adding "It is becoming obvious that the country may face certain isolation from the international community if the government continues to disregard valid court orders. We must respect all statutory institutions of government and pay greater attention to the principle of separation of power. This is the way to go in a democracy."

In October 2007, as Ralph Uwazuruike, leader of the banned secessionist organization Movement for the Actualization of the Sovereign State of Biafra (MASSOB) was on trial for treason, Abaribe and six other Southeastern Senators protested at the Federal High Court in Lagos to demand his release. Again, much later, when other Igbo leaders balked and shirked from speaking against the mistreatment of IPOB by federal security agents, his voice was loud and his support unmistakable. It was a costly gamble to sign Kanu's bail bond, but it was the right thing to do. A good father will never abandon his son. Asked about his involvement in securing bail for Ralph Uwazuruike in 2007, and of Nnamdi Kanu, leader of IPOB, whom he stood surety for, Abaribe explained that when Ralph Uwazuruike was arrested and detained, the Southeast caucus of the Sixth Senate led by the late Uche Chukwumerije decided to go and see late President Yar'adua – whom he called a "great man". With Yar'adua, they made a fairly simple case for Uwazuruike and MASSOB: those talking about Biafra were essentially crying out because of certain policies of the federal government which gave the impression that the Igbo are being treated unfairly in this country. They advised that the best way to deal with such agitators was not to round and lock them up and then throw away the key, rather, engage them in dialogue with a view to discussing their grouses and finding out how they thought such could be remedied. They were eventually able to secure bail for Uwazuruike and they (the South-east Senators) stood sureties for him without any monetary condition being attached to his release.

For the Nnamdi Kanu saga, Abaribe said a whole lot could be said about it. But, according to him, when you look at the basics and the fundamentals, it remains the same. Just like they did with Yar'adua, the South-east senate caucus, now under the leadership of Abaribe, also met Buhari over the detention of Nnamdi Kanu who was ultimately granted bail but with a "humongous figure of N100m surety for each detained person and there were three of them." The Senators rallied round ad perfected the bail conditions.

A consummate politician, Abaribe has been involved in the politics of the Fourth Republic since 1999 when he was elected as Deputy Governor of Abia State. He is known to be vocal, articulate, calculating, and knowledgeable in both the politics of the Senate and legislative affairs. He once said, "The first task of governance is to restore confidence in government and make people believe in government; that government can be responsive to their needs. This will show that you are committed to the people's welfare. Then, the basic thing that an Abia man needs is the common infrastructure. That crunchy experience only served to toughen Abaribe who found space in the then opposition of All Nigeria Peoples Party (ANPP) to contest the governorship of Abia State against Mr. Kalu. Although he lost the election, Abaribe proved that he was a man of steel, principle and character who would not be intimidated to abandon his will and convictions on how to govern Abia State.

An accomplished lawmaker

Senator Abaribe was born March 1, 1955, a Nigerian politician who was elected to the Abia-South Senatorial District of Abia State into the Nigerian Senate in April 2007 on the platform of the PDP. He attended Government College, Umuahia (1974); graduated from University of Benin, bagging a bachelor's degree in Economics (1979) and a Masters in same discipline in 1982. He lectured at Edo State University from 1982 until 1985. From 1985 until 1991, he was SCOA Nigeria's Area Manager for Southern Nigeria. After that, from 1991 to 1992, he was employed as NICON's senior manager for investment. From 1993 until 1995 he was the CEO of Integrated Mortgage Co. Before 2007, Senator Abaribe was Abia State's Deputy Governor from May 29, 1999, after Orji Uzor Kalu's 1999 election as Governor until he resigned on March 7, 2003. He holds many chieftaincy titles.

Thus 2007 came and he had a chance to prove his mettle and convictions through the federal legislature. During his first tenure in the Senate, he served as Vice Chairman of the Committee on Inter-Parliamentary Affairs, a position that gave him a good window of global exposure on parliamentary practices in many parts of the world. He also served as member of Committees on the Independent National Electoral Commission (INEC), Senate Services, and Works during that dispensation.

Abaribe became the chief image maker of the Senate in 2011 with his appointment as Chairman, Senate Committee on Information, Media, and Public Affairs. This position tasked his political sagacity and public service experience especially in those heady days when the Red Chamber made history with the famous "*Doctrine of Necessity*" that resolved the transitional impasse following the illness and eventual death of former President Musa Yar'adua.

He successfully served out that testy portfolio and got re-elected into the Senate in 2015, again as in previous cases, on the platform of the PDP. Until the reshuffle of Committees by the Senate leadership, Abaribe served as Chairman of the Committee on Information and National Orientation. He is now Chairman, Senate Committee on Power and Solid Minerals Development. However, Sen. Abaribe's footprints in the legislature have often been on the political sphere where he does not shy away from his convictions no matter the challenges and threats. For instance, he was the first opposition Senator in the 8th Senate to have openly queried the 2016 budget of President Muhammadu Buhari. Some may have their reservations about the man, but he has shown himself to be a good lawmaker. He was elected to make laws and to exercise oversight over the Executive. On those scores, he has done well. He has contributed to lawmaking and has defended the interest of his people, Ndigbo in a significant manner. He has looked elected Presidents and Governors in the eye and told them the home truth – according to his conscience.

One of Senator Abaribe's major accomplishments in the current senate is his sponsorship of the Public Procurement Act (Amendment) Bill, 2015 which is a culmination of efforts to promote Made-in-Nigeria products in the country. According to his Lead Debate, the Bill "seeks to propose amendment of the public procurement act Cap, LFN 2004. The Public Procurement Act to mandate all sectors of government in prioritizing Made in Nigeria goods to ensure that Nigerian businesses get 'First Dibs' over their foreign counterparts in the procurement processes for agencies and departments of the Federal government."

This amendment, once signed into law, will have ripple effects on the manufacturing industry, as it will assure local manufacturers of a ready and sure market for their products. "Nigerian products must have comparative advantage. Made in Nigeria goods should no longer produce adulterated or substandard versions of foreign alternatives because the market is available. Also, it is high time we pumped the absolute best into our markets to ensure overall consumer satisfaction and building confidence in the Nigerian brands."

More than anything else, the bill is targeted at promoting various goods made in Abaribe's home state, some of which can compete favorably with products from abroad. Abaribe himself is reputed to wear and use materials locally manufactured in his home state. The Bill has been passed by the Senate and when signed by the President after concurrence with the House of Representatives, will be a major credit to Senator Abaribe's stewardship in the 8th Senate.

The popularity of Abaribe in giving voice to the voiceless is a matter of conjecture of which the tweets and other reactions, elicited by his criticism of the President, constitute huge evidence. It is equally on record that an Activist and Social Commentator, Umezulike Desmond-Cruz once directed his petition on the Hate Speech Bill, and its dangerous portents, to Abaribe whom he referred to "as the voice of the common man in in the Senate". The activist specifically urged the Senator to muster his personal and political arsenal to ensure the Senate ratifies the bill.

In all, Senator Abaribe has shown that he is tough, not for the sake of it, but for holding on to beliefs and with good reasons. His stance for supporting Biafra agitations is logical, as the clamor took roots from the imperfections, mostly man-made, in the society. And while he believed in Nigeria, he is of the view that rather than clamp down on those who desire a distinct identity and accelerated progress for their nationality, government should dialogue with them with a view to finding solutions to the imperfections.

Be that as it may, Abaribe has a pointed dislike for autocratic leadership of which he indirectly accused the Buhari administration. He likens autocracy with the *Kabiyesi* syndrome, highlighted by the late Senior Advocate and human rights activist, Chief Gani Fawehinmi. In that syndrome which Gani opposed till his death, whoever emerges as an authority figure is seen as the 'Kabiyesi' whose word is law and who can do no wrong. This notion, as far as Abaribe is concerned, has no place in modern democracy. Therefore, he advocated a practice based on the Igbo culture which he emphasized, extols collective decision-making. Without doubt, Senator Eyinnaya Abaribe is providing a voice for the voiceless in Nigeria.

CHAPTER 17

OBIAGELI EZEKWESILI

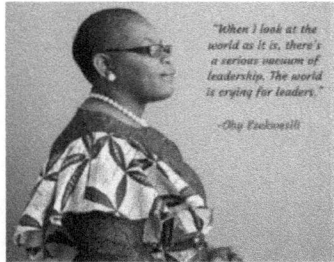

"When I look at the world as it is, there's a serious vacuum of leadership. The world is crying for leaders."

-Oby Ezekwesili

In discussing the role of women in Nigeria's democracy, you cannot ignore Obiageli Ezekwesili - popularly known as Oby. Her name will always ring in the minds of many who are aware of her status as an influential female leader in Nigeria. I have been following her. And for sure, her rise to the upper political echelon in the country will persuade you into believing that politics is no longer a male-only field. She is among the few but influential women that the country can boast of, in spite of the belief in Nigeria that politics is patriarchal.

The African women of today are awake and focused on making a positive change in society. This is a remarkable shift that we ought to recognize. They are speaking for the voiceless and no longer stay on the fringes - as observed in the person of Ezekwesili. You may have listened or watched this towering female figure talking about the usual challenges facing the country; and you probably rubbished her sentiments as a normal political rhetoric. But have you sat down, to ponder over or examine this powerful leader and wondered if given the chance to lead, if she can secure the country and drive it to prosperity!

The Ezekwesili success story is worth celebrating when discussing the achievements of women. She hails from Anambra state and is a well-educated chartered accountant. She has served in various government positions: she was a Federal Minister of Solid Minerals and later held the office of Federal Minister of education under President Olusegun Obasanjo. She is also a co-founder of Transparency International, a global anti-corruption agency, headquartered in Berlin, Germany. and served as the Vice President of the World Bank for Africa. Apart from holding top-notch positions, she has been at the forefront calling out the government on critical issues like insecurity, decelerating economy, and on the increasing poverty in the land. She does not just talk but puts pressure on the government to do whatever it takes to rid the country of its numerous challenges.

With immense desire to take over the leadership of the country from the people she believes has failed, she took the challenge to run for president. Personally, this was a well-thought decision. However, it was ill-fated as she stepped down from the race perhaps because of dwindling chances of capturing the presidency. Nonetheless, that is anecdotal, given that already she enjoyed significant support from people who shared her transformation-centric politics. Again, in politics, especially ideological ones, things can change positively to favor a candidate not considering the party. Contrastingly or rather unfortunately, our politics is emotion-based, party-based, monetized, and tribal to a considerable extent. This makes it a herculean task to defeat either PDP or APC, the two dominant parties in the country. It is the bitter truth that parties considered small, sit on the periphery of power and the chances of a surprise win are slim. Saying this does not make me a doomsayer, or critical of Ezekwesili that I consider to be the voice for the voiceless. All that I am saying is that our politics are not ideological, and we have been made to think only of two parties, yet these perceived 'small parties' may very well be the biggest contributors to the challenges we face today.

On Twitter, she announced that she would quit the presidential race to form a strapping coalition with other parties to get a practical alternative that would floor the ruling APC as well as PDP – the major opposition party. This was a hard decision, but an unavoidable choice for the sake of saving the country from an officious incumbent and ineffective opposition party-PDP according to her. The Allied Congress Party of Nigeria (ACPN) needed to work with other parties. This is to say, she no longer believed either PDP or APC have solutions to the problems facing the country. After all, these two parties have been ruling the country since 1999 when the civilian government was restored. Ezekwesili, in some way, viewed both opposition and ruling parties as hell-bent to win an election, not for service delivery but to satisfy their hunger for power. It was then indispensable, according to Oby for the country to shift from elite bargaining or personality politics to one that is issue-based.

This will remain a hard nut to crack as long as elite personalities, ethnicity, and rotational-based presidency will continue to dominate every election in the nation.

Although she stepped down from the presidential race
in the 2019 general election, I believe that she is capable of
running Nigeria better than the current leadership. Nigeria has never had a female president, though African countries like Malawi, Ethiopia, and Liberia among others have
had female Presidents. It would have been a turning point
for Nigeria to convince the world that it is still possible in
Africa's most populous nation to elect female presidents
in competitive politics. I am not bringing in the issues of
gender as far as Nigerian leadership is concerned, but I
am envisioning how the country progresses under Ezekwesili. Perhaps the situation could not be the way it is right
now where security is deteriorating, the economy is taking a nosedive and many educated young people are stuck
in unemployment. This seems like wishful thinking but is
important is to hold the Buhari-led government accountable for the challenges its ineptitude has caused the country. Given that she is not holding any political office where
she can directly plan for the government on developing
quick solutions for security, she has to pile pressure on
those holding office. She is calculatingly castigating the
government for ineptness and laxity in securing the country, thus this has consequently made her an activist.

The issues Ezekwesili stands for are essential for our
democracy. However, I will not elaborate much on how
security and economy are vital for our democracy. What
will be of my interest is how the former Minister is becoming the voice of the voiceless. She is coming out vocal and

fearless to condemn the weakening state of affairs in Nigeria. She is speaking on behalf of the majority of Nigerians that it should no longer be business as usual. Since the emergence of Boko Haram, many lives and property have been lost and the North-east, Middle belt, and Western Nigeria are becoming danger zones for the masses. The kidnapped girls that prompted Ezekwesili to lead a movement in demanding for the return of the girls who were abducted by terrorists, showed her determination to make Nigeria a safe country for all. As a consequence, she is inspiring Nigerians to ask the government to do more than it is doing presently, to secure the country and lead it to prosperity. We cannot be blissful when parts of the country are becoming uninhabitable. We should demand action from the President and his team. We cannot leave terrorists and criminals to destabilize the country and at the same time think that our democracy is maturing.

An undeterred campaigner of democracy

What I know about Ezekwesili is that she stands for what democracy seeks to achieve in society. I know our memories are invariably preoccupied with the thinking that democracy only advocates for free elections, a line of reasoning I rejected earlier. Instead, we should have a larger perspective of what our democracy should be about. It should be about activism that births change. Not just change, but *positive* change. Ezekwesili is the latest powerful leader to turn to activism. The *"BringBackOurGirls"* campaign is what profoundly defined Oby's activism. The world was in grief as it learned about the "Chibok schoolgirls kidnapping". Book Haram, an extremist set with unclear history and ambiguous mission abducted these innocent girls from Chibok in Borno State to hurt us psychologically, implant grave pains that our hearts could barely hold and at the same time, painting Nigeria as a failed state.

It is at that point that Ezekwesili campaigned and demanded that the government takes swift action to save the abductees from the terrorists. This positive action made her a center of attention worldwide. She stood her ground, energized the already pain-stricken Nigerians to campaign for the release of the girls who were still alive. Unfortunately, some were reportedly abused sexually and even impregnated. Rape, torture, trauma, and bodily injuries are inescapable in the hands of terrorists and that is precisely what the abductees must have been through.

In an informed assessment, this campaign led by Ezekwesili brought the world's attention to Nigeria. The government, on the other hand, had to intensify its rescue operations. It was alleged that there was an intelligence report hours before the attack, but little or nothing was done to thwart it. Ezekwesili did not seize the opportunity for PR but from the bottom of her heart. She consistently spoke about the urgent need to rescue the abducted girls. Although other voices were advocating for same, Ezekwesili was at the frontline of the campaign. This is public knowledge. Ezekwesili spent much of her time demanding the rescue of these schoolgirls. She held peaceful protests. What intrigues me is her resolve and commitment to a cause that nobody invited her. What she did proves that Oby is selfless and willing to sacrifice her time magnanimously for her people. Hence, the global commendation she received was something you and I should not underrate but venerate.

Oby is someone that cares for the people, a trait a majority of Nigerian leaders lack. If we had many leaders of her caliber, I have a firm conviction that as a country, we would have prospered tremendously. She is a stateswoman that we ought to commend. She has proved that she can pursue a cause that ultimately has a positive impact on many people. She left her comfort zone to fight for the release of the girls. It is rare to get such people especially in an era where people are becoming so individualistic. We live in a world where many people look at things selfishly and will not do anything if it will not yield material gains. Nevertheless, there is a flicker of hope when we have people of Ezekwesili's stature on the street, leading peaceful protests against the government.

Protests, picketing or peaceful demonstrations have been used in developed nations. In the United States, for example, we have had prominent African American figures like Martin Luther King Jr, Malcolm X, and Elijah Cummings lead civil rights movement and the results are visible. In spite of a few challenges, the African American community have their rights protected in the constitution. Equally, the pre-civilian rule in Nigeria was terrible. People were tortured or jailed for leading protests against the military government. But ultimately, we were able to execute the transition to civilian rule. In reality, peaceful, non-violent protests or demonstrations are significant. These played an important role in making the US what it is today. In same vein, the pressure Ezekwesili and her followers exerted on the Nigerian government somewhat bore results as some abductees were released.

The health of a democracy is guaranteed when we do not sit and watch the state of affairs worsen without taking substantive action. For Mrs. Ezekwesili, when things are not going in the right way, we should hold the government accountable. We can do that through non-violent protests until the government and its mandarins walk out of their air-conditioned offices to listen to the critical issues being raised. Aside from listening, we must demand an action that will make the government get serious and be committed to the responsibilities accorded to them. In spirit and body, Ezekwesili has demonstrated to us squarely that, it is time that we got on the streets to protest peacefully and perhaps, petition the government to take action that we believe is necessary for strengthening our democracy.

African governments loathe protests regardless of their nature. In most instances, police officers are used to disperse protesters whose goal is to ask the government to listen to their grievances and attend to them aptly. We have recently observed Shi'ite protesters clash with the police leaving some dead. There are instances the police were accused of using force, a situation that in all possibility triggers the initially calm protesters into violence. I do not subscribe to violent protests but will support peacefully protests against the violation of human rights and freedom. The Police could apply teargas and other available security strategies, but not gunfire, only when the protests are not justified by the ambit of the law.

Even so, Mrs. Ezekwesili intensified her activism beyond the grievous abduction of schoolgirls. She is also an anti-corruption campaigner that shares a similar opinion with the other figures of democracy. Corruption is a pertinent issue that everyone is talking about in Nigeria and the world. Having been at the helm of Transparency International, Oby has always had the longing to lead the war against corruption. Since she is not the President and does not hold any elective seat, she has opted to use the platforms she has to ask the government to rescue the country. For Nigeria to realize prosperity, the war on corruption should be won, and nobody should be spared. This war is a pillar of democracy and all arms of government must let the public interest prevail.

During her time in the government, she was prudent at her work. She fought corruption with the slogan of "No Retreat, No Surrender." The Nigeria public sector is synonymous with corruption, owing to a lack of integrity among civil servants. Under her watch, she tried to close conduits that some public servants use to siphon money for their individual use. With her stellar record in fighting corruption in the public service, she has proved that, if given a higher office in the country, she can deliver. She is someone with the willingness to serve the public with diligence and care. There is no doubt that the major challenge Nigeria faces today comes from leaders who lack integrity and commitment to service delivery.

Nigeria needs only good leadership in all arms of government. Ex-Senator Ben Murray-Bruce insists that when Nigeria gets good leadership, the country will head in the right direction. Mrs. Ezekwesili is one leader Nigerians should have elected in the 2019 general election. I saw the Minister-turned-activist as someone who had the competence, courage, and selflessness to lead Nigeria to prosperity and excellence. I watched her interview with CNN's Christiane Amanpour, her calmness and vision for Nigeria is what we need to be a great economy and democracy. With grit, Mrs. Ezekwesili asserted that she was better placed to "disrupt the politics of failure" in Nigeria. She sounded as the problem-solver and someone who commits to promises. I had a feeling that Nigerians would support her unreservedly. Again, the inner voice kept on poking me, reminding me that we are inclined to voting populists. We generally do not vote in leaders who would stand for and with us. The problem of corruption that I keep on mentioning needs a genuine fixer and Mrs. Ezekwesili and few others are up to this task. While I do not want to regret that as a nation, we elected an inept President, but it was our choice. This again brings to the fore, the importance of voters being careful and wise at the ballot. Electing competent leaders will manifestly solve the problems that Nigeria faces today. Mrs. Ezekwesili will help Nigeria overcome the many problems it is facing today considering respect to her record.

Indeed, before quitting the Presidential race, she ran a policy-based campaign whilst other established politicians focused on rhetorics. President Buhari's campaign foot soldiers and himself came out promising to do what they failed to do in their first term. In all honesty, Mrs. Ezekwesili had served the public, transformed, and supported pro-development policies. She is not just a politician, but a good leader and that is something that should persuade us to respect her contributions to Nigeria. In Mrs. Ezekwesili, I see a politician and good leader with the liveliness to steer the country to success. She is not the kind of politician that in every election cycle comes with lies, sweet fanny Adams and populist politics that only lure the electorate into voting but no corresponding result.

It irks me that voters seem not to like good leaders, and I do not understand why this is so. The emotional appeal can deliver results more than ideological appeal. Leaders that sincerely devote their time to serve the public are not usually the ones the electorate elects. This is to say, Mrs. Ezekwesili, despite being a genuine leader, has no chance of winning. Possibly, we need to ask the hard questions about the kind of leaders the voters elect despite having better options. Voters are their own enemies in instances they elect bad leaders as against the voting the ones that will lead with care, love, empathy, and vision.

Ezekwesili has shown that it is ethical to work for people and fight for reforms that will benefit several generations to come. It is on that accord that she engineered policies in the education ministry that centered on girl empowerment. The kind of educational reforms that Mrs. Ezekwesili advocated for are perhaps responsible for putting more girls into school especially in Northern Nigeria.

There is a visible link between activism for the release of schoolgirls and push for educational reforms. This is so honorable on account that a girl or generally a woman can acquire education to have a higher social standing that inspires them into making a change in their communities. The whole issue of female education is not new because that is where the attention of women rights activists' rests. Advocating for female education or championing educational reforms is probably considered feminism but the focus should be to have girls and women go to school for society to stand a chance of alleviating poverty and propping its democracy. More so, no nation can stand with one foot. For the feet to stand appropriately, they must be in pairs.

So, it is for a home or nation to get both men and women educated, to reach higher levels. Though she championed these reforms in 2006, during her tenure as Minister in the Education Ministry, but the impact is magnificent as many Nigerian females have gone to school since then.

In general, the issues Mrs. Ezekwesili stands for are the building blocks of democracy. Activism, which I have widely linked to democracy, is capable of injecting good health into Nigerian democracy only if activists like Ezekwesili are supported. Through activism, female leaders like Ezekwesili can push for true institutional reforms, security and a strong but diversified economy. She fully supports the urgent need to diversify the Nigerian economy to reduce heavy reliance on oil in a future that is getting more obscure today due to the global warming scare.

Amidst cultural or religion barriers, gender-based discrimination, a leader that roots for educational reforms that take more girls to schools is implanting seeds of gender equality or egalitarianism in society. Gender equality must be a protected right in the constitution. When you recognize all people as equals, a leader will be able to see the sense of respecting the rights and freedoms of all and sundry. It is on that basis of fighting for equality, better economy, and democracy that I hold in the highest regard Mrs. Ezekwesili. It will always be my aspiration that Nigeria votes in a female leader like Oby and that will signal the beginning of the end to the many empty promises and failed governance. She is a true voice for the voiceless.

CHAPTER 18

PROF. BABAGANA UMARA ZULUM

B orno State has produced another voice for the voiceless, despite its security challenges. Professor Babagana Umara Zulum has shown grit and focus on fighting for the disadvantaged constituents. Since he became the governor of Borno State in 2019, he has come out as one leader that is determined to do good for his people. His adopts a servant-leadership style of governance. While other myopic and self-centered politicians are busy enriching themselves through dubious means, Prof. Zulum is giving an ear to his constituents as he preaches peace and unity amid endless threats from the insurgents Boko Haram. He is one leader that has set his eyes on national unity. He believes that the strength of Nigeria is hinged on its unity against the common enemy-Boko Haram. There is little that Nigeria can achieve if Boko Haram continues to pose major threats to life and property of the country.

Assuredly, this is a governor that has stood for his people when Boko Haram insurgents remained undeterred. Even when his own life is threatened, he has remained an inspiring figure to his people. He rolled out some development projects and tried to improve infrastructure. At challenging times, citizens want a leader that will stand for them. Governor Zulum has demonstrated to the nation that leaders are supposed to fight for their people. He knew the challenges that stood his way in Borno State and he determinedly shifted his attention to improving security and revamp the state's economy. When leaders become kind and risk their lives for the ordinary people, a healthy environment for democracy to blossom is created. This is why, it is important to celebrate leaders that fight for the downtrodden.

Struggle to keep Borno state safe

Insecurity has been a primary issue of concern in Borno State. In Professor Babagana's quest for power, he campaigned on security agenda. He assured his people that if elected, his attention would be to restore security in a state that for long has been reduced to a battleground. Way before Boko Haram insurgents launched severe attacks on civilians, the security situation in Borno State had not been good. The violent attacks from the Boko Haram worsened the security situation in the state.

In his wisdom, governor Zulum prioritized security. Beefing up security in the state creates a favorable environment for businesses and other economic activities. He rallied all security agencies in Borno and brought many people on board to proffer ideas to help sort the security mess in his state. It is undeniable that this is one of the reasons he was elected. Governor Zulum chose a different approach, to the benefit of the state and the residents. He put politics aside and redirected his efforts to cooperation. His bipartisan approach working with other leaders regardless of their political leanings yielded results. A lot of goodies are coming to Borno State if this governor will not waver. When a leader comprehends the problems of his people, and tirelessly seeks solutions, it is indubitable such actions will create a free society where people are empowered. He has provided resources to the security agencies to ease their work including 70 patrol vehicles to the police, Nigerian army, and Civilian Joint Task Force. He also unveiled for counterterrorism squad to combat other criminal activities that threaten the peace and tranquility of Borno residents. In addition, between June and September 2019 the Borno State government donated 160 patrol vehicles to security agencies and volunteers.

As a servant leader, Zulum regularly visits them physically. This commitment motivates the security forces who are working indefatigably to restore security to this state. In most instances, some leaders fail to achieve because they lead from boardrooms. A good leader is one that occasionally stays out of their physical office to join hands with the people. Governor Zulum himself assured "I have said a number of times that this administration will not hesitate to take any measures or make any sacrifice to ensure peace and ensure that calm returns to our state. As the chief security officer of Borno State, it is my constitutional and moral responsibility to do whatever I possibly can to secure the lives of citizens and doing that, is the whole essence of government in the first place."

This statement provides hope that the governor is ready to lead and solve problem bedeviling his state. By securing this state, people can exercise their rights and freedoms. Movement and assembly have been curtailed in Borno State since it became a flashpoint. Governor Zulum is a workaholic. In his leadership, relative peace is returning to Borno. People are becoming less worried about Boko Haram insurgency. When leaders like Zulum take over leadership in this country, it will enjoy economic freedom and provide the dividends of democracy.

Reconstruction of Borno state

Governor Zulum is reconstructing his state and putting smiles on the residents' faces. The governor is resettling people displaced by Boko Haram by providing relief material and working tirelessly with security agencies to wipe out Boko Haram terrorists. The state has been in dire need of a leader that can rebuild it and get it to back to life. Nevertheless, the threat of Boko Haram to the state is still lingering. With good leadership from Zulum, there is a glimpse of hope that the security personnel in the state will repulse the insurgents.

Before becoming governor, Zulum had worked as a commissioner for Reconstruction, Rehabilitation and Resettlement. As a commissioner he stated, "Governor Shettima told me in September 2015 that he trusted me with so many funds for the rebuilding of hundreds of communities destroyed by Boko Haram, and he was worried about the displacement of more than two million people of the state. That appointment was one major challenge, and I took it up ready to die doing it or trying. Yes, at some point, there was the issue of safety since insurgents can spring surprises, but we had the overwhelming support of the residents, military, and the police in particular, as well as other security agencies, and volunteers."

Through this governor, agriculture, housing, and other many development projects are being rolled out. In his admission, he said "We rebuilt more than 10,000 houses in Bama, schools and hospitals in that local government area, and most others. The ministry is still working and I am sure in few months they will complete the rebuilding, and this is major history for the administration and the people of Borno". A statement like this shows that the governor means business. Gov. Zulum has laid down precedence for other to follow.

Society becomes better when people in a position of leadership commit to serving their people. It is apparent that governor Zulum will continue to inspire Nigerians through his servant-leadership style. At these times of difficulties, citizens want a leader that can inspire hope and commit to serving them. Through this, a society can achieve strong institutions, improved economy, and better lives for the people. Professor Zulum is a man that is inspiring and should be praised for being a man of action. He does not pay lip service, but he delivers on his promises.

⊷⊶ ⊷⊶

CHAPTER 19

AISHA YESUFU

W omen in Nigeria are no longer on the fringes when it comes to socio-political or economic issues. They are participating to bring change to their communities through activism. They are motivated to speak truth to power and defend the rights of the voiceless in society. As a prominent mother-figure, Yesufu is not watching the state of affairs deteriorate in her country but has made activism part of her life. She feels a sense of responsibility as a citizen who is empowered to defend those oppressed by their own government.

Yesufu grew up in Kano, in a patriarchal environment. She had once admitted that at the age of 11 years, she did not have female friends. She attributed the lack of female friends in her childhood life to early marriage which was condoned in her community. Her patriarchal community did not give girls an opportunity to get an education, which would have empowered them. As determined as she was,

Yesufu wanted to fight for her future, she sought education. Through thick and thin, she graduated with a degree in Microbiology at Bayero University, Kano, an awe-inspiring achievement considering the challenges girls in Northern Nigeria face in a patriarchal community that undermines female education. Even though she is not practicing Microbiology, she went into business to create her own wealth. Today, Yesufu is not only a Microbiologist, but a dedicated businesswoman and socio-political activist.

Yesufu's childhood life exposes the many challenges girls face in Nigeria. Some girls are denied education that is necessary for them to build their future. They are rather married off. To set a good example to others, Yesufu had to defy that social construct. Yesufu has seen it all. She has seen the suffering of girls and other members of her community and vowed to bring the necessary change to her society. She does not want to live a life where politicians treat other citizens as second-class. Amid criticism and several broadsides thrown at her for speaking truth to power, Yesufu has remained steadfast and focused on fighting for a better Nigeria. There are those who hate her and could do anything to disparage her.

In society, those who strive to bring change to society are sometimes disliked. Yesufu sure has her own opponents. Intimidation does not scare her as she is determined to defend the values that she stands for. She is fighting corruption, bad governance, police brutality and anything that infringes upon the rights of Nigerians. She is a believer of equal-opportunity-for-all. She wants Nigerian leaders to be held to account on every level of government. In her strong conviction, she believes that Nigeria has potential to grant and protect the rights and freedoms of every citizen. However, those in position of leadership seem blind to the fact that they have a responsibility to defend the rights and freedoms of their people. A country that respects the rights and freedoms of her people does not use the police to brutalize them. Instead dedicates efforts to defend the constitution and rights of everyone.

But the callous nature of a majority of Nigerian politicians is what Yesufu loathes. Citizens are being taken round and neglected by elected leaders, a situation that is infuriating but has inspired Yesufu into socio-political activism. The abduction of girls in Northern Nigeria by Boko Haram insurgents was a clear indictment of Nigerian government. When these terrorists abducted the Chibok schoolgirls, Yesufu felt the need to swing into action to awaken the government from slumber to secure national security which was nearly becoming elusive.

Socio-political activism
and human rights

Yesufu is a force to reckon with. She is one prominent figure that Nigerians look up to when it comes to defending their rights. She exudes unimaginable courage regardless of the danger that can come her way. She understands that the government is not happy with her and can do anything to stop her. As a co-convener of #BringBackourGirls campaign, Nigerians saw a person determined to protect and fight for her people. As someone who understands the plight of girls, it hurt her most that the government could not act decisively to rescue the kidnapped schoolgirls. During this campaign, we all witnessed a person willing to fight for our rights. The voices she gave about the kidnapping of schoolgirls in Northern Nigeria, helped pile pressure on the government to act. Alongside other many supporters, they put pressure on the government to act unfalteringly. Although her critics could think that she was an opportunist, but Yesufu is a kind-hearted citizen who wants the best for everyone. A person who can leave her work for a noble cause is not an opportunist.

Looking at Yesufu's childhood experiences and life, we see a person that is persistent, kind, and consistent. As a selfless person, she does not feel good to see a few people live lavishly, while others are under constant attacks from insurgents. She wants a government that works for the majority, not minority. She is a citizen who does not see it reasonable to be silent, when lives and livelihoods of Nigerians are at stake. Yesufu feels that the government should do its job and protect all citizens. Silence amid injustice is self-destruction. Going silent is never a solution particularly if you are dealing with a government that is callous. African leaders rarely work without civil unrest or protests. People should not go mum, when they are oppressed, but they should speak on top of their voices for their leaders to hear them out. Yesufu does not believe in silence but believes in action. She raises her voice bravely when she feels that the situation is dire. This is something that every citizen should be proud of. Do not mute or allow to be silenced when the government turns against you.

Having a fighting spirit is one thing that is pushing Yesufu to peacefully demonstrate against the government for it to protect rights and freedoms of its people. The very moment when citizens recognize that it is our obligation to 'fight' bad leaders, leaders will respect their offices. If our leaders understand that citizens are empowered and no longer entertain mediocrity, they will work cautiously. Leaders will always exploit an ignorant society. This is the basis under which Yesufu wants Nigerians to demand our leaders to deliver on their promises while protecting and strengthening our institutions.

In essence, the leadership that Yesufu is providing in demanding will determine our democracy. Democracy cannot be built on sand, because it becomes easy for corrupt leaders to wash it away. To build our democracy on a solid rock, socio-political activists like Yesufu are needed. They provide some unthinkable energy that pushes citizens into action against injustice. The energy and inspiration Yesufu are providing to us, is what Nigerians need to better our country. Sometimes, citizens sit back and watch the government trample upon their rights and freedom, because they lack someone to lead them. Nonetheless, Yesufu is providing that leadership. In many protests against police brutality, this devoted figure marched across many streets to demand justice.

Fundamentally, citizens want to be led in protest against a government that is callous. The insensitivity and callousness shown sometimes by government officials require demonstrations, protests and picketing for them to realize that livelihoods cannot be stolen by a few. Yesufu is leading Nigerians who for a long time feel that the government does not care for them. She is enlightening Nigerians to air their grievances to bring an end to the injustice. Through her activism, Nigerians are now speaking truth to everyone in a position of leadership to remember that they are in office not for personal interests, but for public interest.

Yesufu on police brutality

Just in 2020, women in Nigeria stood up to police brutality. For a long time, police violence has been unending a nightmare to Nigerians. Some police officers had relegated their law-and-order role to descend on Nigerians. They brutalized innocent citizens, who they are supposed to protect and treat humanely. Unluckily, due to their power, the police through their SARS unit, dehumanized Nigerians. They never cared about their primary role of protecting citizens and treating everyone equally before the law. At a point Nigerians felt the need to end it even if it could cost their lives. The #EndSARS protests ran through Nigerian streets, even after the army and police tried to submerge the voices of the voiceless. Nigerians marched forwards as President Buhari seemed aloof to listen to his people who put him to office. The mass protests which were met by brute force from men and women in uniform featured some prominent figures that daringly face the government. One of those figures was Aisha Yesufu.

Yesufu moved forward, and never cared about the danger of protests that were repelled by gunfire and teargas from the security forces. What Yesufu wanted was a police force that will care about people, while protecting law and order. In the Capital, Abuja Yesufu was one well-known anti-Sars protester who raised her voice against police brutality. She was tear-gassed, but not scared. She solidly believed that it was time to end police brutality. It was time for Nigerians to have a police force that will protect their rights and freedoms, but not rain terror on them.

With other women, and protesters Yesufu did not scamper to safety. She piled pressure determinedly on the government to disband the SARS unit, which had become torturous to Nigerians. It is her boldness that possibly, energized thousands of young Nigerians to risk their lives in Abuja as they pushed with their #EndSars movement.

One of the renowned symbols that featured in the #EndSars protests was started by Yesufu. While protesting, she raised her fist in the air to symbolize complete defiance to the deadly Sars unit. For Nigerians, these protests were a turning point, and they quickly adopted the symbol of a raised fist to show courage, grit and defiance amid teargas, gunshots and running battles with the police and army.

Yesufu accepts as true that as a woman, she has a role to play to bring positive change to her society. She does not sit back but moves forward with unthinkable bravery to challenge the oppressors. In a BCC interview, she noted "Women have always been the ones who get things done. Any protest that led to change has always been women-led." This statement underpins the strong conviction, Yesufu has in her activism. You cannot doubt, the fact that she is not regretting about her role in protesting impunity and injustices. It is factual that there is power in women when they engage in activism. They bring some endless energy that ultimately brings change to society. It is clear SARS was disbanded because women, this time around, did not sit back. They fought to deliver justice to their community, and this amplifies the fact that Yesufu is on the right trajectory to fight for Nigerians.

She is relentless and will always commit every ounce of effort to deliver meaningful change to her fellow Nigerians. This is the kind of activism that Nigerians have been desiring. There is a lot that good-meaning Nigerians expect from Yesufu. She is going to be a strong voice for Nigerians. Her bravery and readiness to risk her own life for the sake of securing justice and human rights for Nigerians, is no mean feat.

Activism will always be the building block for our democracy. When prominent figures like Yesufu continue to fight for us and call the government out, it is possible for democracy to grow. Though the journey to achieve strong democracy is rock-strewn, with forces like Aisha Yesufu a lot of can be achieved in Nigeria. Citizens need to support any leader or activist that willingly and boldly fights like this great woman for social justice. That will be instrumental in achieving desired change in our country.

⊷⊶ ⊷⊶

CHAPTER 20

ZAINAB GIMBA

It is now becoming clearer that, even in the most patriarchal states in Nigeria, women should have a shot at leadership. When I look at Hon. Zainab Gimba, all that I appreciate is women leadership in the country. Gimba is becoming a political figure in our country determined to lead and inspire women that, it is possible for them to be heard. Times are gone when women could just watch men mess up the country. Gimba believes in fighting for everything that is important to her community and to her country. As a woman of great intellect, she recognizes that women empowerment shall remain a mirage in the country if she, who is educated and enlightened, keeps quiet.

The fortitude and bravery that Gimba exudes has propelled her to greater heights in Nigeria's leadership. Who could imagine that one day, the young Gimba could rise politically considering that her society is deeply patriarchal?

Gimba's life story starts from Kala town, where she was born. The town is in Borno State. She pursued a Bachelor of Science (Public Administration) from the University of Maiduguri. It was from the very university that she was conferred with her master's degree in Public Administration. Later she joined University of Abuja for her PhD in Public Administration and Policy Analysis. This is a woman that knows the value of education, and there has always been a motivation behind her pursuit for education.

She has served in several appointed positions such as commissioner of Poverty Alleviation and Youth Empowerment, Universal Basic Education and Ministry of Water Resources. Having served as a commissioner, she sought a political seat. She was elected as a House of Representative member representing Ngala, Bama and Kala Balge constituency of Borno State. Her election into the House of Representative was characterized by a bruising battle. She fought tooth and nail with men who coveted the position, but as a fighter, she won decisively.

Throughout her life in public service, Gimba has demonstrated her willingness to serve. Personal accomplishments such as working as a senior lecturer at the University of Maiduguri and about ten years in public sector administration in Borno State demonstrate the ability of Gimba to serve. She has worked to empower the youth and alleviate poverty in her state. Though some people could see these achievements as personal, I see her as a role model. In a society, where female education is underrated, a woman who pursues her studies under deeply rooted male chauvinism should be seen as a role model to others.

Her achievements reflect how the Nigerian society is changing. There is acceptance of women in the country's leadership. Citizens are beginning to attach some significance to women leadership. Regardless of her being a member of the ruling party, All Progressive Congress, Gimba is still a leader that Nigerian women should admire and emulate. Apparently, education played a crucial role to her rise in public sector administration and politics.

Anecdotally, young females in Borno State are learning how their excellence can be noted, if they are educated. In a society where women have limited access to education and it is plausible to recognize a few that have it. This will inspire many generations to come, and that is why I am persuaded to consider Gimba an important voice to our society. Everyone wants a society with educated girls, because that is how we can defeat male chauvinism and inequality. Let women and men have equal opportunities if we desire a democratic society. When many women are in leadership, our society can prosper. Women leadership has been proven to lead to more success or positive change.

Women have potentials, and citizens should exploit it to realize real development. The moment the electorate gives women a chance to govern we are likely to bring to a crushing end, the many problems bedeviling our country. I am always delighted when I see women battle it out with men for any elective position. If a woman can win a political seat after running against men, it gives hope that voters are beginning to shift their trust to women leadership. Hon. Gimba has become a testament that women do not need favors but can square it out with men and still win with certainty.

Gimba's political journey and values

Hon. Gimba has confirmed that there is sweeping change in Nigeria's politics. Women are rising and seeking elective positions regardless of the hurdles they are likely to encounter. Gimba ran against four men, and it was not an easy journey. She obviously understood how it was going to be challenging for her. She was getting into a field where men assert authority and control. That did not scare her, but she stood firm, ready to face off with her opponents. Finally, she defeated her male opponents, including the then incumbent House Representative member representing her constituency.

While seeking office, one most notable call from Hon. Gimba was urging calm and non-violent political atmosphere. The honorable is someone who believes that we can compete in a healthy environment, instead of inciting our supporters to fight over us. She ran her campaigns peacefully, despite the isolated cases of interruptions. There was some uniqueness in her campaigns because she was a candidate that solely focused on policies and what she will do to her people. For her, it was not chest-thumping, but it was making realistic pledges to her electorate. Her supporters trusted Gimba right from the bruising primaries.

During the primaries, it was an uphill task for Hon. Gimba. The APC luminaries were not ready to allow the ticket to go to a woman. Gimba admits that the police were used to interrupt her, and sometimes her supporters were bludgeoned. She was not spared in the circus, during the primaries, she was personally beaten by the police and all that captures her struggle to the APC ticket. When she announced her interest to contest for the House of Representative seat, she never thought that she would receive opposition within APC family. However, the police descended on her rallies to clobber them. No police cared about her being a woman, but the issue was to prevent her from winning the primaries.

The challenges Gimba faced before winning the APC ticket reflects the many hurdles' women face in politics. Women are not given a level playground; instead, they are subjected to threats and violence which to some point scare them from seeking elective offices. Naturally, women tend to avoid tense situation that are characterized by violence. On the other hand, men would sometimes want to use violence as one way of displaying their strength and might. Even though that is cruel and barbaric, male politicians particularly in Africa consider such violence something normal. Political mayhem is a demonstration of a fragile democracy. It would be soothing if people can campaign without unleashing violence on their opponents.

When it became apparent that Gimba was winning in the party primaries, she received strong opposition. Nobody was willing to give this woman a party ticket, and they had to use all tricks to deny her victory in the primaries. Fortunately, it was getting crystal clear that in Ngala, Bama and Kala Balge constituency, she was the one most likely to win the APC ticket. The only way to stop her was to use the police to disrupt her and unleash any possible threats that could slow her down.

According to Gimba, there was a directive from "above" that she should not be allowed to fly the APC ticket. This was intimidation and a flagrant assault on the choice of the people. Voters should have the liberty to elect a leader they want. Time to impose leaders on people is gone, people should be allowed to exercise their democratic rights. It is their right to choose a person that they trust will serve them.

In her own statement, Gimba said "I got it on a good authority that some of the local party officials from the three local governments that make up my constituency were given instruction that I must not win and they should do whatever it takes for the incumbent, Mamman-Nur, to win the ticket and retain his seat as the member representing our constituency". This is distasteful and direct attempt to muzzle democracy, ignore the choice of the people. What has been killing or perhaps preventing democracy from growing in developing countries is this kind of behavior. Senior individuals determine who wins the popular party's ticket. When people in authority mess up with the party primaries, in the end, voters end up electing leaders who serve the interests of a few at the expense of the electorate. In this case, voters wanted change when they believed Gimba was able to deliver.

More importantly, democracy prevailed because the senior individuals controlling APC particularly at the constituency level were beaten at their own game. Their preferred candidate lost, and a new face won the party ticket. After winning the dominant party ticket in her constituency it was sure that Gimba was going to win the election to represent her people in the House of Representatives. Looking at her bruised political journey, it instils some hope that women in Nigeria can prevail regardless of the many hurdles they may face. They need to put a spirited fight, and never budge. They should fight hard to claim their positions in elective offices and provide good leadership to this country.

Political violence is detrimental to any democracy in the world. If party officials and those in senior authority are partisan, they force non-performing leaders on the voters. They use violence to subvert the will of the people. In Nigeria, we have witnessed on several occasions' intimidations being used to impose leaders on people. It is one thing that we must not accept but resist by all non-violent means. It is time for voters to speak their mind and vote without any interference. That is the only way we can grow our democracy.

Hon. Gimba preached peaceful elections. She asked her supporters not to interfere or attack her opponents. She wanted to show that for democracy to blossom, people should express their views vocally and freely without fear of being attacked. As a believer of freedom of expression, Gimba never wanted a political atmosphere full of intimidations and abuses. She wanted people to be courteous and honorable. Her belief that elections are supposed to be peaceful is an underpinning of what democracy is all about.

Democracy is pro-peace and tolerant. This is amplified in the way Gimba ran her campaign. She preached tolerance which perhaps persuaded her camp to be respectful and tolerant to everyone. Ultimately, her constituency was able to conduct a peaceful poll that saw her declared a winner. I am not saying that the entire election was peaceful but am driving a point that Gimba showed commitment to promote peace during her campaigns. Her efforts bore fruits, where she finally won without instigating any flames that characterize many elections in Africa even at the lowest elective office.

In the broadest sense, Gimba is a female leader that most young Nigerians should look up to. She is fighting for the rights of young people and women in our society. She is encouraging particularly women, to fight for their position in society. They should seek public offices like men, irrespective of the difficulties they face in a patriarchal society that for long has undermined women. Through her vision and inspiration in the coming years, Nigeria is going to see many women being elected to the senate and other elective offices. She is one woman with the right mind, education, and dream to inspire Nigerian women to participate in building Nigeria's democracy.

⊫⊦ ⊦⊨

CHAPTER 21

DR. PAUL ENENCHE

Paul Enenche is a trained medical doctor and he left his profession for televangelism purposefully to change lives and society. as the Senior Pastor of Dunamis International Gospel Centre, Dr. Enenche is reaching millions of Nigerians. we all agree that the church or religious leaders have a responsibility to play as far as strengthening our democracy is concerned. They are the light at the end of the tunnel in the context that they inspire and direct us on the way we should follow to live graciously.

The moment people including our leaders live decently, they become less corrupt, conscious, and kind. We need a society where leaders understand that they are servants to the people that put them in power. However, our current political leaders need to reflect on their treatment of Nigerian people. At present, very few leaders are committed to serving the interests of the electorate because of insensitivity. These politicians can only reflect if they are preached to, and that is exactly what Dr. Enenche is doing at the pulpit. He understands the plight of Nigerian people, and through his televangelism, he is calling for change that is critical for the democratization of our country.

Religious leaders with many followers like Dr. Enenche have a role to play in our democracy. When a country fails, there is no doubt that the religious institutions would be considered to have failed to save society from collapse. That is why we agree that it is central for the religious institutions to inculcate values embedded in a democracy to achieve a better society. The many people that follow Dr. Enenche's preaching every Sunday or every day are the electorate or leaders. Perhaps his teachings are persuading our leaders to change their ways and become good people. As a religious leader he speaks truth to power, and constantly reminds leaders that they should commit to doing good to everyone.

Enenche's role in building Nigeria's democracy
For the umpteenth time, Dr. Enenche like other religious leaders have been teaching some fundamental values which if observed, our country shall be better off. As a senior pastor, Dr. Enenche has been preaching about kindness, a virtue that is important not only to our leaders, but to all Nigerians. The moment our leaders become kind; they will always have interest in serving their country. However, kindness in this context should not be interpreted in terms of tokenism. One way that I think our leaders go wrong sometimes is believing that providing some material assistance is the only way they can serve their people. Politicians

like offering tokens to the electorate at the expense of real development.

Being kind requires that leaders put themselves in the shoes of the people they serve. If leaders can realize that kindness is not sharing their loot by providing some little aid, they can make laws and advocate for policies that in their knowledge, can serve the interests of their people. We are not saying leaders should not make their direct contribution to people by supporting them directly. Kindness is about being in the shoes of others, sharing and being able to realize that they are in need. People who are in need deserve long lasting solutions that will help revamp the economy and benefit many.

Senior pastor, Enenche is utilizing his platform to inculcate the value of kindness. If millions of Nigerians become kind to each other, they will develop a shared purpose that can have a significant impact on our democracy. Democracy is built by people, and when they lack values such as kindness it becomes difficult to better the society. Nigerians need to discover that for we to become a better society, there must be change of behavior and adoption of some values. If we adopt kindness as a virtue, it is possible for us to be responsible and run our institutions with dignity.

Dr Enenche has also been sharing his comments on integrity is equally central to our development as a country. The reason it is becoming difficult for us to progress as a country is our lack of integrity. If citizens and leaders can exercise integrity in all their engagements, in public or private, I am sure Nigeria will be at a better place. With integrity, we can conduct ourselves honestly. Imagine if our leaders can be people of high integrity. I think there

is a lot we can achieve as a country. Although our constitution stresses on integrity, unfortunately very few leaders
observe it. If institutions such as criminal justice system,
executive, parliament, and many others can exercise integrity, indubitably, we could be a just society.

Dr Enenche's insistence on values such as integrity does
not necessarily persuade many, but I think his millions
of followers are learning something that will benefit our
country. Religious leaders have a role to play in inculcating
values that in the end, will help their country move forward. When leaders with millions of followers spend their
time on preaching about values, anecdotally, some souls
shall be changed. Changing a few people through teachings on important values cannot go in vain.

The hope that this pastor is instilling in his followers
could be the reason some Nigerians believe that we still
have a room for improvement. We may become a perfect
society, but with hope, we can strive to make some improvements, gradually, until social justice and human rights are
observed in our country. Recently, I signed onto twitter and
I bumped into a post that alluded that human life in Nigeria is less than that of an animal. This post got me thinking
about the state of affairs in our country. To some extent, I
seemed to agree with that considering what is happening
in Nigeria. However, we must keep hope alive.

When Dr. Enenche preaches about hope, I usually look
at it in terms of how it can shape our national discourse.
We are a disillusioned people because of bad leaders, and
weak institutions. Nonetheless, that should not mean that
people must stop to hope that one day, the situation will be
better. The future is always bright; this is my philosophy in

life. The ultimate goal of Pastor Enenche is to help us continue to hope for the best. We must agree that hope will keep the fire in our fight for freedom and rights burning. It is hope that is energizing Nigerians to protest injustice like police brutality.

Church and justice

Worldwide religious institutions are separate from government and are supposed to offer proper guidance to society. These institutions mirror society and guide it to light. Churches need to preach to people and persuade them to change their ways to create a fair and just society. The church or any religious organizations cannot go mum when injustice becomes the order of the day. As much as people want to listen to the word of the Creator, they also want the church to speak out if things go wrong. The church acts as a shepherd to guide people on the right way to follow. It is supposed to persuade people to be kind, caring and loving. and when injustice persists in society, the church should not be quiet. It should speak up and call out the leadership of the country to address the grievances raised by the masses. Pastor Enenche is aware of the role his church is supposed to play in promoting governance in the country.

Having understood that the church must guide society and advocate for divine justice, we have witnessed Pastor Enenche seeking to expand his reach. Today, his church owns a radio station and TV station primarily for televangelism. The pastor is using his platforms to tell people about life and how people can live in an organized and peaceful way. In a majority of his summonses he speaks about healing, love, respect, care and treating each other fairly irrespective of status, social status, religious leaning, political affiliation.

Dr Enenche is not the moral police of the Nigerian government, but he is using his platform to persuade his followers to do what is pleasant before God. The church is not mandated to advance social justice. Its major role is to warn society of divine justice and try to persuade people to live righteously. In addition, Dr Enenche does not tell his followers who they should vote. but he teaches his followers to use wisdom to make good choices. The way he has played his role as a pastor clearly shows the role the church should play in society. He has stayed away from interfering with political choices his people make, but keen on changing behavior of Nigerians.

CHAPTER 22

GOVERNOR YAHAYA BELLO

Yahaya Bello is a Nigerian politician and the current Governor
of Kogi State. He was born on June
18th, 1975, in Okene, then Kwara
State, but now Kogi State, Nigeria.
He is the youngest of six children
of his parent. In 1996, Bello was
admitted into Ahmadu Bello University in Zaria where he
read Accounting. He graduated in 1999 but came back to
his alma mater for his master's degree in 2004.

In 2001, he had his NYSC compulsory service at the
Revenue Mobilization Allocation and Fiscal Commission.
He was retained there and later grew through the ranks
and later elevated to the post of an accountant. He was
moved to the Makurdi Zonal Account Department, where
he later became the Assistant to the Chief Accountant as a
result of his diligence. While in Makurdi, Yahaya Bello met
and later married Hajia Amina. The misfortune of both of

them losing their dads at their young age further cemented their relationship. Their marriage is blessed with children.

For some time now, whenever the Kogi State of Nigeria is mentioned in the media, there is a proclivity to allusions, hints, oblique remarks, bashing, and so on about the unassuming and unobtrusive Governor of the State, Governor Yahaya Adoza Bello. I must admit that initially, I also latched on to and believed the media buzz which propelled me to reading and knowing more about this Governor. My findings were contrastingly shocking. I discovered it has all been a calculated deceptive clamor and negative media assault on the Governor. Then I realized, with further confirmation from Mr. Robert Arome Eboh's posit, that I had all these while been tricked by most of the media reportage. Armed with my present knowledge of the Governor's achievements, I write to extol his tenacity, good leadership strides in Kogi State and to declare him a member of the *voice for the voiceless* in Nigeria.

Undemocratic behaviors of the media toward the governor

For a long time, I have been one of the backers of press/media freedom and lack of bias, that is, media neutrality in any society as I once said in one of the pages above. Notwithstanding, I get befuddled and dismayed by the unprofessional predisposition practices of the media these days, most especially on Governor Yahaya Bello. Objectivity has long been thrown under the bus and what we get in terms of quality reportage is below par, evidenced in Yahaya Bello's skewed portrayal.

This, therefore, calls to question what media neutrality and objectivity are and should be. How can the media maintain neutrality and impartiality? Though it is hard to achieve total media impartiality or objectivity, we can start by adding the correct half (side) to one side portion of an issue and chopping the resultant reportage entirety down the center.

The media boasts, and rightly so too, that it cannot tell you how to think, but will tell you what to think. For example, a newspaper's picture of victims in the Vietnam War. The people shown in the photograph could be Vietnamese from the South or members of the Northern Viet Cong but the captions/headline that accompanies the picture has the ability to slant and provoke the mind of the reader for or against. Or if the television camera, trained on a clash between radial students and police shows the violent attack of a wild-eyed student virtually leaping from the camera into the living room, the viewer is likely to look critically at these young people. If, however, the camera shows the police using force to quell and dispel the students, sympathy will flow in favor of the students.

Neutrality suggests that stories be reported in an unbiased, even-handed, and impartial manner amid that journalists are to side with none of the parties involved, and simply provide the relevant facts and information of all. Politics frequently involve questions of neutrality. The mass media should therefore assume a position halfway between the people and the government. We must keep this point in mind when thinking about true neutrality, which is at best a vague concept, usually varying with the case of the moment. This is because mass communications influence society. It does not matter if it is spoken, watched, or printed, the mass media reaches a large heterogeneous audience. The influence of the mass media on society could be positive – information, education, entertainment and can be used for voters, education, advocating human rights, freedom, formation of world views, etc. It could also be negative in that, it can be used to misinform society and can lead people towards crime, violence, poverty, etc.

It is therefore following that; the mass media could become tools for manipulating the people. Media operators can make their message penetrate through the conscious surface of the psyche to subconscious depths. They can manipulate their public's subconscious for their own purposes. The distinction between good and bad, right, and wrong must be made at the macro and micro levels in society. Consequently, mass media must consistently protect the rights of the people and disseminate information honestly and respectfully. It then baffles me when mass media that is the Fourth Estate of the realm and supposed to hold government accountable to the people, deliberately decides to support one party at the detriment of another or supporting a candidate against another. The media should know that this type of nonsense should stop and never be encourage and be fair to all parties in creating a level playing field for all.

Surprisingly, before Governor Bello assumed office, the previous government had embarked on phantom expenditures, including ghost workers, which negatively impacted its finances. Bello, on coming to office was not disposed to such. He made sure that all workers are carefully recognized electronically, a move that the status quo, those who enjoyed the 'pay without work', rejected. They fought back by portraying him as a governor owing to the state workers. Also, on resumption, he observed that the State was sharply and forcefully divided along ethnic and religious lines which were used by the former government to further disunite and create an unhealthy rivalry amongst the people. This further exacerbated the insecurity situation in the state.

Kogi state now and before governor Yahaya bello resume office

Insecurity in the State was at the apex by the time Governor Yahaya came to the office. Kidnapping and robbery were executed with total surrender. Travelers who normally would go through the state to interface the Northern part of the nation were under consistent attack. Even his mother was once kidnapped as well. The Governor, having seen the enormity of work to be done, swung into action, and has done quite well in stabilizing the state and restoring peace and order. Kogi today is perhaps the most secure state in Nigeria as at today. Violent crimes, violations, and kidnapping have been brought to the barest. According to Premium Times of March 17, 2020, the Senate President, Ahmed Lawal commended Governor Yahaya for his exceptional achievements in the area of security and peace of the state.

Health is another area where the Governor has done well. Quality medical services have been improved upon and provision of quality, newer facilities made. Agriculture, which ordinarily should have guaranteed food sufficiency, advancement of non-oil economic transformation, and distribution to other parts of the country, was seriously hit with the insurgency. This also is receiving serious attention from the Governor. The importance of electric power to industrialization is not lost on the Governor. Accordingly, Governor Yahaya Bello has engaged the relevant authorities and the Federal Government on the possible intervention on electrification projects in the state. The Governor is working on correcting gender parity, women empowerment, and education is equally receiving adequate attention. Diaspora engagement is ongoing with a view to attracting investments.

Of late, the financial and economic numbers emerging from Kogi have been extraordinary. Numerous tasks are being carried out in each LGA by this administration. Those things that have been inadequate in the past administration are about to be thing of the past in Kogi state, these are because of the spirit of courage and workaholic attitude of the Governor. Having said all these, let me address some unacceptable impressions and portrayals about the state and the Governor. You see, we will experience all kinds of hurt in life in our drive to achieving our dreams and aspirations. Not all of them will heal. Some may even make us not to realize our dreams. Therefore, the person who triumphs, in the end, is the person who gets up after each fall and pushes onward. The ability to keep on fighting is a matter of the spirit that makes Governor Yaya Bello a voice for the voiceless. He did not allow the 'market noise' to disturb nor wane him. Rather, he focused on what he went to the market to buy, a mark of a true leader, not only for the Kogi people but the entire Nigeria.

The governor concomitant courage
outdazle them all

I believe Governor Yahaya Bello, amidst all oppositions, achieved all these because of what I term 'the special courageous spirit' in him. Courage is especially important in life because it has a crucial bearing on the direction our lives take. The important thing is to have the courage to take a step. No one can escape the realities of daily life. We have to deal with life and its challenges. Life and the world we live in are like a storm-tossed sea. We have to make our way through it, buffeted by all kinds of experiences. There is no other way. This is part of our inescapable destiny as human beings. Everyone has their own hopes and dreams, their own way of life, their own ideals, joys, sufferings, pain, and grief. No matter what happens; however, we have to get on with life. We have to keep moving, working toward realizing our ideals and dreams.

But no matter how wonderful our dreams, how noble our ideals, or how high our hopes, we need the courage to make them a reality. We can come up with the greatest ideas or plans in the world or be filled with boundless compassion for others, but it will all come to nothing unless we have the courage to put those intentions into action. Without action, it is as if our dreams and ideas never existed. If you summon your courage to challenge something, then you can better understand and even defeat it. It is important to take a step of courage than end up wishing: "If only I have had a little more courage". There is no need to worry about what others may think. Be true to yourself. It is your life, after all. The human heart can be very weak, fickle, and ignoble. But it can also be stronger than anything, unflinching, supremely noble.

The great writer, Victor Hugo was forced into exile during his struggle with the dictator, Napoleon III. He was in exile for nineteen years. But he was determined that no matter the persecution, he would stick to his ideal with a vibrant, resolute spirit. Liking Napoleon III to Sula, an ancient Roman tyrant, Hugo writes in the poem "Ultima Verba" (My Last Word):

Even if only one thousand are left, I will hold my ground!
If only one hundred survive, I will still cross swords with
Sula.
When only ten remain, let me be the tenth.
When only one is left, that one will be me!

People that are not afraid to stand alone for their beliefs, gain the support of true, steadfast friends. But today, many people lack ideas and beliefs. No matter what, we must understand that: "We are all born under the sentence of death". The question, then, is: how did we spend the limited time we had? If we are going to give our lives to something, surely, it should be to a noble cause, the cause of eternal truth and justice. If we keep up our efforts, even when the going is tough, we will earn respect. Persevere on the path you have chosen, irrespective of how difficult things become. Those who can do this will emerge as champions and victors in life. They will win in the end. Such people also are true friends. Governor Yahaya Bello is very well-qualified as a great leader and a *voice for the voiceless*.

Those who are strong stand-alone, just as Governor Yahya is doing amid persecutions. The German poet and playwright, Von Schiller (1759-1805) declared that the strong are strongest when acting alone. I have treasured these words since my youth. It is not good to blindly follow the crowd. Going along with something without any real thought, just because everyone is doing it, or being quite content with not having to make any decisions yourself leads to mental laziness and apathy. And that is dangerous.

But we must not be lazy. We must never abandon our commitment to the great standard of living we already set for our mendicant society, and also on peace; our desire to learn, and our love for humanity. Putting those values into practice ourselves and encouraging others to share them, too, takes courage. Courage lies inside us. It is something we must rouse from within. Mindlessly following the crowd is not courage but cowardice. It is fascism, not democracy. In a democracy, we each have to recognize that we are society's protagonists and as such have a responsibility to fulfill. Instead, there is too much self-centered, self-interest, the attitude that "so long as I am happy, that is all matters," and too much bling following, the mentality that, "it is safer to go along with what everyone else says." Only when people have the courage to stand alone can they lead the world in the direction of peace and good. When such courageous individuals join forces and unite in strong solidarity, they can change society, just as Governor Yahya Bello has done in Kogi state. But it all starts with you. You have to be courageous. The rest all follows from that.

Courage is inseparable from justice. It is the determination to do what is right, to build a just society, and to follow the correct path as a human being. It is doing good, taking positive actions, not only for yourself but for humanity and the world as well. To do this, we need the indispensable power of courage. Our efforts may not call attention to themselves, but in reality, they shine with unsurpassed brilliance.

It takes courage to put a stop to bullying, lying, media biasness. It takes courage to endure hardships and survive tough circumstances. It takes amazing courage to lead good, productive lives, day after day. And it also takes tremendous courage to share our opinions with our families and friends, so that everyone, ourselves included, can move in a more positive direction. Those with the courage to do what is right, no matter what others say, possess a "precious sword" of limitless power.

People of genuine courage have no underhanded motivations. They are straightforward and honest, which is why they are often misunderstood and even treated as villains. In contrast, there are others who are skillful manipulators, who scheme and self-promote to gain popularity. Many people are fooled by their apparent success and even envy them. However, others maybe, those who have done what is right, even if misunderstood, scorned, or harassed as a result have a clear conscience. They are victors.

True courage is defined by whether it is motivated by justice and compassion. Confucius once said:

> *It is hard for us ordinary mortals to have compassion.*
> *Emotions get in the way, or we just cannot be bothered.*
> *Though compassion is important, it is difficult for us.*
> *But we can have courage. Practically speaking, having*
> *courage is our way of acting with compassion.*

And in fact, if we act with courage, we find that our compassion for others actually grows deeper. Courage is indeed the highest virtue. May the perfect wisdom of God the Almighty continue with the Governor till the end of his tenure and beyond.

CHAPTER 23

THE FOUNDATION OF THE
CURRENT UNCONSTITUTIONAL
BEHAVIOURS IN NIGERIA

"He who doesn't comprehend the reason for an issue can't fathom it" says an African proverb. Nigeria never truly had a lot of an opportunity to fledge into a new fully functioning country after it gained its autonomy from Britain in 1960. Unlike other Africa Countries, Nigeria is the only country in Africa that did not start the governing systems of the country with the best of its citizens after the independent compare to those countries as Ghana, Kenya, and others. Barely six years after its freedom or independent, the first military coup came into existence in 1966 – the very same year that Ghana encountered its first overthrow. Be that as it may, since Nigeria suffered much longer under military systems (29 years) than Ghana (21 years), the annihilation created by military standard of ruling was unmistakably far more disastrous and broader in Nigeria.

The total destruction of Nigeria began during this period, from: 1966 to 1999 – a period where there were no Constitutions. Military rulers basically suspended them and managed the country by decrees. As such, there was no rule of law and the worst part was the military decree 5, which was enacted to change Nigeria from Federalism to Unitary. A decree that was jealously written and was introduced to the then Head of State, Aguyi Ironsi by his brother, Professor Ben Nwase. Prof. Nwase was the man who drafted the constitution that took away power from the Nigeria regions and handed it over to the central government, a situation that is hunting the Southern Nigerians the most till now. Prof. Nwase did this because his brother Aguyi Ironsi was the Head of State, he reasoned that the Igbo would rule Nigeria forever (Please, do your diligent research before bringing out your venoms). Today, Prof Nwase together with other Igbo and Southerners, are shouting or clamoring for restructuring or Biafra nation from a situation that he helped to destroy. The good people of Nigeria shall not forget.

A Constitution resembles a yarn that weaves the fabric of a general society or country together. It precedes clan or religion and it is what stands between law and progress on one hand and carnage, chaos, and destruction on the other. The Constitution resembles traffic regulations, which all – religion, gender, tribe, or statement of faith must be followed and complied with. During this period, there was no "traffic regulations" in Nigeria. A metaphor that we all need to grapple with. Additionally, badly characterized, or non-existent are the elements of state organs. Under a constitution, Parliament for instance, gives oversight over the executive activities and the job of the judiciary is to guarantee that the standard of law is maintained. But, without a constitution, there is no oversight over the executive, which implies that the Head of State can actually do anything he desires. Further, without a constitution, there is no law for the Judiciary to uphold aside from orders or diktats from the Head of State. Separation of power, democracy rules system, checks and balances are all non-existent without a constitution. Nor are the standards of responsibility, transparency and integrity which disappear totally because there is no standard which stipulates how the Head of State, the Police Chief or the Chief Justice ought to be chosen or considered responsible and by whom.

The absence of a constitution also has deleterious economic consequences. The constitution defines the parameters within which economic activity can take place. Since there is not one, nobody is sure what constitutes a legitimate business activity and uncertainty prevails, which discourages investment – the key to economic growth and development. This creates a situation where hordes of businessmen must seek "approval" from the Head of State before undertaking a venture. And the Head of State, often crooked, may demand a bribe or percentage-share of the business before granting approval. Even business contracts become meaningless. Suppose a businessman wins a contract to construct roads, half-way through the contract, government can decide to arbitrarily cancel the contract. Under a constitution, he may sue the government for breach of contract. But without a constitution, he might take the case to court anyway but there is no constitution which authorizes the court to hear such cases. Or the Head of State can order the judge to throw the case out.

A nation's life hangs in abeyance when there is no constitution. When there are no clearly defined rules or laws, uncertainty prevails. Nobody is sure about what is legal and illegal or how to deal with one another. In such a situation, people or groups may fall back on their traditional (customary) laws, religious laws or make up their own "laws" as they go along. The police, civil servants, armed robbers and even scammers may do so as well. A tapestry of "laws" comes into existence and applied on an ad hoc basis. There is no predictability as these ad hoc laws can change suddenly. Inevitably, a clash of laws frequently occurs. Ordinarily, a constitution resolves such clashes but there is not one, which means they must be resolved by the Head of State. And when one is dissatisfied with his verdict, there is no guaranteed right of appeal. More pernicious and incurably damaging are the effects on the youth. In the absence of a constitution, they grow up without knowing the principles and values that serve as a glue holding the nation together. They do not know what is right or wrong and what is social or anti-social. These young people become increasingly disaffected, confused, restless and lost. They are jobless, poorly educated and they have few role models with moral stature. The value system has collapsed because there are no values celebrated by a constitution. Hard work and entrepreneurship no longer assure success and wealth because what one builds can be wiped out in an instant since there is no rule of law.

Embittered by their very own society, the young become susceptible to radical thoughts and float toward religious extremists — not simply the Islamist fanatics in Northern Nigeria and Somalia, but the Christian groups (the Lord's Resistance Army in Northern Uganda) and the conventionalist (the Mungiki order in Kenya). Some look for escape through rickety boats to Europe. Others get involved in criminal wrongdoing (Internet scams, drug trafficking) prostitution, and radical groups that look for violent change. In sum, the absence of a constitution breeds lawlessness, government dysfunction and retards economic development. Reckless government spending started happening by the vagabond leader who wasted away Nigeria's oil bonanza. There was no constitution or organization to checkmate the government wickedness. State institutions started to decay and disintegrate. Government ministries failed to convey the fundamental social amenities - clean water, sanitation, health care, education, and electricity. The (NEPA), that is, the Nigeria's Electric Power Authority was nicknamed "Never Ever Power Always". Institutions such as the Judiciary and the Police disintegrated. The social fabric of Nigeria – whatever was left of it started to shred, the administration stopped to work, the moral standard and value system began to crumple, corruption became the order of the day and an entire age of Nigerians was lost. In recorded or historical terms, 25 years is commonly viewed as a "generation." Therefore, an entire age of Nigerians was raised without knowing the constitution, its worth, centrality or significance. Around 60 percent of Nigerians today are under 40 years of age, which means most by far were brought up in a constitutional vacuum country or society. Individuals hold the government and the legislature in miserable scorn, seeing the government as superfluous in their lives.

By 1998, Nigeria was 100% affirmed or certified Coconut Republic where good judgment had been butchered and presumptuous stupidity was on the frenzy. There was no standard of law; Lepers and Crooks were and still in control as you read this and the unfortunate casualties, that is, innocent people are in prison. Nigeria, at that point was a completely wasted country, even now. So much potential, so such riches in regular assets, natural resources, and such dynamism in its citizens, yet all wasted. Linus U. J. Thomas-Ogboji, a Nigerian researcher said: "Nigeria, the senseless monster of Africa, may stand out forever as the greatest nation ever to go directly from colonial subjugation to a complete collapse country without an intervening time of successful self-rule. O mase o. So much guarantee, so much waste; such was a mistake, such a disgrace and moron leaders. It makes you sick and debilitated." (African News Weekly, May 26, 1995).

Recall that the situation in Nigeria and many African countries can be described as: Bad driver, bad vehicle, bad roads, and angry passengers are fed up with lack of progress. Changing the driver without fixing the vehicle is pointless as the new driver would also land in another ditch. But since the 1970s, that is exactly what has been taking place in Nigeria. Worst now that the country is in the hands of 'Aliens', those Lepers who know nothing but Sharia, and the Sharia rulings are only to the poor among them, not to the Rankadedes. The children of their so call elites can do anything they like. The dilapidated state vehicle remains kaput or dead.

The people are not the problem

A reasonable differentiation must be made between the individual people and the state of Nigeria. The individuals are not the issue. The state is broken. Figuratively, the state-mobile is completely ruined: brakes do not work; the motor engine leaks oil; the tires are flattened; the battery is dead and the headlights are broken. A failed state is the place where all the institutions of the state do not work. They do not give solid inventory of clean water, electricity, health care, sanitation, or other basic social services and infrastructure. Neither do the military officers and police provide security or harmony. The members of the National Assembly are more interested in giving themselves hefty salary increases and emoluments and the Judges are often on the take. Lawlessness is always the order of the day because the police, supposedly the one the society looks onto either cannot enforce the law or are themselves lawbreakers.

Several Human Rights Watch reports has it that, the genuine sources of power in Nigeria have been the affluent political godfathers who fund and sponsor something like epidemic election-related violence that might have killed hundreds, if not thousands, of innocent people in the several flawed elections conducted since Nigeria returned to democracy in 1999. Discretionary rules were openly ridiculed and voting papers or ballots boxes were no match for the bullets of gangs, hoodlums and even the national law enforcements contracted by government officials and the politicians to rig votes. The conduct of government institutions and many public officials is so pervasively marked by corruption and violence, which makes the process of every election more like a criminal activity than democratic governance. It additionally depicted the severe methods utilized by groups of hoodlums to influence the 2003 to 2019 elections, all of which were set apart by savagery, misrepresentation, and administrative ineptitude.

The crux of Nigeria's problems

The core of Nigeria's myriad of issues comes from an absence of a standard of constitutional law which has led to total government dysfunctions. Therefore, nobody follows the Constitution. The police and the judiciary do not; neither do the politicians or even President Buhari and the previous Presidents who do not "care the slightest bit" about the Constitution. Any abused individual or group can go rogue and unleash havoc to settle scores. As I said before, it is like driving on the road without any *traffic law*. The ensuing result will be wanton carnage, chaos, and deaths, which is what we are all witnessing right now.

The undeniable solution is to uphold the law. ALL must comply with the same traffic regulation; that is, ALL. Regardless of your religion, tribe, gender, or creed, all must obey the same constitutional law. State institutions – the Judiciary, Executive, Legislature, and everybody must regard and comply with the Constitution. It is a socio-political agreement between the state and the people. It characterizes the elements of the state and the rights of the individuals. Above all, and most importantly, the underlying Constitution is a set of beliefs and principles such as equality and justice, freedom; these are what unites a people.

Again, just as transit regulations are required out and about. Six laws might be recognized: Natural, legally binding, statutory, standard, strict, and protected laws. Let us ask ourselves this unique question: What keeps Nigeria together? The shading green color of the flag, the flag itself, our religions, Tribes or What? The conspicuous answer ought to be the Constitution that articulates a set of convictions and principles that all Nigerians believe in. Therefore, if no one follows the Constitution, there is nothing that holds Nigeria together. Nigeria's issues are not because of tribalism, religion, nepotism, or even corruption. They are just indications of a sick nation. The main driver of that malady is the absence of constitutionalism. The Constitution precedes religion, tribe, sexual orientation and whatever else. The Constitution ought to be the incomparable rule that everyone must follow; it is most important and trumps all laws. But at this moment, Nigeria has none but fake constitution. The total destruction of Nigeria started less than 29 years of arrant mismanagement by MILITARY vagabonds and scoundrels, who often suspended the Constitution and later ruled by decree.

Quick solutions in summary

All the Federal Government of Nigeria needs to do now is to effect a complete overhaul of the existing structures and make them function as bottom-top institutions. Hence:

- Reform our legal system, our political arrangements, our educational system, police, security and defence et al.
- Make the Villages and Towns the center of governance. Build the security architectures around the towns and villages, and make the people fully involved in the security arrangements.

- The basic unit of our political system are villages, towns, and cities. Presently, Local Government headquarters have no link to the people. Therefore, demolish them and make Local Governments mere theoretical arrangements, but shift administrations to the villages, towns, and cities.
- Remove the traditional rulers' influences in the political institutions and create town administration. Let every aspiring leader begin from his or her village and keep moving up.
- Create a National Guard as a buffer between the police and the armed forces. Also create border guards, coast guards, and so on. In 2020, the military and the police need Air Wing to operate Drones. Invest heavily in Drones and Drone technology.
- Create a level playing field for everybody and there must never be a sacred cow; everybody must be equal before the law.
- Otherwise, like the regional development commission, every geo-political zone will clamor for its Amotekun because the federal government is not reliable.

Restructuring

Everyone has been talking and wanting restructuring in Nigeria, but the problem has always been the definition, scope, and nature of the restructuring. What exactly needs to be restructured in our system? Is it political, social, economic, or physical (land and territory) restructuring? Is it the functions and the responsibilities that need restructuring? Or is it the devolution of power?

By Olusegun Ogundipe 2019.

Answers to the above questions

1. If Nigeria restructured into provinces -
2. Northern Province
3. Middle Belt Province
4. Western (Oduduwa) Province
5. Eastern (Biafra) Province
6. Niger Delta Province (Atlantic)
7. Central Government at FCT

Ten positive things that would happen within 5 years (primarily due to inter-province competition)

1. The Northern Province will have stronger Islamic laws. Sharia will be entrenched, and this will make the NP become the least corrupt province. The Middle East (Arab) nations will move into partner with them, bringing major development. Jaiz Bank and Unity Bank will become mega banks. Arabic and Hausa will compete with English for dominance in schools. This province will generate more solar power than any other province. After the west, this province will be the 2nd to have 24/7 electricity. They will start exporting food as a major revenue generator.

2. The Middle Belt Province will have a development conference. Focus will be given to solid minerals development/exports, tourism development and food production/exports. This will become

a food hub in West Africa. They will export more food than any other province. Mega mining and food corporations will arise. This province will have foreign inflows through tourism development greater than any other province. It will host the most beautiful places to live in Nigeria.

3. The first province to experience economic explosion would obviously be the Western Province. The Oduduwa Master plan will be revealed. There would be trans-regional 4G internet fiber connection/ rail/subways/highways/power grids etc. Yoruba will become the 2nd official language. They are relatively united. They have oil. They own academia. They have mega corporations. The WP would be the first to have stable 24/7 power supply! Foreign money will flood the province. More Forbes recognized billionaires will arise. Some of them will be internet billionaires. Lagos will be relieved a little from overpopulation as railway lines from other states will make living elsewhere and working in Lagos a breeze.

4. The Eastern Province will transform into the Auto Industry Hub of Africa. Indigenous manufacturing of vehicles that will start competing with foreign vehicles will commence in earnest. This will grow to manufacturing of airplanes, helicopters, tractors, cranes, heavy duty construction equipment etc. Forbes recognized billionaires living in Anambra will arise. The Biafra agitation will fizzle out since formation of the EP will be seen as a Biafra success in another form. There would be so much develop-

ment that villages (as we currently know them) will quickly cease to exist. This province will be the first to semi-urbanize all their rural areas as all Igbo living abroad will rush back to take advantage of the changes.

5. The Atlantic Province will take the Uyo blueprint and run with it. An abundance of oil wealth and opening up of major seaports at Rivers and Uyo will enable this region to revamp their infrastructure quickly. There will be more monorails here than anywhere else. This will be the 3rd province to achieve 24/7 electricity generation in Nigeria (mainly from gas turbine technology).

6. With provincial indigenous security forces in control, kidnapping, Armed robbery, Boko Haram, Fulani herdsmen and the Niger delta militancy attacks will all fizzle out. Nigeria will become the most secure and peaceful African nation; thus, attracting more foreigners.

7. Each province will have their own airline professionally managed. And with better roads/rail, air and land transport costs will crash.

8. With the rapid development occurring all over, Nigeria's GDP will shoot up. Obtaining visas to travel out will become easy as more people will want to come in than go out. A worldwide immigration into Nigeria will commence, as Nigerians living abroad will be struggling with foreigners to enter the country. "Nigeria will become the most desirable Nation to live in".

The central government at the FCT will become smaller and less powerful. There will be a mini exodus from Abuja to the provinces as the action is now elsewhere. The out-skirts of Abuja will no longer be overpopulated. Abuja will become awesome again.

Therefore, can we go ahead and do the needful by restructuring the country accordingly. The more we delay on this the nearer the country is moving toward disintegra-tion. That will be too bad.

━━╬ ╬━━

CHAPTER 24

FIGHTING CORRUPTION AS A BASIS FOR A DEMOCRATICALLY STRONG NIGERIA

For many developing countries, corruption has been the greatest cancer to democracy, security, and economic growth. Nigeria, as the biggest economy in Sub-Saharan Africa, is 'blessed' with human and common assets. However, the country is in abject poverty due to massive corruption in government institutions. Corruption has become so common that poor service delivery, misallocation of resources, mis-governance, insecurity, and infrastructural decay in the country have hindered economic growth. A state of affairs that is leading to poverty, despite the country's huge oil wealth. Corruption in Nigeria is seen as dishonesty among the people entrusted to hold public offices. It is deeply rooted in the judiciary, legislature, and executive arms of the government and by extension private sector.

It is common knowledge that there have been many scenarios that indicate corruption is pervasive in Nigeria. There has been rampant embezzlement of public funds running into billions of dollars. The private sector, long been believed to be corruption-free zones, has also hit headlines for being used by government officials to launder stolen public monies. Moreover, foreign firms like Sagem have been involved in corruption in the country. These pieces of evidence are clear indicators that Nigerian public officials have continuously used their power of office for their gain. Furthermore, Transparency International positions the country as perhaps the worst nation on the planet.

Government officials are named or chosen into public workplaces to contend for the privileges of their constituents. For example, the current ruling party won elections with the promise of ending corruption in the country. However, the government has been criticized for encouraging more corruption. More than a trillion Naira has been used to try to subsidize the importation of fuel, yet the nation boasts of four 'dead' oil refineries. A democratic regime should address issues it promised its people and not escalate the problems. A corrupt system continues to violate the established rules for personal profits and gains. The common evidence is bribery among the officials. Entrepreneurs evade taxes and cannot get permits and licenses without giving unnecessary gifts and bribes to public officials. Many people bribe their way into jobs through nepotism. The corrupt public officials use their power to favor their friends and relatives into the offices without the correct credentials and work experience needed for those jobs.

This approach has led to poor service delivery and incompetence which is a major contributor to economic stagnation. This has affected the health and banking sectors where fraud is common. The major cause of this problem is that employees are lowly paid. So, they use this chance to receive bribes. They take bribes to facilitate the provision and procurement of public services. In some cases, crucial files have ended up missing because those in charge were not bribed. Graduates are jobless and many educated people are leaving their lucrative private jobs to join politics, to gain wealth through corruption.

Corruption is rampant among politicians and bureaucrats, undermining democracy. It is more likely to flourish in institutions that exhibit weak democratic foundations. Populist politicians are at the center of corruption and cannot deliver their services without favor or bribes. Such institutions cannot monitor or sanction corrupt government officials leading to economic inequality. Democracy is all about representing the relevant people in a just and fair manner. It helps to prevent autocratic rulers, promotes human development, and encourages prosperity through fair income, education, and health. Therefore, when corruption infiltrates a democratic nation, all these benefits are lost.

The democratic regime in Nigeria since 1999, rescued the nation from decades of military rule. Such governance promised positive impacts on social, economic, and political systems. However, corruption got in the way. Many cases go unsolved or case files with enough pieces of evidence to prosecute corrupt officials go missing. Moreover, elections across all levels of governance are rigged in favor of particular people who will be able to sustain personal interests across different public offices. The Nigerian public corporation generates huge funds that can promote economic growth but fail to remit the funds to the public treasury. Parliament cannot account for all the crude oil production and shipments. The funds are embezzled through corrupt ways.

Furthermore, such huge revenues are laundered through the private sector. They collude and transfer the public funds to personal business investments and accounts, thereby defrauding the nation. Moreover, government projects are given to the highest bidders who bribe their way into the bidding process, or the contracts are given to private companies that belong to senior government officials. As expected, government projects slow down for quite a long time prompting helpless conveyance of administrations to individual people. Nevertheless, there have been instances of public corporations being handed over to fictitious foreign companies without paying the concession price. Also, many government projects are advertised and approved just for publicity and as a formality. The contractors embezzle the funds, leading to poor quality works across the country.

Security agencies are mandated to prevent corruption and uproot corrupt officials from society. However, in Nigeria, security officers are at the center of corruption. At the border checks, bribes or gifts are given to security officers to allow contraband goods into the country. Moreover, military operations against militia groups like Boko Haram are compromised by corruption. It comes in form of kickbacks, misuse of security budgets, awarding of non-competitive contracts, and using military resources to generate personal profits. Moreover, security personnel recruitments are unfair since most people bribe their way through the recruitment process. Furthermore, on the roads, traffic officers take incentives and bribes to allow unroadworthy vehicles on the roads and illegal goods, thereby risking the security of the road users.

All these forms of corruption are due to several factors. First, since Nigeria's independence, there have been generations of greedy and corrupt leaders. Leadership posts and what the roles entail are no longer to serve the overall population that elected them in the first place. Such greedy elites eye these posts to benefit themselves from the government contracts or the powerful positions. They use political platforms to campaign with the promise to fight corruption when elected, but after winning these posts, they create loopholes within the anti-corruption systems to cripple their efforts in fighting corruption. These loopholes are opportunities for rent-seeking, and such greedy and corrupt leaders walk scot-free even when found to be involved in corrupt practices. The exemption from prosecution extends to their network of clients, friends, and family. Some even seek and occupy these leadership posts through perjury and forged certificates, undermining the performance of the public corporations.

Bad policies promote corruption alarmingly. For example, the ban on the importation of used cars above five years from their manufacture dates encouraged corruption. Importers found their way through this policy as it negatively affected their business. They opted to bribe the customs officials who allowed such cars into the country. Such a policy did not consider the negative impacts on the business owners and the government. Besides, it increased the number of illegal routes into the country making the business more lucrative for corrupt officials and businessmen. The policy also made the government lose huge import duties to corruption. Other policies like the international laws on illicit drug control have also promoted corruption in Nigeria. The laws have only increased the number of underhand dealings among drug dealers, smugglers, and producers.

Corruption in Nigeria is deeply rooted to limited job opportunities. Many job prospects like graduates have limited access to economic opportunities. This situation allows many people to go through corrupt systems to gain access to job opportunities which are limited. Nigeria suffers from the type of culture in which more stress is put on economic success as a major life goal. There is also evidence of "ghost workers" which gives a blurred indication that all posts are filled, but instead, they are allocated to specific people and a network of clients within institutions through nepotism. Also, such limited opportunities encourage crime especially among people that cannot afford bribes.

In addition, poor reward systems encourage corruption. Many government institutions lack appropriate reward systems for top-performing government officials or public workers. In equal measures, there are no tangible consequences for poor performance or wrongdoing, especially for the elites. Remunerations in the public service are low and, in most cases, not paid as at when due. Furthermore, contracts that involve public institutions are either not paid or not paid on time. All these factors contribute to low productivity level among workers. Since these workers have needs and responsibilities to their families, they develop unethical practices to achieve the missed incentives. Nigerians are aware of this situation and still take the job offers with the hope of getting something extra through corruption.

Family pressure remains a great contributor to corruption. Nigerians believe in an extended family system in which successful family members are expected to provide for their less successful members. To meet the demands of extended family members, public servants go the extra mile to acquire wealth to please their relatives. Such pressure has led them to circumvent rules and anti-corruption efforts to have the advantage of accumulating funds through corrupt dealings. It also links corruption to feelings of obligations that must be met. Moreover, many family members view public jobs as a means to amass wealth and access job opportunities, thus encouraging nepotism and favoritism. Society's attitude towards this vice and how it is handled by the state creates a favorable environment for corruption to fester.

Moreover, the efforts to end corruption have been rendered useless depending on how corruption charges are prosecuted by the judiciary and other arms of government. The quest for wealth is overwhelming. With the current tough economic times, the urge for wealth through corruption is frightening. Society is obsessed with expensive lifestyles. Instead of incriminating corrupt officials, they are idolized and seen as heroes and heroines. Many have forgotten the principles of democracy, life principles of honesty, justice, and fairness. Ignoring such social norms has created breeding grounds for corruption. Society has also seen corrupt officials being released on bail and still allowed to lead government institutions. This has encouraged corruption as many people are aware that they can get away with corrupt deals so long as they have money and know the right people among the elite group in society.

The war against corruption has been long stalled by various factors. First, the government lacks the political will to end corruption. Different regimes have been previously elected based on their promise to end corruption but come out worse than their predecessors. There are no proper mechanisms to track government's service delivery or to monitor and track corruption incidences. Corruption should be handled across all levels of government with steadfast laws and guidelines that ensure that all factors - social, cultural, and political - are considered. Implications of corruption are insecurity, poor economic growth, poverty, increase in the cost of development, impunity, and poor corporate structure in public institutions. It also stops people in the public arena from making the most of their basic liberties and opportunities. It is therefore essential to strengthen the rule of law as this will help to prevent corruption for sustainable development.

The primary methodology is to zero in on education. The syllabus and education policies should focus on providing a conclusive curriculum that is updated with modern societal changes to reinforce positive social values in students. Education should not only be formal but must factor into the process, informal mechanisms by involving both religious and community institutions. Moreover, students should be exposed to real-life scenarios by engaging them with political institutions, vocational opportunities, and public participation. These will help bridge the gap between the young generation and political institutions and ultimately, promote productive relationships in society. It will also help in educating the public about different forms of corruption in different social contexts. Eventually, a culture of integrity will be created in society. Therefore, the private sector, civil servants, and political elites are better able to professionally deliver quality service to the people. Consequently, dignity is birthed, no underhand dealings and no one is above the law.

Society has a role to demand accountability from their leaders concerning their campaign promises and targets. Leaders complicit in corruption deals or that have failed to deliver their promises as demanded by their roles and responsibilities, should not be allowed to hold future positions. Rather, they should be prosecuted and were found guilty, sent to jail. Incentives should be given to those who report corruption incidence. Nigerians should develop a culture of openness and oppose bureaucratic systems that encourage secrecy. The press as the fourth estate of the realm also plays a major role in enlightening the public through anti-corruption campaigns. Campaigns should also target the minority, the illiterate, and vulnerable groups within the society by delivering the campaigns through local dialects. This way, more and more people are reached. Civil servants should be provided with comprehensive reward systems - financial and non-financial incentives - to improve their morale and productivity. It will help to reduce bribes and incompetence within the public institutions and will ensure equal opportunities for everyone. Eradicating corruption will lead to improved security, democracy, and living standards for a better nation.

CHAPTER 25

FOOD PRODUCTION: CATALYST FOR AFRICAN DEMOCRACY

Africa has such an issue with food production deficiency and to grasp it, one must take a close look at all factors and stakeholders. Government of each nation in Africa has the challenge of finding harmony or striking a balance between beneficial exports and providing enough food to the countries or states. A few perspectives have been negative in the advancement of this equalization, and it is an intense challenge to get Africa back to the normal order of doing things altogether.

Right from the time Africa was 'settled' by the different European nations, no base framework was set up for the continent to progress in the African ways. European countries utilized these colonies for nothing but to extract raw materials for their own continents or purposes, that is, the purpose of colonialism only profited the mother country. When the European nations got what they required or wanted, they abandoned the continent as a depleted land.

One of the most destructive choices that the European countries made was the introduction of crops good for Europeans but not for African nations. Europeans ensured that Africans planted cash crops that would profit them. In other words, the crops that were only good for Europe were the types that the European colonies taught the African farmers to grow. They lied to them that they would get as much higher income if they would plant European crops, which are on high demand in European countries. Hence, that was the kind of crops the Africans have knowledge of and produced.

Another challenge African farmers faced was the production of cash crops from Europe which did not fit well into the continent's ecological circumstances. The farmers in these regions would need to manage the distressing climate states of their territories, for example, flood, dry season, and in some cases, high temperatures with different difficulties that these harvests were not used to. A large portion of the cash crops, e.g., tobacco, and cotton are unstable. These resulted in low yield for the farmers, who expended a lot of lands, time and energies that could have been utilized for other crops that would have yielded better harvest on the terrain. Of the crops the farmers were producing, larger part is being exported to the European countries. The European settlers were setting up tobacco and cotton cultivations all through Africa and the yields were being shipped over to Europe. This makes an extremely lopsided framework wherein no supportability is made for the African nations. This left nothing for the individuals of Africa with the exception of the depletion of assets and deficient farmland. Due to this poor foundational framework, the mainland is yet to overcome the circumstances it began with. The accomplishing of food security in its totality is a challenge for the ever-expanding population of Africa.

Therefore, my recommendation is that, if the ever-increasing population of the African nations is to be fed, mechanization of every agrarian community must be embraced, and this should be our contention for now. The significance of food security to any country cannot be overstressed. The issue of food security got unmistakable during the 1970's and had been given impressive consideration from that point forward. The World Food Program reported in 1979 "Conceptualized food Security", by likening it with an "affirmation of provisions and a balanced supply/demand situation of staple food in the universal market". The report showed that the expansion of food creation in developing nations is a remedy to food security.

The idea of food security suggests that food supply must be accessible, available, and moderately affordable in the societies, when and where it is required in an adequate quantity, and that, this condition should be sustained. It is a circumstance wherein adequate food is accessible consistently in the correct amount and quality, at a reasonable procedure. To achieve this, we should have a production system or program that will produce enough foods in the short run, feasible in the long run and does not put undue dangers of stress on the agricultural producers. It must react quickly to interruptions in the food supply chain due to natural disasters, civil disturbances, disease epidemics, environmental imbalances or other reasons that may come our way. In the light of these, different efforts at the local, national, and international levels had been set up before now at different levels as a way to help the agricultural production to make food accessible to the ever-increasing world population, mostly in the continent of Africa.

"Sustainable Development Goals" (SDGs) established to end hunger and malnutrition by 2030, ensuring all individuals particularly children have adequate and nutritious nourishment all year round. This includes advancing a reasonable agricultural system, supporting little scale ranchers and equivalent access to land, innovation, and markets. It furthermore requires all-inclusive cooperation to ensure interest in infrastructure and development to improve farming productivity. Achieving zero hunger challenge should be taken seriously because it is a shared commitment. With the 2030 SDG Agenda for the whole world and Africa in particular, the United Nations member-states have focused on complete, coordinated, and universal changes that will be of benefit for us all. The agenda is individual-focused and dependent on human rights and social equity. Mirroring the incorporated thought of the 2030 agenda, Zero Hunger Challenge (ZHC) propels approaches that respond to the various interconnected purposes that is behind hunger and absence of solid sustenance. This requires thorough efforts to guarantee that each man, woman, and child make the most of their Right to Adequate Food. Women must not be left behind, they are to be engaged, and total priority must be given to family farming just as it was in the primitive past, but in a modernized way that is compatible with our world of today. It requires a revived focus on the most ideal approach to respond to crises, while all the time creating limits and adaptability inside individuals' and networks' long-term and proactive systems that pass on for people and planet. Experience has indicated that, with the correct blend of arrangements, political initiative, and with everyone doing their job, to end hunger and malnutrition will be easy.

Former President Olusegun Obasanjo has once called for total change of mind as a priority for all Nigerians, demanding a multi-partner and multi-dimensional methodology to accomplish the objective of zero-hunger nations by 2025 ahead of the UN-expected 2030. The Zero Hunger Challenge was launched by UN Secretary-General Ban Ki-moon in 2012, as his vision for a world without hunger and a global call to action in other to achieve zero hunger in the world. Additionally, Minister of Health, Professor Isaac Adewole portrayed the Zero Hunger as a well-planned activity and as an empowering influence for others in the nation. The Minister expressed his trust that the zero-hunger activity will encourage the execution of the National Policy on Food and Nutrition in those territories that were as of late, affirmed by the Federal Government.

It must be comprehended that the Zero Hunger vision reflects five components from within the SDGs, which when taken together, can wipe out lack of healthy sustenance, and can likewise end hunger and fabricate comprehensive and economical nourishment frameworks. ZHC has added to a changed story. It has propelled activity at the national level and added to guaranteeing that nourishment and sustenance security and practical farming have remained high on the worldwide advancement motivation. It has urged all to cooperate towards ending hunger.

Reflecting on the intertwined idea of the 2030 Agenda, ZHC advances strategies that react to the different, interconnected purposes for hunger, and non-attendance of sound sustenance. The breadth of the methodology mirrors the truth of the difficulties that individuals face everywhere as they look for better agriculture and nourishment systems that convey improved nutrition, sustainable and flexible provincial communities. It recognizes the activity of sustenance structures in protecting the environments and biodiversity and also advancing climate equity. It is the right of everybody to have sufficient, safe, and nutritious food.

The process of a mechanized agriculture
Agricultural mechanization suggests the utilization of different kinds of power sources and also to improved farm tools, instruments, and hardware in other to lessen the drudgery of individuals. It also drafts animals, upgrade the precision, cropping intensity and timeliness of efficiency of different crop inputs and diminish the losses at various phases of harvest. The end target of farm mechanization is to upgrade the general efficiency of productivity and production at the most minimal cost. It upgrades biological and chemical production, irrigation system inputs of the high yielding seed, mechanical energy, pesticides, and fertilizers.

The term mechanization is tragically and narrowly misunderstood, but it is genuine reason, is to upgrade the efficiency of land and labor. Indeed, an agricultural mechanization technique should be an agrarian innovation methodology and general farming improvement procedure. In any case, while formulating a genuine agricultural mechanization procedure for the state, the different decisions for overhauling land and labor benefit must be well understood, together with their economic and financial related action. Any rural development programs must take into consideration the future needs of agricultural mechanization.

In some cases, rather than supporting mechanization of explicit exercises, the elective choice may be dynamically appealing. It is then seen that rural mechanization is critical in the battle against hunger and poverty which will likewise address the normal and wellbeing concerns of the citizens. In this way, past mistakes are avoided via the formulation of viable mechanization procedures.

Rural dwellers that are involved in farming lack the fund to practice large scale farming required for food security in Africa. Various Governments must make available funds in their annual budgets for agricultural inputs and loans to farmers through a Development Agricultural Bank. However, experience shows that, if made available, the funds always go to the wrong hands, or on getting to the farmers late. Since agricultural operations are timed, the money is used for different purposes instead of addressing the food security issues they are meant for. These and other factors are limiting the quantity and quality of agricultural produce produced annually by African farmers.

Farm Power consists of equipment and machinery, manual labor, agricultural tools, tractors, draught animals. While a large portion of the problems facing food security in Africa is due to the population increase, some improvements can be made in agriculture. Instead of using expensive irrigation equipment and chemical fertilizers, the farmer can find a crop that fits better into the growing environment, and he/she will be able to produce much higher and stable yields at a much lower cost, allowing abundant food for the masses. There will also be much less threat of natural influences affecting harvest because the crops are much more suited for the area. For example, where a farmer might grow corn because it has a higher market price, he might plant a much more drought-resistant plant, such as sorghum. It is still used for the same types of food but is much cheaper to produce and sell. To make the transition to the more suitable crops, the farmers will need some government incentives, seeing that the transition of crops is awfully expensive. If governments support these programs by making these alterations in policy, the administrations throughout Africa might have a much greater chance at dumping starvation.

Once the officials and the general public understand the importance of the crisis they are currently in, the next stage is attempting to stop the challenge before it gets completely out of hand. With the proper planning and programs, the nations throughout Africa will have a strong chance at surviving starvation which is one of the leading causes of death on the continent anymore.

══╪ ╪══

CHAPTER 26

CONCLUSION

Anatomy of Nigerian problems and why democracy should keep up the fight?

From all the personalities I have covered in this book, I can summarily say that they are advocating for similar goal. They want to rid Nigeria of bad leadership, corruption, human rights abuse, insecurity, and poverty which are undermining the country's democracy. They may not be saints, but their ideas are fundamental in the transformation of this oil-rich country. The challenges we face as a nation today arise from poor leadership, which in my reflection, can make the situation worse if we sit back.

As a developing nation, Nigeria faces lots of social, economic, political, and cultural issues that have in no little measure influenced the prosperity of its people. However, Nigeria as a country is not an exception to the challenges ailing Africa. With a population of over 200 million, Nigeria is Africa's largest country in terms of demography. Joblessness in the country keeps on increasing regardless of the unlimited human and natural assets accessible in the country. Never-ending youth joblessness is prevalent. This joblessness has transformed into a vital issue tormenting the lives of the Nigerian youth and this points to a certifiable risk to the Nigerian prosperity. Joblessness causes dissatisfaction, downfall, desperation, and reliance on relatives and companions who likewise have their very own issues to battle with.

This tricky circumstance has left the young people in an endless loop of neediness that is on a daily disintegrating their hopes, confidence, and future. The magnitude and expansion of poverty in Nigeria and the threat it poses make it one of the biggest challenges in the nation today. The prevalence of urban wrongdoings in Nigeria is an impression of hardship, underestimation, and breakdown in foundation and amenities that are supposed to manage or control wrongdoings among urban occupants. Hence, it is noticed that the developing gap between the rich and poor is a ticking time bomb situation.

I passionately believe that these affirmative reasons are enough to give us a voice to demand better living conditions and a working economy for all Nigerians. The truth is, for forty years, we have not only failed to improve on our basic social amenities but also succeeded in creating worse conditions. Today, our communities are facing numerous challenges like unreliable public water supply. Just imagine a setting where there is no single water-bearing pipe within a ten-kilometer radius!

Security is no longer guaranteed, though there are efforts to restore it. The public power supply is epileptic to the point that we battle daily with the cacophony of noise and carbon monoxide emissions from generators. The current scenario is worse than what I witnessed growing up in the '60s, 70s and partly 80s. Yet, I have heard stories from those much older that the seemingly better situation I witnessed from the 60s to the early 80s was worse than what was obtained under colonial rule.

What saddens me is the thought that the social amenities and industries of our nation have so badly deteriorated over the last five to six decades. With the current sad state of affairs, what and where is our pride as a sovereign nation? Is it not paradoxical that we are sovereign and still suffering? Up until this morning, (60 Years since Independence!), our leaders at various levels of government are still "promising" water, power, security, and roads, but year in, year out, it is looking increasingly beyond our politicians to find a solution to our social problems, owing to the lack of political will. But whatever argument in the manner of excuses our leaders, past, and present can throw up, they are not only unacceptable, but objectionable. The failures of several past administrations have made it pertinent for us to wonder whether our breed of politicians can ever produce the set of leaders who can fix these problems once and for all. I am in no way a pessimist. But it does not look like we are any closer to joining the comity of nations with people-oriented functional social amenities.

My greatest wish and joy will be to see a Nigeria where these amenities become free-flowing dividends, rather than far-fetched privileges. I hate to nurture, even for a fleeting second, the thought of the probability of not witnessing anything different in my lifetime. Now, my strongest hope is drawn from what I have read over and over in the Bible: "Nothing is impossible for God to do". A majority of our leaders have failed the citizenry and has thrown us into despondency. Maybe it is time to turn to the colonial master to come and re-colonize us. But no, we do not need re-colonization. We need a breed of leaders like Senator Dino Melaye, Sheu Sani, Femi Fani Kayode, and their likes to stand up against bad leadership and empower citizens to challenge autocratic and corrupt civil servants and state officers.

Nigeria is a country of diverse people, cultures, religion, and political groups. The country achieved independence from the British colonialist in 1960 and in October 2020 marked 60 years of post-independence. The journey so far has not been an entirely smooth one since self-determination. The country has had to face several challenges. It is becoming a laughing matter anytime somebody mentions some problems facing Nigeria today. The obvious rebuttal from your listeners or readers would be: what solutions do you have to be able to solve those problems? While the suggestive solution is an answer to a problem, the implementation of such a solution is openly at stake. In other words, a problem is unsolved until you implement the suggested idea or solution. Most Nigerians will cite bad leadership, as the number one problem that is facing our country. The simple solution to such a problem is electing good leaders, but the challenge is: will bad ones allow democratic institutions like an electoral body to run elections independently? With the unwillingness of leaders to support genuine electoral democracy, our dilemma is when will Nigeria get good leaders! It is said that since 1960, either the military coup lords have ruled the nation or the puppets that were hand-picked by the outgoing leaders through rigging them into power. Nigerians have never had the chance to choose their leaders through reasonable and free decisions, except that of late MKO Abiola in 1993 - but was foolishly and sinisterly annulled.

Accordingly, our initial step to solving the political leadership issue in Nigeria is to establish an electoral system that will guarantee genuine, free, and reasonable elections. Can this be possible? Indeed, YES, it can. Although such may not be actualized because any party in power uses the chance to propagate its authority. The ruling party rarely sees a need to support electoral integrity for fear of losing power. As a result, it manipulates the election results to win back power deceitfully at the chagrin of Nigerians yearning for better leadership.

In the same breath, another situation that I covered extensively in this book is concerned with its economy. My view is that Nigeria's over-dependence on oil may prompt its defeat. How? A nation with a monolithic economy may not likely be able to endure any little unfriendly happenings in the global economy. For example, the Nigerian economy suffered massively during the crisis that befell nations that depended mostly on their oil deposits between 2008 and 2010. It is generally prudent that nations ought to broaden their economies. This normally enables a country to maintain a strategic distance from financial downturn. With the uncertainty of the economy, Nigeria can expand into agriculture, manufacturing and development of human resources as envisioned by ex-senator Ben Murray-Bruce.

Also, security which I have exclusively highlighted to be one of the major vices that are deflating the realization of true democracy in Nigeria at the moment is worrisome.

Only joint efforts with collaboration and exchange of ideas among the Nigerian States will enhance the efforts that will be designed towards the handling of the country's insecurity. Although no actual society is immune to insecurity, committed leaders work round-the-clock to protect property and people. Sadly, violent, and non-violent conflicts are commonplace in developing countries and sub-Saharan Africa. Regardless, created social orders are unmistakable in their methodologies to check the heightening of instability by guaranteeing that culprits scarcely get away with their crimes. In contemporary Nigeria, deep disappointment is joblessness among graduates and non-graduates. No doubt, several Nigerians involved in the violent conflicts such as armed robbery, smuggling, political thuggery, assassination, ritual killing for wealth, human trafficking, and the likes must have been frustrated to join criminal gangs to fend for themselves. Theoretically, they such to satisfy different commitments in the public eye, for example, marriage, parental obligations, helping their dependents and adding to community ventures. Yahoo-Boys not only use spiritual means to acquire economic benefit for their fraudulent, criminal activities but also use the same diabolical spiritual insurance for their safety so that no harm may befall them while carrying out their criminal activities.

This statistics is frightening when the security, economic and social implications are considered. Youth unemployment has been linked to various social and economic vices, such as theft, robbery, thuggery, smuggling, kidnapping of prominent politicians, business executives, top public, and private sector personnel. Similarly, they have been linked to terrorism since they are easy targets for recruitment into terrorist organizations.

Such baffling issues in the country fuel corruption, youth joblessness, and the orderly rising wave of wrong-doing which have real repercussions on national advancement. Corruption is noteworthy contributing component to the internal insecurity in the country. A common referenced impact of police corruption on the general public is loss of lives through extrajudicial killings, capture and illicit confinement of citizens. The reason for these abnormalities includes insufficient or unpredictable welfare packages for police, low degree of demonstrable skill within the force and interference from the political class.

Mention any societal or institutional ills in Nigeria that is not sustained by the negative and selfish attitude of the Police or the Judges or both at a time. The two institutions, besides politicians, represent the actual satanic temples of evil desire from where the bitter water of sorrow flows endlessly into the country. Anyone interested in reforming the negative vices of the nation but failed to notice this fact is an alien in the Nigeria social system. In Nigeria, corruption is rampant in the justice system and police. Until a surgical operation is performed on the criminal justice system and other institutions, nothing substantial will be accomplished when trying to reform the decayed Nigeria system. Corruption flourishes in Nigeria for the fact that the Police and Judiciary are made up of many operatives without conscience. Corruption is without a doubt boundless and endemic in Nigeria.

The country must stay together so that the forces of darkness attempting to overpower the nation right now would be crushed by speaking with one voice. It is then that those vices, such as harassment and killing by the criminal herdsmen, kidnapping and other crimes that are now looming in the country would be eradicated. What is so troubling is that the vast majority of herders that are executing these crimes are affirmed to be non-Nigerians, but transients from some West African nations. We should also know that the answer to the present security difficulties in the nation lies in the rebuilding of the federal system. This is mostly because the central government is just too powerful. The executive powers perhaps should be reduced.

Every aspect of our nation requires reforms. Education is considered as a human right that ought to be accorded to every human. Incomprehensibly, in spite of her gigantic natural and human resources, Nigeria's education framework is bedeviled with the difficulties of underfunding, poor infrastructure; laboratories, inadequate classrooms, and teaching aids such as projectors, libraries, computers, poor or polluted learning environment and paucity of quality teachers. The nation's educational system is additionally tormented by various social mis-norms like cultism and infant-hooliganism as well as examination malpractices. The derailment of the nation's education happened in the late 80s when the then Minister of Education brought in a "catch up" program into the already well-established educational system in the country. No time to go into details of this now. Alas, this satanic program by Senator Jubril Aminu when he was the Minister for Education then, had since set this country on the path of abyss.

How do I come to this conclusion?

At the passage door of a college in South Africa, the accompanying messages were posted for consideration: *"Destroying any country doesn't require the utilization of nuclear bombs or the utilization of long-range rockets. It just requires bringing down the quality of education and permitting cheating in the assessments of the examinations by the students".*

Solutions to these issues are to scrap the quota system out of the nation's education programs. Improvement of education, strengthening the school administrations and execution of Schools Management Committees (SMCs) is equally essential. Another approach would be the empowerment of educationists through the employment of professionals (qualified teaching staff) and allocation of adequate resources for the sector.

Can you also imagine that many Nigerians never enjoy electricity for twenty-four hours in a day? Many areas are without power supply for half a month or even months and little is done to fix the problem. The terrible performance of the electric power sector in the nation has been a critical obstruction to private investment and economic growth. Let us remember that the power sector like in most economies of the developing nations is run by state-owned power plants, such as Power Holding Company of Nigeria (PHCN) - and some time ago, the National Electric Power Authority (NEPA).

Nevertheless, neo-expansionism or dominion is another issue confronting Nigeria. This is an outside factor of Nigeria's underdevelopment. It is the most conspicuous type of exploitation by the British on their provinces after independence. Nigeria has contributed so much to its own economic backwardness, as it promotes the upkeep of foreign domination and improves neo-expansionism and the booming of subjugations.

Imperialism has consistently been an exploitative marvel, which was the underlying motive in colonization. Nigeria has been viewed as a dumping ground for most British or foreign products, making it hard for the nation to produce anything. Likewise, the fact that we are the primary producers with fewer technicalities to refine our crude materials into finished products mirrors our myopic leadership. For instance, in the area of crude oil, Nigeria is the biggest nation with unrefined petroleum. It is the least fortunate nation because of a lack of technical capacity to change its crude oil into refined oil or gas, a situation that continues to plunge the country into fuel shortage.

According to John C. Maxwell, "Authority is about the impact" and Niyi Adesanya sees it as "not just impact but as well as motivation". These difficulties we are facing as a nation today points to Nigeria's bad leadership which was founded on egotistical interests. The issue of poor leadership is the contributing factor to corruption and self-centeredness. Instead of service delivery, leaders make laws to favor their actions, and would always amend the constitution to suit their political parties' purposes. Sadly, politicians make empty promises during election campaigns, only to snub the citizens when elected. "We got to change; we can't continue like this". With this, I conclude that dignity and ethical morality are values we need to base our actions on going forward. These values are absolute and impossible to exchange them for anything else. Our consciousness of human dignity ought to make us feel humble.

Human nature does have dignity, but its dignity is precarious and never complete.

A human being is dignified insofar as he is altruistic, compassionate, loving and devoted to other fellow living beings and the universe. He is undignified insofar as he is greedy and aggressive. The readiness with which we allow ourselves to be greedy and aggressive is humiliating and the poorness of our ethical performance is made more humiliating by its contrast with the brilliance of our cunningness. Our present situations ought to make us humble as I mentioned above, and this sense of humility ought to spur us to achieve the dignity without which our lives have no value, without which our lives cannot be happy. Human dignity cannot be achieved in the field of greed and corruption, in which Nigerians are experts. It very well may be accomplished uniquely along moral and ethical considerations, estimated by the degree that our activities are represented by sympathy and love, not by voracity and hostility.

May the Lord heal the foundations of Nigeria!

⊨⊰+ +⊱⊨